THE TIGERBELLES

THE TIGERBELLES

Olympic Legends from Tennessee State

AIME ALLEY CARD

LYONS
PRESS

Essex, Connecticut

An imprint of Globe Pequot, the trade division of The Rowman & Littlefield Publishing Group, Inc.
4501 Forbes Blvd., Ste. 200
Lanham, MD 20706
www.rowman.com

Distributed by NATIONAL BOOK NETWORK

British Library Cataloguing in Publication Information available

Library of Congress Cataloging-in-Publication Data
Names: Card, Aime Alley, author.
Title: The Tigerbelles : Olympic legends from Tennessee State / Aime Alley Card.
Description: Essex, Connecticut : Lyons Press, [2024] | Includes bibliographical references and index. |
Summary: "The epic story of the 1960 Tennessee State University all-Black women's track team, which found Olympic glory at the 1960 games in Rome"— Provided by publisher.
Identifiers: LCCN 2023023746 (print) | LCCN 2023023747 (ebook) | ISBN 9781493073887 (cloth : alk. paper) | ISBN 9781493073894 (electronic)
Subjects: LCSH: Tennessee State University—Sports—History. | African American women athletes—Tennessee. | African American women Olympic athletes—Tennessee. | Olympic Games (17th : 1960 : Rome, Italy)
Classification: LCC GV691.T47 C37 2024 (print) | LCC GV691.T47 (ebook) | DDC 796.04/309768—dc23/eng/20230711
LC record available at https://lccn.loc.gov/2023023746
LC ebook record available at https://lccn.loc.gov/2023023747

♾️™ The paper used in this publication meets the minimum requirements of American National Standard for Information Sciences—Permanence of Paper for Printed Library Materials, ANSI/NISO Z39.48-1992.

Dedicated to the Tigerbelles, the Temple family,
and all the young people they continue to inspire.

Special thanks to Dwight Lewis, Tracey Salisbury, New
Hope Academy, and Edwina Temple for so generously sharing
access to their work and their personal archives.

Contents

Contents

He's made me a wonderful woman, he did that for all of us.
All of the Tigerbelles feel like that, the legend Tigerbelles.

—Barbara Jones

Content guidance: The following quotes have been gathered over the course of more than sixty years, ranging from immediately after the events to looking back decades later. Some details may be misremembered over time, but the essential story has not changed. Language used and subjects discussed portray racist incidents and slurs, reflecting the era and events that occurred.

L to R: Isabelle Daniels, Barbara Jones, Lucinda Williams, Wilma Rudolph, (seated) Ed Temple. Special Collections and Archives—Tennessee State University

Chapter 1

Origins

The year is 1960, and the host city is Rome. A grainy black-and-white video is shown on televisions around the globe for the first time in Olympic history. It is the moment when the world was forced to sit up and acknowledge that women can run.

The 4x100-meter relay is one of the most exciting events in sports. The race takes less than a minute. In those seconds, anything can throw a team off their game. Most track events are for individuals. Each athlete measures their strength and speed against their opponents, but the relay depends on the collective. The connections between, the coordinated steps, the matched speed, and ultimately, the smooth handoff of the baton between each leg are what make the critical difference. Four runners each sprint 100 meters, carrying and passing a baton for one full lap around the track, two straightaways and two curved around the edges. Each runner has been placed according to their own strengths and trained accordingly. They must work like clockwork—each pass of the baton at breakneck speed takes the highest level of precision.

The gun cracks, and the starter for Team USA springs off the blocks into the curve. As quick as she is, her competitors are as well, and they reach the end of the leg in a close pack. She approaches the second runner, who turns and starts her sprint, glancing behind her as she climbs into a run, waiting for the handoff.

The starter reaches out and lands the metal cylinder directly in the second leg's outstretched palm within the passing zone, and the second accelerates to top speed. She runs through the straight like lightning and pulls ahead by the time she meets the third leg for a clean handoff. The third takes the curve, maintaining the lead.

The packed crowd at the Stadio Olimpico rises to their feet, stomping, screaming, and cheering for their team.

The third leg runs her final strides, her arm stretched to meet the anchor's hand. The last leg watches the third approach, waiting for the baton. Then there is a hesitation. The third leans forward at the waist, reaching out with the baton, and there is a bobble. The runners seem too close and the baton waves through the air, without a clear landing in the anchor's hand.

There is a collective murmur and gasp in the crowd as time seems to stop.

The two square miles in Nashville were described as a little utopia. There were four historically Black colleges, churches that were regularly visited by civil rights pioneers, restaurants, stores, swimming pools, movie theaters, and music venues. A town within a town where everyone knew each other and the children roamed free until the streetlights came on. It was a place where excellence was expected, and big ideas were floating in the air. A safe refuge from the Jim Crow South—or so it seemed.

The campus of Tennessee Agricultural and Industrial State University was in the middle of it all. Perched alongside the Cumberland River and approached by a long drive into a quad of imposing structures, it was a rolling, grassy campus dotted with oak trees and redbrick buildings with white columns. Howard Gentry Jr., a self-described campus brat who was the son of the school's athletic director, said, "I was on campus every day of my life because you couldn't go anywhere else. Tennessee State was my world. We didn't have to deal with a lot of the damage from segregation, especially at the younger ages, because we had TSU." Gentry and his friends regularly took advantage of the two swimming pools, bowling alleys, campus movie theater, and especially the wide-open spaces of the 600-acre campus. "TSU was a big farm. We had cows and horses; I've been riding horses all my life."

Tennessee State's president, Walter S. Davis, firmly believed that excelling with athletic programs was the key to increasing attention and support for his school. With the dominating success of the football and basketball programs, a co-ed track program had been added to the lineup, almost as an afterthought, when President Davis heard about a similar program at one of their greatest competitors, Alabama's Tuskegee Institute.

Davis was a "dyed-in-the-wool football fan," but he saw potential in the idea. His marquee sports were limited to segregated competitions, and while his teams regularly won national championships, they were only allowed to compete against other Historically Black Colleges and Universities. Track was the exception to the rule. It was the only desegregated collegiate sport, and it allowed both men and women to compete.

Historian and TSU alumnus Dwight Lewis wrote, "Dr. Davis knew that we would hardly be able to convince people that we were equal to other folks if they kept us separated. He knew that as long as you kept white people playing in one area and never let them play together, nobody would ever know how good we were."

Although President Davis added a track program to the school's portfolio, it didn't mean that he was willing to invest any funds in its success. One of the first track coaches, Tom Harris, who joined the school in 1946, said, "When I came to Tennessee State, there was no track. There was only a horseshoe-shaped walkway-like path around part of the football field." One day during practice he waved down a couple of passing dump trucks filled with dirt and persuaded them to dump some of the rocky debris onto the field, smoothing and raking it into some semblance of a track surface.

Being resourceful by nature, Harris used his skills to recruit both male and female talent. He found two young track stars from the Harrisburg, Pennsylvania, area, Edward Temple and Leroy Craig. Harris had "a good line of gab on him," Temple said. He talked up Tennessee State until Temple was interested, then he pulled a fast one. He told Craig, Temple's biggest rival, that Temple had agreed to go to Tennessee State, and he told Temple that Craig had as well, before either of them had actually decided where they would go.

"If Leroy was doing it, I knew it had to be the best," Temple reasoned. Craig must have thought the same of Temple, and the tactic worked. Ed Temple and Leroy Craig boarded a train from Pennsylvania to Tennessee. "We got on the train heading south and had to go to the back of the train," Temple said. "That's the first time it hit me. That's the first time I was ever segregated. Because up there you ran into problems, but it was never 'you had to drink out of this fountain,' or 'you had to sit here.'"

When Temple and Craig got to Tennessee State it was even more of a shock. They thought they'd been swindled when they saw the state of the facilities. "We had three-quarters of a track, and when it ended, it was a dump from there on back."

The Tennessee State team couldn't host any meets without a track, so they had to travel through the Deep South for all of their competitions.

"We were ready to turn back," Temple said of his reservations, "but we were down here, and we stuck it out." It was a sentiment that Temple would see echoed by his own recruits for years to come.

Temple had a strong athletic career at Tennessee State and also made his mark as a student with a healthy social life. While in physiology class his senior year, a young lady caught his eye by the name of Charlie B. Law.

Charlie B. was a leader on campus who was elected Miss Sophomore and chosen as a member of the prestigious Queen's Court. Charlie B. didn't know what to make of Temple at first. He was handsome and stylish, but also guarded, and she never knew exactly how he felt about her. She asked herself, "Is he worth fooling with?" But after spending many long afternoons talking in the campus hangout, The Spoon, Ed and Charlie B. cemented their bond. The two secretly married after their graduation in 1950 before Charlie B. went to teach in her hometown of Hartsville, Tennessee, and Temple stayed on campus, looking for a coaching job.

His coach, Tom Harris, was leaving to be the athletic director for Virginia Union in Richmond and suggested Temple should stay on as a coach. Over the four years Harris was at Tennessee State, he had not only focused on his male recruits, but he'd brought in three women who outperformed the men and competed on the international level. Harris believed that Temple had the drive and discipline to see how far the team could go. President Davis agreed, because "he saw something in him. He had a hunch he could do well." Harris tracked Temple down to tell him that the president wanted to see him the next morning in his office.

"The first thing I thought," Temple said, "was what did I do wrong?" He worried that he was being called out for staying past graduation in the dormitory.

Instead, President Davis said, "I'd like you to do three things: Run the post office, go to graduate school, and coach the women's track team for $150 a month." Davis included an upgrade to a larger first-floor dorm room in the deal. It wasn't the football or basketball coaching gig he'd hoped for, but free tuition, room, and board, with a little cash on the side, seemed workable for the young graduate.

"I didn't have nothing else," Temple said, "so I said, 'Well, okay,'" and Temple's fate was sealed.

President Davis "wanted to give women a chance," Temple said. "Of course, he had no idea, and I had no idea either, that they were going to go as far as they did. . . . If he had had any idea it would ever surpass football, he wouldn't have turned it loose."

Once he agreed to do something, Temple was all in, and he took on the challenge. It was a way for him to stay in school and earn a master's degree and eventually be reunited with Charlie B.

Temple started with a $64 budget and about five men and women on the team.

"That year, we didn't go no place," Temple said. The budget was intended to cover all expenses, including travel for competition, so it was either shoes, equipment, and uniforms, or an out-of-state meet. The track was still in rough shape. He described it as "one step above a cow pasture." It had been updated with sparse cinders, but still only went halfway around the football field, ending in a pile of debris near the pigpen for the agricultural department. "Running a 440 was out of the question, and on hot days down there by those pigs, you sorta lost your motivation to run much of anything."

They finally scraped together the travel budget to compete in the Tuskegee Relays and were outmatched on every level by the tough competition. "They killed us," Temple said. "My goodness, we've got a long way to go."

Temple loved to win, and his competitive nature suffered the defeat. While there was some talent on his team to work with, he was determined to gather more, and set his sights on Mae Faggs, a high school phenom and already an Olympic veteran. In 1948 Mae had qualified for the US Olympic team at just sixteen, along with two Tennessee State students, Emma Reed and Audrey "Mickey" Patterson. Mae and Mickey both competed in the 200-meter, and while Mae didn't make the podium, she saw Mickey win the bronze, becoming the first Black woman ever to win an Olympic medal. Mae knew she had that in her, too.

In 1952 Mae made the Olympic team again and led the 4x100m relay team in the 1952 Olympics in Helsinki. Mae's personality, confidence, and no-nonsense approach allowed her to take charge of the even younger relay team. Mae was a quick study and knew from her experience in the 1948 London games not to rely on the designated coach. The women had to take care of themselves, and Mae leaned on her "natural talent" to survive. "Mae Faggs was about five-foot-two and cocky," Temple said. It was an attitude that helped her every bit as much as her power on the track.

The weather in Helsinki was dreary, with a cold, misty rain, and the women on the team had lost any hopes of winning. No one expected the US women's team to put up any results against their stronger competitors, and so far, they hadn't. Their last chance was with the 4x100m relay, and things were not looking good. None of the women had run together before, and Barbara Jones, just fifteen at the time, was refusing to practice.

Mae had to resort to bribery to get the child out on the track, promising to style Barbara's hair if she would practice with the team. Mae knew that without even the most minimal practice between the four legs of the relay, they had no chance to compete against the favored Australians, or the Russians.

The friction on the women's team did nothing to change their image of being lightweight "cream puffs," but Mae pushed the relay contenders out for practice every day in the bad weather until they had smoothed their timing and baton passing. Mae's leadership seemed to put the fire under the team that they needed, and they qualified for the finals.

But on the night before the race, Barbara Jones—disoriented with jet lag and the "six months of light," when night never truly falls in the Helsinki sky—woke to the midnight sun and thought she might as well start her day.

"So, when I woke up it was light, and I heard the carnival," Barbara said, referring to the Helsinki Fair near the Olympic Village. "And I got up and I walked out of the Olympic Village, and I was just having a ball. This was the same day I had to compete in the Olympics. But I was walking around, enjoying myself, [at] two o'clock in the morning."

Mae Faggs heard that she was missing and was frantically searching the Village for fifteen-year-old Barbara Jones.

"I'm on the Ferris wheel," Barbara said, "so when I come down, there's Mae Faggs and Floyd Patterson, the boxer, waiting for me."

One of the guards had tipped off Mae and Floyd[1] as to Barbara's location, and their fury at finding Barbara roaming free in the middle of the night before a race was immense.

"So, they whipped me all the way back, and I learned quickly that I had to stay in place and not act as a fifteen-year-old, but as a woman."

At the start of the race, Mae, being small and quick off the blocks, took the starting leg and passed off to Barbara, with a solid lead. Barbara increased the lead when she passed off to Janet Moreau of Providence. Janet, overpowered by the competition's strong power third legs, fell behind before the final pass to Catherine Hardy of Fort Valley, Georgia. Australia, England, and Germany were running first, second, and third.

Then the unexpected happened, and Marjorie Jackson of Australia, the favorite to win the event, dropped the baton in the handoff to the anchor leg.

The US team anchor, Catherine Hardy, capitalized on the Australian's critical error and charged ahead, catching first the German and

---

1. Floyd Patterson, nicknamed "The Gentleman of Boxing," was a two-time heavyweight champion boxer between 1956 and 1962, and won a gold medal as a middleweight amateur in the 1952 Olympics.

finally the English runner mere feet from the finish line, passing her to break the tape first. The four American women who no one had taken seriously had just set a new world record of 45.9 seconds, winning gold for Team USA, and Mae had gotten them there.

Mae Faggs became a gold medalist before she even started college, and Barbara Jones became the youngest woman ever to win Olympic gold in athletics. "When I was standing on the platform in Helsinki, waiting with the other three girls for presentation of our medals," Mae said, "I guess I was the happiest girl in the world."

Mae Faggs was a superstar, and Temple knew if he could convince her to come to Tennessee State, it would be a game changer for his program. But Tuskegee was after her too. Alabama's Tuskegee Institute, now Tuskegee University, was a powerhouse for track and field, and the only school in the country offering full scholarships to women for track. Temple, however, had never been one to shy away from competition.

Mae Faggs. Special Collections and Archives—Tennessee State University

Temple went to work convincing Mae to join his program. Mae remembered recent graduates Emma Reed and Mickey Patterson as standouts from the 1948 Olympic team, but that was more due to their individual talent than any kind of enduring program. Temple was never sure what did the trick, but something worked, and Mae signed on to his team. Temple's best guess as to why she settled on Tennessee State was that it was closer to Bayside, New Jersey, where Mae had grown up. He was able to offer her free tuition in exchange for a spot on the team and two hours of work on campus a day, called a work-aid scholarship.

"Tuskegee offered her a scholarship, and we offered her a scholarship. Of course, it was a work-aid, but we called it a scholarship. You don't offer no work-aid to come down here," Temple said, laughing. "We didn't tell her about the two hours a day until she was already here." Temple had learned a few tricks from his old coach, Tom Harris.

Mae was the thing that gave the team the "spark" in 1952, and Temple said, "We were lucky to get her." But the transition wasn't so easy for Mae. "We almost lost her that first year because she couldn't adjust. It was hard."

The workload and the culture change between New Jersey and Nashville came as a shock to Mae, the same as it had for Temple, and he understood it as well as anyone. When she wanted to go to a movie downtown, she discovered that the main entrance was "Whites Only," and she and her friends had to walk down the back alley and up several flights of exterior stairs that resembled a fire escape in order to see the movie from the balcony. A burger and a shake at the joint next door was out of the question.

If that humiliation wasn't enough, she was denied the funds to travel to the national meets. "They just didn't understand what was at stake," Temple said. "President Davis didn't know a thing about indoor track. Shoot, we didn't even have an outdoor track at TSU at the time, so why would he think indoor track competitions were important? They just didn't understand."

Temple fought the administration hard for more of a budget, but they still didn't give him enough money to send Mae back to the national championships she was regularly winning, and she missed the chance to defend her title.

"We were going to one to two meets a year," Temple said. "She was ready to go home. I really had to talk to her, wasn't no doubt about it. She was used to running in Madison Square Garden and running up in them big meets and she come down here and we don't have nothing."

Temple, just a couple of years older than Mae, leveled with her. He had a vision for the team that Mae could help them achieve. Together they could build something. Something that would support young women. They were both embarking on a new journey, and they would be stronger together.

Mae listened and set her mind on doing what it would take to stay. She began to put the program at Tennessee State on the map.

Mae was now internationally recognized as a champion, but she didn't use her newfound status for herself; she was bringing the team along with her. While Temple was the coach, Mae was the leader. The two worked together to bring more women on to the team and to teach them all the discipline and skills to succeed.

Temple favored a strategy he had learned from his father that concentrated on repetition and focusing on technical details. It was a grinding, workhorse approach that had worked well for him in his own athletic success, and he strongly believed it would translate to others. Mae brought with her the experience of national competition. There were things she taught Temple and her new teammates that they'd never been exposed to before, and she provided the motivation for the team to reach for the highest heights. She showed them what was possible.

"I was already a national outdoor champion," Mae said. "I was a national indoor champion, [and] I had been to the Olympics. My teammates, all they cared about in practice was running past Mae Faggs. You couldn't let your guard down at all because if one ran past you . . . they turned around and gave you one of those looks that said, 'Uh-huh, I got you now.'"

But as much as they competed, they also leaned on each other.

Temple said, "To build this track program at all was a challenge from the start. It took many with pride and determination to do the job. It required a lot of caring, too—none of this everyone-for-herself business. . . . If a girl was having a problem, a teammate cared enough to see me or C.B. and ask for help. We all worked together." Temple's new wife, Charlie B., was ever present as a resource to the women, and they considered her a mother figure during their time away from home.

In 1955 Temple took the team in three station wagons to Ponca City, Oklahoma, where the Amateur Athletic Union (AAU) Nationals meet was held on a high school track with only around fifty people in the stands. "Because, you see, this was the girls' championship, and at that time everything was separate," Temple said, and women's track wasn't drawing the spectators. Between the three cars, Temple was able to bring a junior team of new high school recruits as well as his senior team of college students. Mae Faggs captained the team that included Isabelle Daniels, Lucinda Williams, and Wilma Rudolph, as one of his youngest team members. Together, they won their first national championship.

It was the first national championship that Tennessee State had ever won. They had won the Black championships for football and basketball, but never an integrated national championship.

"It was a great thrill for me," Temple said, "but it was a disappointment, too."

It was a major accomplishment, one that had never been achieved, and Temple was sure that when he got back to campus there would be the same level of excitement that he saw for the other teams and felt for his own, but "there wasn't," Temple said, "because it was the women."

He was "on cloud nine," but Temple and his team still weren't fully appreciated for what they had accomplished. Tennessee State was used to winning championships, but for Temple, winning the first integrated championship carried new meaning that he felt should be recognized. "Really, we just advanced too fast for the school at the time. There is no doubt about it," Temple said.

Despite the lack of recognition from the administration, the women were gaining clout on campus. The school's sports information director, Earl Clanton III, coined the name "the Tigerbelles," and it stuck. It was

1955 National Championship: Mae Faggs (holding trophy) and Ed Temple. Temple Archives

a combination of the men's team mascot, the Tiger, and a Southern belle. Temple knew he was facing an uphill battle when it came to female athletes being taken seriously, and he believed that in order for them to maintain the respect of the community, they had to hold themselves up to the highest standards.

According to longtime sportswriter for *The Tennessean*, F. M. Williams, "Earl Clanton III is the man credited with naming the school's women's track team 'Tigerbelles,' but it was Coach Ed Temple who set the standard under which a girl can properly be called a 'Tigerbelle.' Not only is being a 'Tigerbelle' special, it's an honor and a testimonial to having been the best."

Temple told them to "Look like a lady, act like a lady, and run like a man."

The national championship didn't bring in any more money, so Temple still had to stretch his budget in 1956 to buy gas for the old station wagon for the Indoor Nationals at Madison Square Garden. Mae's leadership role was more important than ever. She carried them through while Temple was still learning himself. "She was the backbone," Temple said. "She put the fight into the team."

Temple brought along a second coach, often Samuel Abernathy—affectionately known as Mr. Ab—to share the driving so that they could avoid stopping on the long trip from Nashville to New York City, and they drove around the clock. There were a number of reasons to avoid stops; first, of course, was the cost of hotel rooms, and second, he could never be positive where they would be safe. "We had to pack a brown-bag lunch of a peanut butter and jelly sandwich, and an orange or an apple." Even on the shorter drives to Tuskegee they filled up with gas in Nashville and drove straight through, only stopping to relieve themselves "alongside the road."

The AAU provided rooms for the athletes at the Paramount Hotel in New York, but there was a circus being held at Madison Square Garden the night before the race, so the team, cramped after the overnight drive, "ran up and down the halls at the Paramount to loosen up their legs after all that driving."

Other patrons of the hotel, hearing the thundering footsteps up and down the hallways, opened their doors to see what was happening. They immediately jumped back when confronted by the elite athletes charging at top speed past their faces. "We were flying up and down the halls," Temple said. "We didn't want to go that far to lose."

They got up early the next morning to get used to the feel of their spikes on the curves and the banks of the indoor track. "On the day of the meet," Samuel Abernathy said, "he'd try to be the first one there." Temple left nothing to chance, and neither would his team. Never mind that they had to "unload from cramped car seats and perform against college teams that had scholarships, hot food, and first-rate travel and housing."

It was the first time the team had seen a bank track, an indoor track that had raised curves around the corners. Mae taught them how to use the corners to push off instead of slowing. "We had never run on a bank track—we didn't know what a bank track looked like, but Mae had experience."

The team had prepared for the indoor meets by running laps and very short sprints in the gymnasium. They "couldn't wear track shoes indoors because we were practicing on the gym floor," Temple said. "So, we didn't put track shoes on till we got to the place where we was going to run."

Despite having to travel in less-than-ideal conditions, practicing in the hotel hallways, and learning new surfaces on the fly, the Tigerbelles dominated their events and finished the meet with a hard-earned victory. But when the competition was over, there was no time to celebrate. After the last race, "we'd have to get back," Abernathy said. "We had to get back after four days if it snowed or whatever. We didn't have a whole lot of money in our pockets."

They were fighting on all fronts: for funding, for respect, for their rights. It seemed that nothing was in their favor, but still they won.

Chapter 2

Growing a Team

Temple's strategy was bearing fruit and the program grew under Temple and Mae's leadership. Every year they earned a slightly larger budget. "We went from $150 to $300, $500 to $1,000, to $1,500," Temple said. It wasn't nearly as large a budget as that of most of their competitors, or the men's teams at Tennessee State, but it was something.

Temple always had his eye out for new talent and used a summer program for high school girls as a sort of minor-league farm team for the college team. "I'd go to Fort Valley to see the top girls in Georgia, would go to Birmingham to see the top girls in Alabama," Temple said, but placing in the Tuskegee Relays was the best way for the young runners to gain his attention.

The first summer, in 1955, he recruited Lucinda Williams and Isabelle Daniels, and the second, in 1956, Wilma Rudolph and Willye B. White.

"Every girl I recruited, I went to her home and met her parents. I wanted to see where she came from. I wanted to sit down with her parents in front of her and go over my program." Temple went over the rules and the goals carefully, making sure his new recruits heard the message. He felt that he was able to pull more people on to his team because the parents "knew what they were getting, and [that their daughters] would be safe." The priorities were first, to get an education, and second, to run track. "Track opens doors," he said, "and education keeps them open."

Temple's hard-and-fast policy was three strikes and you're out. The rules were strict and consistent. Ten p.m. curfew, no riding in cars with

L to R: Mae Faggs, Wilma Rudolph, Lucinda Williams. Special Collections and Archives—Tennessee State University

boys, no misbehaving of any sort. He felt responsible for their safety as well as their souls. He was bringing these young women away from their homes, most for the first time in their lives, and none of them could afford any missteps. If someone fell out of line, Temple responded quickly. "When I call you in the first time, I'll tell you what you did wrong. Warning. Second time, I'll also call the parents. Third strike, you're on the bus going home. I'll buy you a Greyhound ticket."

After he finished his talk with the parents, they would nod their heads, and he knew they all understood each other. They all had the same goals. For nearly all of the recruits, it was their only opportunity to go to college, an opportunity afforded to basically none of their own parents, and one that would change all of their lives.

By the time Temple chose the athletes, they already had the talent. They were each used to being the best where they came from. But when they got to Tennessee State, they were just one in the crowd. They could no longer count on being first. If they still wanted to be first—and he made sure they did—they'd have to work harder and harder to get it. "Coach Temple brought in champions," Margaret Matthews said. "If you just ran track, that wasn't enough. You had to be a champion. And everyone who was there was a state champion."

At first it was difficult for most of the women to understand the point of all of the pain and suffering, but the older teammates pulled the younger ones along, encouraging them and challenging them to dig down and keep going.

"That first summer in Nashville was the only time I wanted to go back home," Lucinda Williams said. "It was difficult. It was hard. But then, it was also somewhat fun because the older Tigerbelles—Mae Faggs, Cynthia Thompson, and Pat Monsanto—because those young ladies were there and in college, they just kind of took us under their wings and guided us through."

If they didn't know that they had what it took, Coach Temple surely did. He knew that each of them was capable of more than they had ever dreamed, and he was determined that they would see it for themselves.

"He was a visionary," Lucinda Williams said. "He saw within us what we probably didn't realize was within ourselves. He saw the potential of not only being great women athletes, setting the stage, opening the doors. He also saw the potential of being contributors to society. Being able to be strong Black women and strong role models. He saw that in us at an early stage."

Of all of Temple's recruits, Wilma Rudolph was special from the beginning. Instead of being spotted in the usual places, such as the Tuskegee Relays or one of the national meets, Temple first saw Wilma while he was refereeing high school basketball games in nearby Clarksville, Tennessee. It was a side hustle for him, a fun way to earn extra cash: $15 for calling high school football games, and $7.50 for each basketball game of a two-game set, when the girls' and boys' games would be back-to-back.

Wilma was young on the team, and not the best player yet, but Temple saw a raw potential in her. She was all arms and legs, earning her nickname, Skeeter, and like a mosquito was always buzzing around. She had the easy smile and ingratiating spirit that often comes with being doted on as a baby. But underneath all the charm was an electric energy reminiscent of an unbroken filly being set free in the field. A kind of undirected power.

Wilma was "the young Rudolph girl" that Clinton Gray, the basketball coach at Burt High School in Clarksville, had given Temple the heads-up about, wanting him to take a look at her.

"She had to be five-eight or five-nine by then," Temple said, "and she was so thin, she looked like Olive Oyl—you know, from *Popeye*."

Pulling her aside, Temple told Wilma that with her height, she should be jumping much higher than she was. He pointed to a mark on the wall and told her to jump twenty times a day until she could reach it, then tell him when she'd reached the goal.

Wilma took the challenge seriously. She was already pestering Coach Gray for extra time on the basketball court, so having an official directive just gave her one more excuse. Wilma wanted to run, jump, and play more than your average child, and for more of a reason. It hadn't been very long since her left leg had been in a brace and she hadn't been able to run at all.

Wilma was born too fast; after her mom had a fall, Wilma entered the world early. Being premature left her weak and vulnerable to everything, and she fell victim to all of it. From whooping cough to double pneumonia, and finally polio, she couldn't remember a day before she turned twelve when she was fully healthy. Her leg was crooked and her foot turned inward from polio, so she walked with a limp and a drag that caused the other kids in town to tease her and call her a cripple.

While the other children were in school, Wilma stayed behind, listening to Billie Holiday records on an old Victrola player in their small wood-plank farmhouse on Kellogg Street in Clarksville. "I would sit around and dream about what the rest of the world was like," Wilma said. When she was well enough to go play in the neighborhood, she was often teased to tears, until she decided not to take it anymore. Wilma said, "Okay, someday I am going to show them all; someday I'll do something that will put them all in their places." Wilma was craving the other children's acceptance, but instead, they gave her the drive that she needed to push beyond her perceived limitations.

Blanche Rudolph was determined not to let her young daughter fall behind. With time and money they could not afford to spend, Mrs. Rudolph and Wilma traveled together by bus from Clarksville to Nashville for weekly treatments at Meharry Medical Center. Wilma's treatments included a brace to help straighten her stride, along with massage and physical therapy. Wilma said, "My doctor told me I would never walk again. My mother told me I would. I believed my mother."

The travel between Clarksville and Nashville for Wilma's treatment was in and of itself a struggle. The Clarksville bus station had a separate ticket counter and waiting area for Black passengers. "You didn't even get near the white people who were making the same trip," Wilma said. She and her mother were expected to sit in the back of the bus, and when the bus got crowded, the white passengers would sit toward the back, forcing people out of their seats to stand crowded in the aisles. The bus driver would enforce the rules, correcting anyone who might be out of place, though in all the years Wilma made that trip, she never saw anyone challenge him. "It affects you inside," Wilma said. "It makes you think less of yourself, destroys your self-esteem."

Money was always short in the Rudolph household. Wilma was the twentieth of twenty-two children, one of eight from her father's second marriage to her mother. Mrs. Rudolph used all her available resources to take care of the family, sewing her daughter's dresses from flour sacks on an old sewing machine that she pedaled by foot. A leftover economy from the Depression era, flour sacks of the time were printed with floral patterns, and Wilma's mother would gather extra used bags from the store for all of her girls.

In addition to making her family's clothing, she also helped in the kitchen of a local restaurant, bringing home extra food, and worked as a housekeeper on Saturdays, where she was asked to serve her white employers coffee in bed while they slept in. That particular indignity enraged Wilma more than all the others, and she told herself, "I don't know yet what the escape is going to be, but Wilma, it's not going to be like this forever."

Suffering the cost and discrimination of the weekly trip to the medical center proved worth the effort, and Wilma, with her improved health, began to outpace all of her peers.

Temple continued to watch Wilma's improvement until he saw her put fifty points on the scoreboard in one game and told her coach he wanted her for his summer program. However, Temple faced some resistance in the Rudolph household to the idea of Wilma spending the summer away from home.

"I went to visit her parents, and her father, he was not receptive [to] her coming here. He didn't want her to leave because she had been in a brace, and for a long time, she'd had a hard time walking. He got real close to her because the rest of them were out playing and she had to sit at home with him. He wasn't for her coming, but I could tell Mama was."

Blanche Rudolph knew what a college education would mean for her daughter, an opportunity they never would have been able to afford otherwise.

Temple went back to the house two or three more times, explaining the program and how carefully he watched over his team. "I explained that she would be in the dormitory, and she would have to be in at ten o'clock, and she couldn't be out running around or anything, so I finally got him to say yes, although Mama was the big factor that pushed it."

Wilma was finally allowed to join the summer program at Tennessee State in 1956, along with nine other junior runners to test her mettle. "It was rough, no doubt about that. It was rough," Temple said. Wilma was coming in as any other runner to compete against the best, and it just happened to also be an Olympic year. The stakes had never been higher.

Though mostly inexperienced, the team was stacked with talent by 1956, and Temple knew he had some serious contenders for the Olympics in Melbourne. Mae Faggs was the only "old pro" on the team, having been on both the 1948 and 1952 Olympic teams. Temple judged the group against Mae's standard, using her as the benchmark and the leader, a skill that came naturally to Mae. She wasn't afraid to be tough when she needed to be, and she had an intuition about each of her young teammates' talents, motivations, and weaknesses. Mae could use that

1956 Tigerbelle Junior and Senior Teams. Temple Archives

knowledge to either exploit in her challengers or encourage in her team-mates, and it was a critical component to the success of the team.

"Mae Faggs was just a person that you wanted to do well for," Lucinda Williams said. "She would say you gotta do this if you want to be part of the 100 or 200, and every sprinter wanted to be on the 4x100-meter relay. That meant you had to work every day as hard as you could and never let up. That was motivation in and of itself. Just being around each other and talking about what we wanted to be when we did excel, and everybody knew who we were."

In an Olympic year, the top performers from the Nationals championship would be invited to the Olympic trials, and then the top three for each event at the trials would make the US Olympic team. The first step was Nationals, and as always, travel was the first thing Temple had to work through.

The 1956 Nationals were held in Philadelphia, followed one week later by the Olympic trials in Washington, DC. "We couldn't afford to make both trips," Temple said, "but we couldn't afford *not* to make them. So, we made two trips in one." In 1956, as in previous years, the same challenges applied—money and segregation. Lucinda Williams said, "We'd travel around the country, and we couldn't stop many places. We had to go to the bathroom in the bushes along the road and sometimes we slept in the car. I remember once we went to a restaurant in Baltimore. The owner chased us out saying I don't serve n****** here! Stuff like that. I didn't let it get me down. I made it motivate me."

Lucinda Williams had just finished her freshman year at Tennessee State, having been invited to join the team after running in the summer program in 1955. As with Wilma, Lucinda's first summer was the hardest to get through. She had been desperate to quit and go home, but her pride, and the prospect of a college degree, forced her to stay. Like Coach Temple had said when he'd sat down with her parents, offering her the spot on his team, her speed got her to college, and her degree would serve her for the rest of her life.

The first time Lucinda said good-bye, it was such an occasion that nearly one hundred of her friends and family drove the twelve miles to the Greyhound bus station in Savannah to send her off. Her mother had packed a basket of cold chicken, pound cake, and a jug of water for the long ride to Nashville, and she was wearing her "Sunday best," a dress sent to her from her aunt who worked as a housekeeper for a wealthy family in Palm Beach, Florida. When the family's daughter tossed her old clothes, Lucinda's aunt saved them and sent them to Lucinda, along with a suitcase for her journey.

Each neighbor whispered words of advice and best wishes to her as they pressed a coin or two, or sometimes a dollar, into her hand. Lucinda climbed onto the bus and walked straight to the back, where she would stay for the entire journey. Her mother said, "You know your place. Don't give anyone any reason to trouble you."

Lucinda waved at her parents, her neighbors, and members of her church, all cheering for her as the bus drove away. She was proof as to what was possible. She was part of a new generation capable of achieving more than any of her community had ever dreamed possible. All of their hopes and dreams were quite a lot to carry on her thin shoulders, but she was determined not to fail. "It was not easy," Lucinda said. "I was home-sick, and it was so hard, but I knew that everybody was counting on me. I couldn't quit. I knew I had to make some hard choices. I couldn't let those people down. I couldn't let my family down, because I was the first person in my family to go to college."

Lucinda learned to depend on her team the same way she had on her family and community at home. The older runners on the team "continued to encourage us," Lucinda said, "but they also made it known that we were there to work. You learned time management, number one. You learned how to take care of yourself and your teammates, because the team concept was born with the Tigerbelles in taking care of each other and being sure everybody got about the same thing, to a point."

Together the women pooled their resources, sharing clothes and meals, doing each other's hair, and making sure that they each had what they needed.

"We didn't have very much," Lucinda said, "but what we had, we shared."

CHAPTER 3

The 1956 Nationals

TWO STATION WAGONS HEADED NORTH FOR THE 1956 OUTDOOR Nationals competition with Temple driving the lead car. Wilma sat up front next to him with a book of maps, struggling with the massive, folded sheets. She tried to navigate for the first time in her life, with Temple chirping in her ear until she got it right. Earl Clanton followed in the car behind, and the pair traveled through the night, stopping only for "gas, restrooms, and hamburgers when the packed lunches ran out."

The rest of the team crowded in among all of their gear and luggage, but they didn't let the cramped quarters get in the way of their appearance. They fixed themselves up for every single stop. "We had our hair in rollers," Lucinda said, "then before we would stop, we'd take the hair out of the rollers, comb our hair, make ourselves presentable, and straighten ourselves out."

Any time they showed themselves in public, they were dressed to the nines. Temple's goal, which the women shared, was to be mistaken for a choir group or a debate club. Appearing to be female athletes did not meet the standard of the day, and they had to hold themselves even higher than the highest standards.

The team held a meeting before they ever left campus. "He had us all sit down," Lucinda said. "Went through our dos and don'ts. The expectations." Coach Temple told them, "You're here representing Tennessee State. No foolishness. Do your best, and that's what you're here to do."

The expectations went further than just physical appearance; they included physical performance as well.

Lucinda fully understood the expectations. "We knew if there were three of us in an event, then that meant one-two-three. Nobody comes between you."

With Mae Faggs as their captain and leader and the rest of the team chasing closely behind, there would hardly be room for the competition.

The events started with Junior Day, the championship for the high school girls on the team, including Wilma Rudolph and Willye B. White.

Willye—who had changed her given name, Willie, to include the "y," to "stop being mistaken for a boy"—was a standout high school athlete from Greenwood, Mississippi. Willye was known in her town as the girl who ran everywhere in high-top shoes and overalls when most of the girls were wearing dresses and patent-leather shoes, with bows in their hair. She considered herself a misfit because of her green eyes, light skin, and short red hair that her grandmother put in "nine thousand little braids."

"I was wild, buck wild, wild weeds, and very unattractive. Parents wouldn't allow me to play with their children. So, I was just an outcast," she recalled.

Willye entered school late, at nine years old, and struggled to catch up.

"I didn't have the basics of reading and writing and arithmetic and things like that, simply because my grandparents were, you know, they were not lettered. So, I suffered there," she said.

But Willye found refuge in a place she truly excelled: sports. She played every sport she could, as a way to stay out of the house and out from under the thumb of her strict grandfather. The more she ran, the faster she got. By age twelve she was on the varsity track and basketball teams. Actor Morgan Freeman, one of Greenwood's most notable residents, once joked to Ralph Boston that he didn't run track in high school "because he'd have [had] to run against Willye B. White, and he didn't want to lose to a girl."

Ralph Boston first saw Willye running in the state high school track meet and wondered, "Why is this girl running barefoot?" He knew she was fast then, but had no idea what was in store for this local girl he saw beating everyone in her bare feet.

Temple competed with Tuskegee to recruit Willye to his summer program, and like Mae Faggs, Willye chose Tennessee State because of its distance from her home state—the difference being that Mae had wanted to be closer to home, while Willye wanted to be as far away as possible. "The only thing that I knew when I got there on May 28 was, I was missing all the cotton. That's what I was so happy about."

Willye lived with her grandparents on a large farm she called a plantation in Mississippi where not much had changed since emancipation. Her grandfather worked for the owner of the land, training the horses. Every day during cotton season Willye joined the other children and workers on the cotton truck before sunrise, earning $2.50 a day for twelve hours of hard labor. Her grandfather's theory was that the work would not only keep her out of trouble but also provide the motivation for her to work toward a better life for herself. He told her she had two choices: to either "go to college and get out of Mississippi, or stay home, get pregnant, and pick cotton the rest of her life."

When Willye arrived at Tennessee State, the only thing the other runners were talking about was making the Olympics and going to Melbourne, Australia. It was the first Willye had heard of the Olympics, and traveling to Australia might as well have been to the moon. Before that summer, she'd never even left the Mississippi Delta. The thing that stood out to Willye was that the competition would be held in November, so if she made the team, she wouldn't be home until all of the cotton was gone. No one thought that Willye would be able to make the team; she was as green as a runner could be, untrained and untested. "But see," Willye said, "they didn't know that I had a mission. And my mission was that I didn't want to go back to the cotton fields."

While most of the team concentrated on the sprints, Willye trained for the long jump, because she thought it was her best chance to make the team. She figured out how far she needed to jump, and she jumped over and over again until she'd pushed herself past that length by sheer will. On Junior Day at the National AAU Championship, Willye had six jumps, each surpassing the Olympic qualifying standards.

When Wilma Rudolph saw Franklin Field on Junior Day, she "nearly fainted." It was by far the biggest, most important competition she'd ever been a part of. She was entered in the 75, the 100, and the 440 relay. It was an all-day event, and, including qualifying heats, Wilma raced nine heats and finals, winning every one of them. Tennessee State swept the junior division with five runners on their entire junior team, competing with more than fifty girls in each event.

Coach Temple allowed Willye to participate in the senior competition because of her results, but he had serious reservations, and told her so. Willye was singularly focused on making the Olympic team, but he didn't believe she was ready. He considered her a wild card, and he wasn't sure if she could handle the big stage. Temple told her, "The boat is going to sail without you," and that served as an even greater form of motivation for Willye. She said, "I just decided, but shoot, I'm not going to let that boat sail without me." He told her that she would not qualify and would have to go back home if she didn't jump 16 or 17 feet at least. "I wasn't going home," Willye said. "So, I jumped over 19 feet."

Tennessee State won both the junior and senior championships and then drove to Temple's parents' house in Harrisburg, Pennsylvania, to stay for a few days and train for the Olympic trials the following weekend, in Washington, DC. Willye still had a spot on the team, and she was having a ball.

"I'd never eaten in a restaurant, you know, and it was an experience. We went from Philadelphia to DC, and we were living in this hotel, and we ate in these beautiful restaurants—well, they were cafeterias, but still, they were beautiful."

One's performance in the Olympic trials was the only chance to make the team, regardless of past results. The pressure was intense, and some handled it better than others. To qualify, each competitor had to meet the international standards for the event and place in the top three of the finals. Barbara Jones, who had earned international acclaim by her record-setting performance in the 1952 Olympics with Mae Faggs in the 4x100-meter relay, was considered "one of the all-time greats among American sprinters." She ran for the Catholic Youth Organization in Chicago under the direction of Bishop Sheil and was a favorite for the 100 and the 200. But Barbara wasn't only fighting against the up-and-coming Tigerbelle team; she was also fighting against herself. "High-strung, nervous, always on edge," she warmed up too early, burning crucial energy. "She probably beat herself more times than any of her opponents by sheer worrying," a teammate said.

An injury may have also played a role in Barbara's performance in the Olympic trials, but whatever the cause, the result was that one of the fastest known young women in America, and the youngest gold medalist, was shut out of the chance to compete in the 100 meters in Melbourne.

Mae Faggs, Isabelle Daniels, and Lucinda Williams came in 1st, 2nd, and 3rd. An all-Tigerbelle upset. Right off the bat, three Tigerbelles made the US Olympic team, qualifying for the 100 meters.

The long jump competition was just as fierce. Willye knew it was her only chance to keep going with her team. She stood at the edge of a cliff with the long jump being her only lifeline. If she went out now, she'd have to go back home, and the cotton was way too high in the fields for that to happen.

Willye lined up at the end of the slender strip of cinders in the infield and looked down the runway to the sand pit at the end. One good jump would change her entire future.

The home where Willye lived with her grandparents was in Money, Mississippi. The cotton trucks that picked up Willye and her neighbors every morning the previous summer also carried a fourteen-year-old boy by the name of Emmett Till, who was visiting his cousins in Money during the summer of 1955, the year before Willye came to Tennessee State.

It was common between Greenwood and Money, Mississippi, for children to work in the cotton fields, and Barbara Murrell also lived in the area at the time.

"That year I was a junior in high school, trying to figure out if I could get out of Mississippi," Barbara Murrell said. "In my little neighborhood, cotton was king. There weren't any jobs or anything for young people, so [you'd] get on the trucks, early in the morning and go chop cotton all day. So, by five or six o'clock in the afternoon you'd come back, but you'd have a pocketful of money, what young people call money. Well, my mother wouldn't let me go, and I would be so upset because all of my friends would be going and then they had money, and I didn't have any."

Barbara's mother eventually let her spend some time in the fields with a man they knew in a sort of trial run for the work. "They took me out there. Well, I was ready to leave by noon." There was no doubt how hard the work was, how hot out under the Delta sun. But Willye and Emmett Till both worked that summer.

Coming home one afternoon with extra money to spend, Emmett Till went into Bryant's Grocery and Meat Market to buy some bubble gum. Being from out of town, he was unaccustomed to the manner in which he was expected to behave by the store's owners. He didn't know that he wasn't allowed to be a kid, to have a personality, to be himself.

A few nights later, Emmett was pulled from his bed, beaten, dragged down to the Tallahatchie River, and shot in the head. But they didn't stop there. These men—men that ran the local grocery store in Willye's back-yard—had tied him with barbed wire to an old metal mill fan and sunk his body in the water. Despite a trial, a trial where Emmett's own uncle, Moses Wright, had risked his life to testify, those men were still walking free, and the woman who worked behind the counter and had accused Emmett of inappropriate behavior, stood beside them.

Barbara Murrell had gotten a job at a Greenwood funeral home with an aunt, and they heard the talk right away. About two days before the news was printed in the papers, "we were starting to hear that somebody was found in the river," Barbara said. "That's the kind of town we lived in. Very segregated. When they found Emmett Till, he wasn't the only one they found in there. That's the only one that you heard about because his mother made a complaint, but there were other people that they found. That wasn't something that was unusual in that little town, because it was just that kind of place."

The community had to work out a scheme to get Emmett's body prepared for an open casket and out of Greenwood. "They used the Pullman porters from the City of New Orleans train to slip that body on there so it could get back to Chicago."

Barbara Jones was in Chicago when Emmett Till's body was brought home for the funeral. "I actually went to the funeral and saw . . . oh yes, the distortion of his face," Barbara said. "And how it was blown up. Because they wanted the people to see what he looked like. I never will forget that."

It was an assault on the entire community, but the impact on Willye was acute.

At the 1956 Olympic trials Willye White started the run toward the long jump pit, gaining speed, faster and faster, until she launched high into the air, flying over more than 19 feet of sand before her feet landed in the pit and she bounced up and kept stepping forward. She didn't even have to look back to know that it was enough.

"My first jump, I qualified for the Olympic team. And then she [Margaret Matthews] came behind me and jumped farther." Both Willye and her Tennessee State teammate placed first and second, for a total of five Tigerbelles qualified for the United States Olympic team. The jump also set up what was to become a long-running battle of fierce competition and psychological warfare between Willye and Margaret.

The 200 was up next and Wilma Rudolph hadn't earned her spot, so she leaned on Mae Faggs for help. "Mae Faggs particularly mothered Rudolph," Temple said. "When Faggs and Rudolph got together they looked like Mutt and Jeff." Wilma was tall, at nearly six feet, and Mae barely cleared five, but while Wilma had the height advantage, her age and inexperience were showing. She was barely sixteen years old and a bundle of nerves. "I was just all to pieces," Wilma said. "I was real nervous."

Mae took pity on her. She sympathized with Wilma particularly because she had also been just sixteen years old when she had gone to the

1948 Olympics. Mae knew exactly how intimidating the whole process could be.

Mae said, "Skeeter, baby, you want to make the United States Olympic Team?"

Wilma said, "I sure do."

"Now look," Mae said. "If you're gonna make this boat I'm going to tell you what to do. When that gun cracks, I want you to lay right on my shoulder. If you stay right on my shoulder, you can make this team."

Wilma murmured something in response, and they lined up by their blocks. Wilma was in the third lane, with Mae a few lanes over, another factor that added to Wilma's concern, as the two were used to training side by side. The gun fired at the start, and Mae was off the blocks first. Wilma said, "I looked up to find her and she was a long way in front of me, so I said to myself, 'I am going to try to catch her.'"

Mae stayed out in front for the first 150 yards, then Wilma started to catch up, right on Mae's shoulder, where she was supposed to be.

"Coming down that straightaway . . . it looked like a big truck pulling up beside a Volkswagen," Temple said. "Mae was just churning those little legs."

They ran around the last turn and Wilma pulled slightly ahead. Mae said, "As we came off the turn, Skeeter was in front of me. But she turned to look back, and when she did, I beat her to the tape by just inches." It could have been that look, or it could have been the lean at the tape that Wilma hadn't yet learned, but both Wilma and Mae finished the race at 24.1 seconds, tying the American record, with Lucinda Williams coming in third, all three qualifying ahead of former Olympian Barbara Jones again. Mae and Lucinda had each qualified for two events, and Wilma had earned her spot on the team.

Mae couldn't let Wilma's challenge go. After she jogged down the track a bit, she came back with her hands on her hips, staring Rudolph down.

"Now look. I told you to stay on my shoulder. I didn't tell you to act no fool and try to pass me," Mae said. "When I tell you to stay on my shoulder, you stay on my shoulder. You act like you wanted to pass me!"

Mae Faggs edges out Wilma Rudolph in the 1956 Olympic Trials. Special Collections and Archives—Tennessee State University

"I'll always believe to this day that if Rudolph had really wanted to go on and pass her—and [had] had the confidence and experience—she could have passed Faggs," Temple said. "Rudolph was a big, strong girl then, but she just didn't have the experience and finesse to be an outstanding runner at that time." After all, she was just sixteen running against a two-time Olympic veteran.

Barbara Jones came up short again in the 200-meter, ending her opportunity to travel to Melbourne with the US Olympic team. Barbara was shocked and devastated. Four years after she'd been the youngest Olympic gold medalist, when she was supposed to have been in the prime of her career, she was out.

Barbara was nursing a leg injury that may have slowed her down, but it was hard for her to understand how quickly her status had changed. "The reporters called me wonderful, fantastic, great, beautiful, all that when I had broken the world's record," Barbara said, "and when my leg didn't heal, all of a sudden, I was a has-been. I was a fluke."

Barbara had depended on Mae Faggs during the 1952 Olympics with outstanding results, and again in the 1955 Pan American Games in Mexico. "She taught me everything I should know about my starting blocks, the starts, everything," Barbara said. "Now, Mae Faggs, mind you, was five-foot-four. I'm five-seven-and-a-half. I'm still trying to use Mae Faggs's steps in the starting blocks. I'm trying to use her stride, and I'm trying to do everything that Mae did, because she was so great. And I beat her in '55."

Barbara asked her friend for advice.

Mae responded honestly. "The thing for you to do is to come on down to Tennessee State and learn what training is all about," Mae said.

It was advice that Barbara took to heart.

"When I was running for CYO [Catholic Youth Organization], I was running against the Tigerbelles," Barbara said. "I would see Mr. Temple, and I would see the discipline he had toward the Tigerbelles. It was awesome to watch him, and it was awesome to watch the girls. He didn't have to do anything, he would just nod his head, and I noticed the girls would know exactly what to do."

It would be four more years before Barbara would have another chance to redeem her status. But she was determined to try.

At the end of the Olympic trials, six Tigerbelles were placed on the US Olympic team, a feat previously unheard of. At best, most programs could hope to send their top competitor; no single program had ever sent such a large contingent. No one had thought it was even possible.

It was time for the Tigerbelles to prepare to travel to the opposite ends of the earth, for the biggest competition of their lives.

Each of the women had their own preparations to make, so after being congratulated in Nashville by the president of Tennessee State, Walter Davis, with the local press, they each went to their homes to rest and regroup for the month before training began.

Edward Temple did his best to help them get organized, writing out training plans and giving instructions, but he would not be making the

1956 Olympic Tigerbelles L to R: Mae Faggs, Wilma Rudolph, Lucinda Williams, Margaret Matthews, Isabelle Daniels, Willye White, Ed Temple. Temple Archives

trip with them. The coach for the Olympic team was chosen by the AAU, and Temple, being a relative newcomer, was not considered for the job.

Sending his team off on their own was excruciatingly painful for Temple. He had to trust that someone else would take care of each of them the same way that he would, when he suspected, even knew, that they couldn't. His only solace was that the coach of the women's team would be Nell Jackson,[1] a former Olympian from 1948 and a Tuskegee graduate.

Jackson would have a lot on her plate, being the first Black woman to coach an Olympic team with the short resources Temple knew would be available to her. It wasn't just a matter of keeping everything straight—schedules, locations, training, meals, lodging, travel, equipment,

---

1. Nell Jackson won two national collegiate titles in 1950 (200m and 4x100m relay) after her participation in the 1948 Olympic Games. She was the first Black coach of a US Olympic team in 1956, and was inducted into the US National Track and Field Hall of Fame in 1989 for her contribution to the sport.

35

uniforms—all the hundreds of tiny details they weren't used to managing on their own. It was also about sending the young people who had been entrusted to his care off to the most challenging competition of their lives on the other side of the globe, where anything could happen to them. Mae Faggs was the only Tigerbelle that had traveled out of the country at all, so Temple depended on her more than ever.

Wilma was the youngest of a group of very young and inexperienced travelers and needed everything from a passport to appropriate clothes for the various events. Word spread through Wilma's hometown of Clarksville about their local Olympian, and the community showered her with support. Knowing Wilma's humble circumstances, one family called her high school coach and said, "Bring Wilma downtown, let her buy some clothes and some luggage so she can go to Melbourne in style, and we'll take care of everything."

Leaving the Nashville Airport for Melbourne L to R: Lucinda Williams, Margaret Matthews, Isabelle Daniels, Willye White, Wilma Rudolph. Temple Archives

Temple helped secure Wilma's passport and gave it to Mae Faggs for safekeeping, telling her, "Wilma, you lose this little thing, and you may never get back home." Mae was also given the responsibility of the hot plate, straightening comb, and curlers for their hair. Temple told her, "You take care of these girls' heads." Isabelle Daniels said, "She did, and she washed our hair in the dormitory and got [us] fixed. Our hair would look nice because Mr. Temple wanted us to look like young ladies."

Temple brought the team to the airport with a fair amount of fanfare for their send-off. They were dressed impeccably as they headed to Los Angeles, where they would train before going on to Melbourne. A photo captured the moment, the women lined up and proud, ready to go off into the world, representing their community well.

"I think we looked kind of cute when you see that picture, the six of us," Margaret Matthews said. The last thing Temple said to her revealed one of his main worries: "Take care of Skeeter."

Temple sent them off with a letter to be opened when they arrived. He wrote, "Always remember what you are out there for. Don't forget people want to see you fail. I want them to envy you. So, win."

CHAPTER 4

Melbourne

THE TWO-DAY FLIGHT TO MELBOURNE WAS THE FIRST TIME ON A PLANE for most of the group, but Wilma especially was racked with nerves. She didn't touch the food on her meal trays, worrying that she would have to pay for it, and being too nervous to eat anyway. Mae and her other teammates happily helped themselves to her tray, picking at her food every time they walked by.

As the hours passed over the Pacific Ocean, Wilma thought she was in a dream. "It was only a couple of years ago that I couldn't even walk right, much less run. It was only a couple of years ago that I was going back and forth from Clarksville to Nashville for treatments on my leg. Now here I was on this big, chartered jet going off to another country as one of the fastest women in the whole world."

It was clear that Wilma was overwhelmed. The women's track and field team traveled with the men's basketball team, and captain Bill Russell, the standout all-American inventor of the alley-oop, knowing Wilma was the youngest on the entire team, looked out for her like a daughter.[1]

Willye B. White, also sixteen, was just as naive and inexperienced, but her scrappy nature kept her from appearing vulnerable to the group.

---

1. Bill Russell graduated from the University of San Francisco in 1956 as a two-time national champion and signed with the Boston Celtics. He delayed his official start with the Celtics to play on the Olympic team, where he could have also qualified as a high jumper, having tied gold medalist Charlie Dumas in the 1956 West Coast Relays. Russell was considered the first Black superstar in the NBA and one of the all-time greats, winning eleven NBA championships over the course of his career.

"I thought I would never get home," Willye said of the flight. "When you [woke] up, you were over water, when you went to sleep, you were over water. And when you landed, you landed in water." Willye's first time seeing the ocean was flying over the vast expanse of the Pacific. She had never heard of Australia before the trip and had no idea where she was going or what it would take to get there.

Even for Lucinda Williams, who at eighteen, with her first year away in college under her belt, had gained a little more independence, the trip was "unsettling." She wrote to her mother confessing she was homesick, and wondered if this really was what she wanted after all. This was a rare moment of doubt for Lucinda, whose steady drive almost always outweighed any hidden insecurities. "We didn't know that this [was] big league," Lucinda said. "That the world was watching."

Isabelle Daniels couldn't believe how far she had come. "Who would have ever thought this girl from Jakin, Georgia, would end up in Australia?" she said. Isabelle's childhood, while modest, was probably one of the most secure of her teammates. Her father was a successful farmer of corn, tobacco, peanuts, and cotton and drove a school bus. Her mother had gone to college and was a respected schoolteacher. Isabelle was the youngest of nine children and loved to roughhouse with her brothers, who nicknamed her Tweety, because she chirped like a bird as a baby.

Tweety was taught to behave like a proper little girl and discouraged from running and playing outside with her brothers. One summer a pig got into their garden, wreaking havoc on their summer vegetable crop. Her father called to two of her older brothers to chase down the pig. The boys each tried unsuccessfully to pin down the animal, until Tweety begged her father to let her have a try. She was the one to finally catch the errant beast, with her brothers and her father looking on, wondering where little Tweety's speed had come from.

Isabelle Daniels's speed became well known, and eventually earned her an invitation to join the summer program at Tennessee State after a stunning performance at the Tuskegee Relays. She was taught the basics of race techniques by her high school coach, Miss Scott, things as simple

Isabelle Daniels. Temple Archives

as being ready for the calls of "On your mark, get set, go." After she raced at Tuskegee, Isabelle noticed that her coach was visibly "teary-eyed." She was worried that her performance had made her coach upset, and when she asked her mother about it, her mother assured her that she was crying because she was so proud.

Isabelle Daniels and her mother caught a ride to Nashville with a couple of other teachers headed in the same direction, and Edward Temple met them outside the freshman women's dormitory, Wilson Hall. Her mother spent a couple of days with her, helping her get settled before she took the bus back to Jakin, content that her daughter was in good hands.

Coach Temple's rules were taught to Isabelle, and she remembered them in a slightly different format, emphasizing her own spiritual focus. "When I got to Tennessee State," Isabelle said, "Mr. Temple put down the rules of what we needed to do, and he made it clear that we were there first of all to honor God. He took us to church on Sundays. And the second reason we were there was to get our lessons. The third reason was to run track."

Isabelle trained hard back home in Jakin, running barefoot alongside her father's school bus to get in extra miles. But she leveled up when she joined the Tigerbelle program. When she finally got her first pair of spikes at Tennessee State, her feet hit the cinders so hard that sparks flew up behind her.

Isabelle Daniels and Lucinda Williams both came to Tennessee State the first year of the summer program, both earning work-aid scholarships and both becoming the ideal that Temple sought out for his team: dedicated, motivated young women who could be role models and leaders. They also had the tendency to leave their peers in a wake of dirt.

Once the team settled into the Olympic Village, their fears began to dissipate, and new views on the world challenged their perspectives. For Willye, it changed her life. "I came out of a totally segregated area where that fourteen-year-old child had just been lynched in my hometown. Blacks and whites didn't associate. If they did meet, it was always in a confrontational manner, and the Blacks would always lose."

When Willye got to the Olympics, she got a taste of another life— another world that she had never known existed. A world where no one told her which water fountain she could use, where she could eat, or who she could eat with. Willye saw Black and white people living, eating, and dancing together. Before she got to the Olympics Willye "thought the whole world consisted of cross burnings and lynchings. After 1956 I found there were two worlds, Mississippi and the rest of the world." The rest of the world was a place she hadn't believed was possible, but she found it there in Melbourne among young athletes from countries around the globe. "Where Blacks and whites, they were friends. They touched. They were your roommates. You cried with them; you hugged them."

At the Opening Ceremony, Wilma met Betty Cuthbert, an Australian record holder who seemed poised to win, capitalizing on her experience and home-field advantage. Wilma was in awe of everything about her, most especially her custom spike shoes made of the softest kangaroo leather that cost between $20 and $30 a pair. The shoes felt as soft as melted butter, and Wilma would have given anything to run with them, but they were not in her budget. "I just ate my heart out," Wilma said.

Nell Jackson from Tuskegee was the women's coach, and the Tiger-belles all agreed that training with her was easier than it had been at Tennessee State, but they missed the discipline and structure that Temple kept around them. "I do think there was a psychological letdown in not having Coach Temple there," Wilma said. "All of us sort of felt it."

Mae did her best as a stand-in. But it was hard to keep the young women in check. Wilma hardly ate anything but hamburgers and soda, and Larry Snyder, the coach of the men's team, complained that the US women's team was keeping the men's team up late. It was true that the American women took advantage of the dancing in the Village. Isabelle spent most of her free time teaching "the bop" to the Italian and Canadian teams, most likely encouraging Willye White's antics while away from the stern gaze of Coach Temple.

But Wilma said the blame rested with the Australians, who lived up to their reputation as the life of the party. "Actually, if people want to know the real truth," Wilma said, "most of the girls in the compound weren't interested in men at that point; they were there for one reason— to do their very best, and maybe win, in the Olympics."

The Australians and the Russians loomed large as intense competitors. Isabelle, who qualified for the 100 meters, said, "I was nervous when they said, 'Take your mark,' but I had a scripture that I always read, 'The Lord is the light of my salvation, whom should I fear?'" Isabelle placed in the top three of each of the heats to make the 100-meter finals, where she placed fourth, barely missing a medal. The third- and fourth-place finishes were so close that Isabelle was brought to the podium for the bronze medal before the photo finish was consulted and she officially placed fourth.

Isabelle Daniels was the fourth-fastest woman in the world, and she became the first Tigerbelle to qualify in the 100-meter finals in the Olympics, because Mae had not been at Tennessee State for her prior two Olympics. "That's history right there for me," Isabelle said.

Lucinda put in her best effort, and that's what she had gone there to do.

"Well, you did your best with the competition because the Australians were there and the Russians," Lucinda said. "Because it's as emotional as [it is] physical. The mind-set is to be continually focused on the job at hand. Remember who you are representing and do the very best that you can. And have faith."

Both Lucinda and Mae Faggs were beaten in the early heats of the 100-meter.

Mae Faggs had another chance at the 200-meter but was busy keeping Wilma Rudolph from losing her nerve. Mae tried to calm Wilma by telling her to do everything she did, to follow her every move, and Wilma grabbed onto her like a lifeline.

"If I bent over to touch my shoes to limber up, she bent over and did the same thing," Mae said. "If I raised my arm, she raised her arm." Mae kept Wilma by her side for the 200 qualifying heats, believing her strategy was working.

During the race, Mae broke her own rule, turning her head to find Wilma coming up behind her, and called, "Come on."

Wilma replied, "I'm coming."

"I mean, she was blowing down that straightaway," Mae said. "I had to reach back and get some of those horses I didn't think I had to beat her." The two qualified for the next round, but were beat out by the finals, leaving Wilma more shaken than ever.

"I blew it," Wilma said. "I felt terrible. I couldn't eat or sleep. I felt like I had let down everybody back home and the whole United States of America." Wilma beat herself up for the next couple of days while she sat in the stands watching Betty Cuthbert win the 100, the 200, and the 4x100m relay, earning three gold medals. It was a feat Wilma believed she was capable of herself, and she set her mind on proving it. Wilma said to herself, "You've got four years to get there, but you've got to work hard those four years and pay the price."

Willye White and Margaret Matthews were competing in the long jump, and the rivalry between the two outsized egos had become more heated than ever. Margaret thrived on riling up her competitors, chirping and "goading her rivals into mistakes." And she also didn't apologize for wanting to win.

Willye, who had come in second only to Margaret in the Olympic trials, was out for revenge. "I didn't want to beat but one person," Willye said, "and that was Margaret."

Margaret Matthews was two years out of high school and running with Barbara Jones at the Catholic Youth Organization in Chicago before she was invited to the Tennessee State summer program in 1955, and she stayed on for the school year. While technically just finishing her freshman year, Margaret had earned some life experience by that point that helped her confidence on the team and in the Olympics.

Margaret was born in Griffin, Georgia, where her father was a farmer, but when the family moved to Atlanta, their survival was a struggle. Her mother was the main breadwinner, working at a laundry, and her father found intermittent work as a day laborer. They lived in a shotgun house in a tough neighborhood, and their lack of education hurt their job prospects. As a child, Margaret was often sick with a series of major viruses, including measles, whooping cough, and the mumps. She was the first of three siblings, and as soon as she could, she helped to earn money for the family. Margaret wore her mother's handmade flour-sack dresses and hand-me-down shoes.

"I really didn't know I was poor until I got to Tennessee State. There were so many students there who came from families with money. Some of them had a lot of nice things."

But Margaret was scrappy—a fighter, and a survivor. She was also surrounded by family and was well liked at school. Her mother was the oldest of twenty-five children, and her extended family lived in every other house on their city block. "She was a member of the King family," Margaret said. "Everybody in the community knew us."

She learned quickly that school was going to be a way forward for all of them, and she threw herself into as many activities as she could. She was the head majorette; the captain of the basketball team, winning All-State for three consecutive years; a member of the National Honor Society; and elected "Miss Howard High." Margaret became the first person in the entire family to graduate from high school.

"I have always wanted to be the top person in whatever I did," Margaret said. "And I don't mind working hard. I have worked hard from the first time that Coach Temple let me on that campus, and I have never stopped."

At the Olympics in Melbourne, however, Margaret seemed to have left her attitude in the States. Willye was also riddled with nerves, so she turned to the Bible. "I read the verse about have no fear, and I relaxed. Then I jumped farther than I ever jumped before in my life."

"For I, the Lord your God, hold your right hand; it is I who say to you, 'Fear not, I am the one who helps you.' "—Isaiah 41:13

Willye took her first three jumps and qualified over Margaret Matthews. Three more landed her into the top twelve. After her final jump Willye was in first place for a precious few minutes until she was edged into second by the reigning Olympic champion, Elżbieta Krzesińska, from Poland.

"Let me share something with you about the Olympic Games," Willye said. "The hardest thing in the world is to make an Olympic team. That's the hardest thing to do. The second hardest thing to do is to get in the top twelve. And the third hardest thing to do is to get a medal. Now, when you make an Olympic team—you've made the Olympic team. And then everything else is a bonus. And then, when you get there, you just say, 'Oh, god, please, let me make it into competition.' So, then you say, 'Oh god, please, just let me get a medal.' You don't care what color it is."

Willye earned a silver medal, making her the first American woman to ever medal in the long jump at the Olympics. "I didn't know what I had accomplished," Willye said. "I had no idea. The only thing I knew was that I was not in the cotton fields. That was it." The feat was all the more incredible because Willye was just sixteen, at her first international competition, in her first year of any competition outside of Mississippi.

The final event was the 4x100m relay. One of the runners with a bout of nerves had to be replaced at the last minute, allowing all four members to be Tigerbelles. Mae Faggs, Isabelle Daniels, Wilma Rudolph, and Margaret Matthews were on the relay. Mae, of course, took the lead. The last-minute change left little time for practice, and the team had trouble getting the baton pass right. They hadn't driven through the hundreds of necessary details to perfect and were passing blindly at full speed. Wilma said that if Coach Temple had been with them, "he would have been all over us the way we were passing the baton."

They made it through the qualifying heats in the morning, but they were a mess. They knew they could do better. Mae said, "Skeeter was upset. She thought she had run out of the passing zone. Margaret and Isabelle were down in the dumps because of our slow time."

So, Mae grabbed the team together, pulling them to a practice track, "and I said some terrible words to them. I said I didn't come all this distance just to go home empty-handed. You'd better move. I'm not playing with you." Mae knew what they needed was confidence, because they had it in them to compete. "Mae was the spitfire. I mean, she put the fire in 'em," Temple said. Isabelle Daniels agreed. "When Mae spoke, everybody listened."

The relay team pulled themselves together, and Mae got out of the blocks with a good start, handing off to Margaret Matthews. Margaret handed off to Wilma, who remembers passing two on her leg before landing the baton with Isabelle Daniels in the anchor leg. In another close finish, Isabelle nearly reached second place. All three medaling teams broke the world record.

The all-Tigerbelle 4x100m relay team earned a bronze medal, "which was doing pretty good for three inexperienced girls and one city girl." Temple said.

Lucinda Williams left Melbourne without a medal, and they all felt that they could do better. "Wilma wasn't happy with that bronze," Lucinda said. "She said it didn't shine like the gold." The long flight home from Melbourne left plenty of time for reflection. "That's when we set the goal. Okay, we'll be back in four years."

The 1956 Olympic Games were over, and the Tigerbelles came home with one silver medal for Willye B. White, and four bronze medals for the all-Tigerbelle relay team. They exchanged little gifts with new friends from around the world, hugging and saying tearful good-byes. It would be four years before they had the chance to meet again, and in four years of an athlete's life, anything could happen. Some would retire, many would get married and have children, begin their careers, suffer injuries. Some would not be able to make it back, but some knew in their hearts that they would.

Wilma didn't know where the next Games would be, but "I did have this feeling that wherever they were held, I was going to be in them."

The Tigerbelles wrote a letter to Coach Temple from the plane.

Greetings from seventeen thousand feet in the air. . . . Maybe we could have been faster, but . . . we were more proud to get our bronze medal than the first two teams were to get their medals. We really stood high on those steps.

Everyone wants to know, "WHAT DAY IS PRACTICE WHEN WE RETURN?" Smile.

Signed,

Isabelle "Tweety" Daniels, your anchor leg (I shall never be removed)

Wilma "Skeeter" Rudolph (your future star)

Aeriwentha Mae "Assistant Coach" Faggs (smile)

Margaret Matthews (your third leg, I shall not be moved)

Willye B. "Red" White (I'm in no hurry to go home)

And last but not least, your starter, Lucinda Williams (hope to stay there too!)

Tennessee State was quick to send out a press release upon their return, heaping praise on their Olympians:

The fabulous six scored three outstanding firsts in the history of the Olympics:

This was the first time that any school or club had had six members to qualify for Olympic competition in any sport.

This was the first time that all four members of the women's relay team came from the same team.

This was the first time that three teams broke the world's record in the same event.

Mae Faggs, Isabelle Daniels, Margaret Matthews, Lucinda Williams, Willye B. White, and Wilma Rudolph

In summarizing his team's activities, Coach Temple pointed out that notwithstanding Russia's Olympic top scoring (gained particularly in sports

1956 Olympic Team showing off their medals L to R: Willye White, Margaret Matthews, Mae Faggs, Ed Temple, Wilma Rudolph, Lucinda Williams, Isabelle Daniels. Temple Archives

where we had no entries), not once did a Russian girl top any of our girls in the competition they entered.

The 1956 Games was Mae Faggs's final Olympic competition. She decided to retire the moment she made the team, telling Wilma, "I think you've made it. You're ready to replace me now. You really beat me in that race. What took you so long to get there?"

"You see, Mae Faggs was like the mother of the team. And Mae had a philosophy: If you graduate winning, you didn't help anyone," Barbara Jones said.

"They broke the mold when Mae Faggs was born, because she helped all of us," Margaret said. "She was something like a second coach to us."

CHAPTER 5

Beginning Again

LUCINDA CAME HOME FROM MELBOURNE WITH A NEW PERSPECTIVE from her travels. "We had an opportunity to set goals," Lucinda said. "We knew what the Games were about now. We knew that we had to train just a little bit harder. We knew we had to focus, and we knew that we had to really put our mind to what we needed to do and how we needed to do it. So, we trained hard."

The young Tigerbelles moved on and went back to their lives. They had seen the Olympics and the path that was available ahead of them. They were more motivated than ever, and they knew what they had to do for the next four years.

Willye White went back to high school, having earned a new status as an Olympic medalist. People in the town of Money and at Greenwood High School expected that Willye would come home changed, and she did. But not in the way that they expected.

"I was still the same little wild teenager that left," Willye said. The teachers and administrators felt that she had elevated herself and shouldn't be hanging out with "the derelicts, and the drunks, and the lower standard of people," but Willye had a nose for authenticity, and she didn't sense it coming from the high-society people in Greenwood. "I would sit on the corners, and I would talk. . . . I would go down to the joints where they were hanging out, and that was taboo. . . . That created a lot of problems for me." Willye chafed against society's rules and felt that if she had earned anything through her experiences, it was the right to choose who she wanted to hang out with, and when.

Wilma went back to Burt High School in Clarksville and took advantage of her newfound popularity. She began dating her childhood sweetheart, Robert Eldridge, and the pair were king and queen of the school. Robert was a football star, and Wilma strutted around campus wearing his letter jacket with her straight skirt and bobby socks. They danced together in *American Bandstand* contests at school and had a ball.

Lucinda Williams, Margaret Matthews, and Isabelle Daniels went back to Tennessee State to finish their year and continue their training, and they found a new teammate waiting for them.

Barbara Jones had watched the Tigerbelles go to the Olympics without her. When she returned home, she discovered that her advocate in Chicago, Bishop Bernard James Sheil, had lost support for his program among political clashes within the Church, and her scholarship to Marquette University was revoked. Scholarships for all of the boxers and track and field athletes were transferred to gymnasts and swimmers, predominantly white sports, by the archbishop. Barbara was faced with the realization that she no longer had the support she had counted on, and she needed to reconsider her options.

Barbara was the youngest in her family, the only girl, so she was doted on at home—"spoiled," according to Coach Temple—and after her Olympic wins, she received special treatment from everyone, so when things turned on her, they turned hard.

Mae had given Barbara good advice when she hadn't qualified for the team, and Barbara listened. Losing the scholarship was the final insult that pushed her into what she knew was going to be a challenge, though she had no idea how much.

Barbara and her mother both knew that training with Ed Temple at Tennessee State was where she needed to be, but her mother did have some reservations. "One of the things my mom feared was for me to go from Chicago down south, because I was a person who would speak my mind," Barbara said. Her mother worried that her frank nature would put her at risk in the segregated South.

Despite her reservations about the location of the school, Tennessee State's undisputed success won out. Barbara's mother called Coach

Temple saying that she was looking for a new team, and Temple said, "Put her on the train tomorrow."

Barbara's parents were her biggest cheerleaders, but they also kept her feet planted firmly on the ground and guided her conscience. They lived in the Ida B. Wells projects in the South Side of Chicago. Barbara's father worked in a meat casing factory and earned a gold watch at his retirement for never being late or missing a day of work. Barbara's mother was able to stay home to raise the family, and she was the kind of mother, Barbara said, "who never missed a track meet."

Even though Barbara was the recipient of her parents' adoration, they expected big things from her. After her first Olympic win, her father had said, "Okay, what's next? If you're still doing the same thing this month that you did last month, then you're not growing."

After her gold medal win in the 1952 Olympics, Barbara had been the one to watch. Not only her family, but her entire community and the track and field world, had great expectations for her. Jesse Owens[1] gave her a medallion that she kept with her as inspiration, and he told her, "Always follow your dreams and do your best. Never settle for less."

That's what kept her moving, and that's what was going to get her back to the Olympics and her chance at redemption. Barbara resolved not to be left behind again.

Her father told her, "There's a time that you have to get out of the starting blocks and start being who you are as a person."

When she arrived at Tennessee State, Barbara thought her new teammates were going to be thrilled to see her on the team. She would be the new queen of the Tigerbelles. She was always the fastest and used to being the diva on her team. "And when I got there," Barbara said, "all of these divas are there. All of the women I ran against. Any one of us could have won that day, that's how fast everybody was." Barbara was just one in the pack of elite women.

---

1. Jesse Owens earned worldwide acclaim by winning four gold medals at the 1936 Olympics in Germany (100m, 200m, 4x100m, and long jump) and was considered one of the great all-time sprinters and a trailblazer for Black athletes.

Barbara learned pretty quickly that she had to earn her spot on the team just like everyone else had, and she wasn't going to be the superstar anymore. They were all superstars.

"Mr. Temple was the type of person who didn't stand for anything. You had to follow his rules," Barbara said. "I mean, what kind of man could have all those divas and be able to stay in control?" Temple's presence and dominance loomed large over Barbara, so much so that she hardly noticed that he was less than a decade her senior. "We thought he was 100 years old, the way he trained us," she said.

"It took her awhile to get adjusted to us," Temple said, but she became well-loved on the team. The team wasn't set up for divas—they were taught, and coached, and shown how to lift each other up.

"We were no longer CYO and PAL [Police Athletic League], this team versus that team," Barbara said, referring to the clubs some of them used to run for. "Now we were a team."

Temple was certain he would get more funding after their outstanding performance in Melbourne, but he was denied once again. The school was proud, the community was proud, the Tigerbelles were proud, but Temple was as frustrated as he'd ever been. He had gathered and trained the fastest women in the world, but when they got home, he had nothing more to give them. "You can't eat applause," he said. They still had to complete the work requirements to earn their tuition, and they still had to train on their dirt-and-cinder track. Meets were sparse, and travel even more so. Somehow, they had to stay at the top of their game, with resources gathered from thin air.

"It doesn't matter which area of the sports world you're talking about," Temple said, "high school, college, or international level—the women have always been deprived. It galls you twice as much when you're accomplishing so much, proving yourself, and still have to take a backseat, whether at home or abroad."

The administration heralded their accomplishments, but it was still the women and still track. There was money in the budget for football and basketball, and that's about it. Those were the sports that packed the stadiums and brought in the receipts. Those were the sports that people talked about and wrote about. Not women running around a track.

It seemed at times as if they were running in place, and their loads were heavy. But Temple was determined to make it work, and so were the Tigerbelles. In addition to coaching, Temple taught two sociology courses, and ran the campus post office with his wife, Charlie B. The Tigerbelles kept up their grades, worked two hours a day to pay their tuition, and didn't miss a single minute of practice. They were back to the daily grind. The unglamorous work that built will, stamina, skills, and that created champions.

Even though they were Olympians, they were students first. Lucinda Williams took her schoolwork every bit as seriously as her running. She was entering her sophomore year, and already setting her sights on graduate studies. "Well, it was kind of tough," Lucinda said, "but I knew even as a youngster that the way in which I could get a college education and travel, which I had always dreamed of, was to stick it out. There were many days when I wanted to quit, and go back home, but I did not want to disappoint my family."

During her childhood, Lucinda's parents were janitors at the segregated school for white children in Bloomingdale, Georgia, and Lucinda would tag along with them sometimes while they worked after school. Even as a young child, Lucinda was aware of the differences between the school she and her friends went to and the one reserved for the white children. While she helped empty the wastebaskets, she would fish out pencil stubs that had been casually thrown away, bringing them home to share with her friends the next day. Lucinda believed deeply that education was the key to a better life, and she put in the effort to keep her grades high.

"When you came to know her," Temple said, "you realized she was going to be an achiever. She has proven it on and off the track." Lucinda took great care with her personal appearance, leading the team to always act and dress as ladies. Her dorm director commented that she was always perfectly pressed and presented, and Temple said she deserved a "Miss Clean" award. It was the kind of attention to detail and dedication that set Lucinda apart and made her a leader among her peers. This level of self-control and discipline had been so ingrained in Lucinda that she brought it to every aspect of her life, excelling on all fronts. The flip side to perfectionism is often anxiety, and Lucinda gained comfort from her family, both those at home in Georgia, and her new family in Tennessee.

Temple was aware that having to stay over the summer for training put extra pressure on the women. They could be with their families, helping out at home, or earning some much-needed cash for the school year, but these women had a higher calling. Truth be told, he liked having them over the summer because they had the entire day to work, as opposed to the school year, when there were so many other things they had to do. Some of them even squeezed in time for a social life and a sorority, although he couldn't imagine how.

The summer practice started with a boot camp so intense that it would not even be allowed in today's college programs. The team woke up at five a.m. and ran a five-mile cross-country trek, repeated twice more in the day for two solid weeks, all in high-top sneakers, to add just a little bit more pain. Boot camp was followed by hill sprints, midday hauls in the suffocating Tennessee summer heat, and hours of tedious drills on the track.

The hills around Nashville create a kind of bowl of humidity that traps the heat near the ground. Running day after day in this soupy mess wears anyone down. Still, Lucinda didn't believe Coach Temple was mean or hard; he just didn't play. He'd often tell them, "I already got mine, now you gotta get yours."

Three times a day they ran miles and miles on dusty trails in the suffocating humid heat. The high-top Converse basketball shoes they had to wear didn't help, either. Wilma claimed she weighed them once, just so she could finally see what kind of torture she was having to endure. They weighed two pounds. Each. Lucinda was prone to shin splints, so she taped up her legs every morning to fend off the pain, and peeled the sticky, sweaty mess off every night. Lucinda's daily taped ankles earned her the nickname "Lady Dancer," because she ran taped up like a racehorse.

In between laps they stopped to drink out of the hose by the Ag building that was used to water the pigs, and in the late afternoon when their uniforms were already drenched with sweat, they ran circles underneath the sprinklers until they were soaked with the cool water, making their socks sag around their ankles. Then they headed right back up the hill.

"At first, everybody does everything. It doesn't matter if you're a sprinter, middle distance runner, long distance runner, high jumper, long jumper, or whatever, you'll work out in heavy shoes running the hill and cross-country," Temple said. They ran cross-country not for competition, but to build their endurance. Even sprinters needed endurance. In a big meet, they would run several events in a day, and to maintain top speed from the beginning to the end of the day took as much stamina as any distance run. At that speed, each run was as hard as a solid mile.

Cross-country running in weighted high-tops would challenge the resolve of even the most dedicated, so Temple followed along in the car with his binoculars to keep tabs on the group and make sure they weren't cutting corners.

"You know, we did not have weights," Barbara Jones said. "We were not in a weight room, never picked up weights. Our drill was running through the cow pasture. They had hills, they had a fence you had to go through. You had to pass the cows, and you had to, at the end, run up a steep hill. Now what made this very difficult for us was that Mr. Temple was on top of the hill with binoculars, looking down. If you stopped, you had to do it again."

Teammate Shirley Crowder said, "One day we thought we were going to get slick on him. We were running through the cornfield, and we sat down for a while and chatted, played around, then we're going to finish the course. We start up the hill, and who should we see standing up on top of the car? Mr. Temple with his binoculars. As soon as we got there, he said, 'Hit it again.'"

"We didn't know at first that he was looking at us," Barbara said, laughing. "We thought, well, he's way back there, so we're talking and having a good time, and when we got to the hill, we were"—Barbara huffs and shakes her head, mimicking how tired they were claiming to be—"oooh, that was hard, Mr. Temple. And he said, 'I know, but just do it again.'"

Any fooling around was automatically met with extra laps. They'd been caught, and they understood the consequences. It was always more running.

"We knew then if you stopped, you had to do it again. And it was like twenty-five minutes." Barbara shook her head at the memory. "That was such a steep discipline that it almost made you want to quit. Because at the end, you're tired, and you have to run up this steep hill, and there he was. There he was."

"There's a song the girls sing while they do their warm-up exercises," Temple said, "and the phrase they keep singing is, 'It's so hard to be a Tigerbelle. . . . It's so hard to be a Tigerbelle' Well, let me tell you something. It's awful hard to be a Tigerbelle coach," he said, including always having to stay one step ahead of any antics.

"Oh yeah, I resented a lot of things Mr. Temple did," Barbara Jones said, "but you never told him that. You just felt it. But, like I said, it was awesome. And you almost had to be there to understand how he could train. He was so laid-back. He said very few words, but his eyes said everything. His actions of his head, you know." Barbara cocked her head to the side with a look that seemed to say *You'd better get yourself in line, and quick.*

For the first two weeks they worked hard, "rough training," Temple agreed. Then they dialed it back a little to focus on the details. Two weeks of twenty miles a day made them strong enough to handle anything Temple threw at them.

"We ran hills and mountains," Willye said. "The first day at practice, we had run this hill. I said, I don't believe this. There was nothing there but squirrels and raccoons. . . . So, you run up one side of the hill where you hit the cows and you ran down the other side where there were chickens and pigs."

Temple also started a rumor that there were snakes in the grass in those far fields, to make sure they didn't slack off when they got out of sight. They couldn't afford to slack off. Temple knew that they would have to work harder than anyone else, and behind every cut corner lurked lost opportunity, failure, or anyone wanting to trip them up.

Ralph Boston was on the men's team, and while they didn't practice with the women, they ran on the same hill down to a water tank in the distance. "Going to the tank from the campus, it was not tough, it was basically downhill," he said. "It was returning back to the campus from the tank that was tough. You coming up that hill . . . mmm. You've expended a lot of your energy, a lot of your chutzpah—oh wow."

Hard work for its own sake wasn't the motivation of all the suffering Temple put his athletes through. Temple used that dreaded hill for a specific reason: "I want them to know what it feels like to go up to it being tight. Then I want them to come down the hill loose and relaxed. I want them to see how it feels to run and let their body drift. This is the feeling I want them to transfer to the track." That effortless glide that the Tigerbelles seemed to all have in common was the result of hours and days running up and down that cursed hill on the Tennessee State campus. Only they would know how much effort it took to achieve the effect.

"How much pride does it take? Enough to sacrifice," Temple said. "You've got to hurt. This means that when you can't possibly run any further, you reach back, get something else, and keep on going. When the average person feels like she can't keep going, she stops. 'I'm tired' is not the time to stop—it's the time to push. Giving all isn't enough—you must learn to give just a little bit more."

CHAPTER 6

Blood, Sweat, and Tears

BARBARA JONES WAS ALWAYS DRESSED TO PERFECTION WHEN SHE strutted across campus. She wouldn't be caught outside her room without being fixed up, unless she was at practice. "We were confident, competitive, and very cocky on the field," Barbara said, "but off the field we had to be ladies." The priorities to Barbara were clear, and she ticked them off on her fingers: "Had to have your hair beautiful, go to school, go to the library, then ten o'clock in the dorm." People on campus would say, "Here comes Barbara with her gloves and her hat and purse going to church."

But there was no amount of primping that could protect her feet from the brutal miles at boot camp. The heavy Converse basketball sneakers they were forced to run in irritated Barbara's feet, and she became hobbled with angry, swollen toes. Barbara had logged hundreds, maybe thousands, of miles, and it wasn't the first time her feet were bloodied. It was the work behind the glitz and glamour of being awarded medals and being doted on by famous athletes like Jesse Owens. Making the Olympic team again would make all the suffering worth it, so she pushed through. She was desperate to reclaim her former glory, ingrown toenails and all.

Barbara showed Coach Temple her injuries and he sent her to the doctor, telling her to get one ingrown toenail cut out at a time. But between his directive and the excruciating procedure, she was second-guessing her coach. Why should she have to double the pain when she could get it all done at once?

So, Barbara watched as they pulled the nail away from her flesh on both of her big toes, slathered them with ointment, and wrapped them up in big bandages. She shuffled back to practice, her bandages broadcasting her choice like a flashing white light.

Temple caught sight of her and raised his voice in a high, slightly mocking voice. "Oh, but you got both feet done. I told you to get one."

"I didn't see the need—" Barbara started, defiant.

"Oh, but it's practice time," Temple said.

"Mr. Temple, I can't run—" Barbara said, pleading for his sympathy.

"Oh, yes, you can."

Temple refused to give her an inch. He left practice, going straight to the gym and returning with a pair of men's basketball shoes, big enough to cover her bandaged feet.

"Here, put these on." Then he pointed to the track, pushing her right back into practice.

Barbara called home crying and told her parents she was quitting, as she admitted she did every couple of months. She had been working hard and thought she had earned the right to do whatever she wanted, but she was no longer the person in charge.

Her mother said, "Okay, well, you can come on home, but let me ask you a question."

Barbara said, "Yes?"

"Mr. Temple asked you to get only one foot done at a time, right? Do you know why he asked you that?"

"No. I didn't see the need to be in pain twice," Barbara said.

"But what about Nationals. Isn't that coming up?"

"Yes," Barbara said, her voice slightly less adamant.

"Doesn't he depend on you a great deal for the hundred and for the relay?"

"Yes," her voice even quieter.

"Well, do you think you're being fair to the team? Doing what you want to do?"

"No," Barbara stuttered out her answer, knowing that her mother spoke the truth.

"Well, you have to pay the consequences for what you did. He was right. You have to practice. If you had done only one foot, you could have scooted. But you did both. So, who do you think is right?"

Temple described Barbara as being hotheaded at times, and thought one of the main things she needed to work on was her attitude. He knew about all the calls home and relayed a harsher response from Barbara's mother when Barbara complained about Temple specifically. He said Barbara's mother wrote, "Shut up and stop complaining. You just have a bad case of Temple-itis, and you're staying."

Barbara stayed, as she always did, and suffered through the work. She was earning the training and discipline Mae Faggs told her she lacked. It didn't come easily, but Barbara was making progress—even if it didn't feel like it every day.

Each day the temperature rose with the sun, and all the dew on the ground evaporated to make the air as thick as mud. "It was so hot you couldn't walk on the ground in your bare feet." Willye said. This was something coming from a girl who was famous for running barefoot in races all through high school in the Mississippi Delta.

Temperatures were regularly in the high-90s range, and the tiny cinder pebbles of volcanic rock that were smoothed along the track's surface would absorb the sun's heat so that their skin would burn if they touched it directly. "The sun was so hot down on that track that they had to put tape on their knees and tape on their fingers to get down on [their] mark. That's how hot it was out there," Temple said.

It was the kind of work that developed the inner grit that couldn't be taught. Willye said that if a person was working that hard, they weren't part of the norm. "Nobody is gonna force you to get out of bed at five o'clock in the morning; no one is gonna force you to perform when you're injured. This is inbred, this is inborn. This is within you."

Every now and then, an afternoon storm whipped through the campus and forced the practice indoors. They didn't have an indoor facility for training, so they used the gymnasium.

Practicing in the gym irked Coach Temple. Most of the other clubs and schools they competed against had an indoor track. He hardly even had one outdoors, but his girls had to make do. "You just have to do the best you can with what you have, so I refused to let the girls use the poor condition of the track for an excuse," Temple said. "Being used to inferior facilities means that we can only go up when we run somewhere else." Temple knew the extra challenges gave them grit, but it was tough to overlook the potential disaster of the makeshift facilities. A wet streak on the hard wood of the gymnasium could cause a devastating injury.

Injuries meant lost practice time, and sometimes even critical competitions missed. Ralph Boston first came to Tennessee State in 1957 and saw Wilma rehabbing from a pulled hamstring from a meet in Philadelphia. "I remember seeing Wilma walking around the track with an umbrella when it was drizzling. I hadn't heard of her then," Boston said.

The sight of Wilma, walking alone in the rain, spending time on the track in whatever capacity she could, even though she was injured, helped to set the expectations that Boston would carry through his own career. He wasn't aware, but must have sensed from the melancholy scene, that Wilma hated to be sidelined, especially with physical limitations. For those that did know Wilma's history, which included polio and a leg brace, even the smallest injuries were cause for concern. "I remember them sitting there watching," Boston said as Wilma was "working on that bad hamstring."

But time was short, and they would work where they could. Everything was preparation for the big meets and there was no time for complaining. When a storm passed through campus Temple and his assistant coach, Samuel Abernathy, Mr. Ab, hurried the team inside where Howard Gentry Jr. was often playing in the gym. "When the track team came into the gymnasium," Gentry said, "everybody had to leave. I'm talking about students, coaches—if you weren't a track person you had to get out of there and they closed the door and they would practice."

On one rainy day Mr. Ab came in to clear the space. A couple of kids shooting hoops quickly complied with the request, along with a handful of students spread out on the benches with their notebooks out for study.

Everyone made way for the team. They were the queens on the Tennessee State campus.

A group of children, the offspring of faculty and staff, scampered away, but Howard Gentry Jr., known by the Tigerbelles as "Little Howie," decided he wasn't going to leave. He stayed in the rafters of the stands and watched the practice. He knew Temple saw him, but he didn't put him out.

"Gentry." Coach Temple singled out the boy. Temple knew him as the son of athletic director Howard Gentry, the man who determined his annual budget.

"Gentry, come down here," Temple called to him.

Gentry rushed down to the court, sure he was in trouble.

"You think you can hold the door for us?" Coach Temple sized him up as if measuring the strength in him.

"Oh, yes, sir!" Howie stammered, standing up straight and tucking in his stray shirttails.

The first pair of sprinters lined up in the far hallway. Howie's fist gripped the door handle like his life depended on it.

One side of the basketball court to the other wasn't long enough to measure even the shortest sprint, so the women kneeled down against the far wall of the basketball court, ready for the start.

Coach Temple fired off starting gun, the crack echoing off the walls, and the pair pushed off against the gym floor and ran.

They sprinted across the length of the basketball court, straight up the middle. By the time they reached the door that Howie held open, they were at full speed, rushing past him mere inches away. They flew at such a speed that the wind from their wake nearly pushed the child backward, but still he held on.

Temple explained the extraordinary practice simply: "We had to run through open doors to practice a 50-yard dash," Temple said, "and then you had to hit the wall within 10 feet. That's something else when you're running all out."

The women didn't compromise their speed at all in the short space. The only thing they had to adjust was their wind-down at the end of their sprint. Perspective in all things matters, and just like bringing a race car indoors, the intensity of the speed the Tigerbelles maintained was highlighted at such close quarters.

Little Howie considered the moment one of the greatest honors in his life. Not only was he allowed to hold the door open, but he was able to tell the grown-ups and older students that they couldn't come through.

"They would fly by," Gentry said. "I got to see women who were the fastest women in the world fly by my face at full speed. When I tell you they flew by, I mean, you could feel the wind." It was a moment Howard Gentry Jr. would never forget.

After two weeks of distance running in high-top sneakers, there was a buzz among the team when they finally moved to the track work. This was where they wanted to be, to fine-tune their skills. Their basketball sneakers could be traded in for spikes that ground into the cinders with a satisfying crunch.

Temple had each of the women try all of the events, even if they were sure they were better at one or the other. Things could change, and it helped to have a versatile team so they could cover a range of events, earning points across the board in competition. Eventually a natural split occurred that tended to separate the jumpers from the sprinters, or the sprinters from the longer distances.

In each event, there were plenty of critical skills to perfect, but the most complicated was the jumping. Whether hurdles or long jump, it took the highest level of skill to make a body sail through the air. To make it appear easy was a combination of strength and repetition; in other words, hard work.

Willye White studied the different types of jumps and practiced each to determine which was best for her. "There's a sail jump, a hitch-kick jump, and a hanging jump," Willye said. She described the hitch-kick as "you walk in the air," and the sail as "you put your feet out and you sail." Each jumper had to find her style by body type and natural instincts. Willye's jump was shifting from the sail to the hang as she perfected her form. "I learned the hitch-kick," Willye said, "only to find out that [this] was not my jump, because when I got in trouble, I would revert back to the hang." The combination of study and practice were exactly what it took to hone each athlete's craft.

It came from studying other performances, trying new techniques, seeing what worked, and making the most minute adjustments. Anything that would gain an inch would be tried by adjusting footing, ground speed, air positions, and landing positions.

The Tigerbelles didn't have a dedicated field event instructor, and Temple spent most of his time with his power sprinters. Not for lack of caring, but sprinting was his background; it was what he knew best. So, the long jumpers and the hurdlers were often left on their own, teaching each other, pushing each other, and comparing strategies—a practice that had to intensify the competition between Margaret Matthews and Willye White. Both Margaret and Willye were very strong sprinters, but they stood out with their power and lift with the jumps.

"Everybody can't be a superstar, I realize that," Temple said. "But I also realize that everybody can put forth a tremendous effort. And there is no use being here if you can't make a contribution." Temple was looking for "pure hearts and mental toughness," and the hard work they had to do served to "separate the weak from the strong."

If the jumpers didn't have exactly what they needed, they could band together, help each other, and figure it out.

CHAPTER 7

What Does It Take?

IN THE SUMMER OF 1958, THE TEAM PREPARED FOR ANOTHER SEASON of major competition. Though they now had five Olympians on the team, with Mae Faggs's retirement, the team still skewed to the young and inexperienced side. Temple had redoubled his recruitment efforts and had gathered several more promising prospects. People always asked him how he found his team, how he picked the winners, but it was more than just picking the fastest runners for him. It was spotting that elusive characteristic that a person could only be born with. It was a fire in the eye and in the belly. It was a sparkle that made someone stand out above any of the others.

What he would find was a quality that if trained and guided could make others follow, and then they could share that light that they had within them with others in their world. He saw what was special about them, no matter how much the world tried to drag them down. If they could see what was special in themselves, then they would never forget it, and they could teach others to find the special qualities within themselves, and on and on their light would shine.

The new team showed a lot of promise. They were pushing each other hard at practice, and the competition was fierce. Barbara worked hard to keep her ego in check, but Margaret Matthews loved to tease her. "I am really going to give you a beating today," Margaret would say, with Barbara getting "so rattled, her teeth would chatter."

Taunting or "woofing" between the teammates was a common occurrence at practice, but was absolutely prohibited in competition. The team was expected to show their dominance, not talk about it before or especially after the races.

Martha Hudson and Anna Lois Smith had both joined the Tigerbelles in 1957, and both came from Georgia. Martha was a sprinter, tiny and fast like Mae. "Why, you are shorter than I am," Mae said when they first met. "I have a name for you: Pee Wee." The name stuck, so much so that decades later, her friends had trouble remembering her as Martha. Isabelle Daniels was considering her own retirement, and glad to see a new crop of runners coming in fast. "Pee Wee is a loving person," Isabelle said. "She will do anything she can to help you."

"Pee Wee!" Ralph Boston said. "She was the tiny one. You wondered, how does somebody that small run so well. But she did. They raised them well down here in Georgia, oh yes, they did."

Temple had a scout in Georgia, Marian Perkins Morgan, who sometimes worked at Tennessee State with the summer program while she earned her master's degree. During the school year she was a coach in Atlanta at David T. Howard High School, a perch that allowed her to keep an eye out for talent. Temple called her "one of the best women coaches I ever worked with," and said he "learned a lot from her for her very calm, but firm approach. She was really tops." Morgan promoted Lucinda Williams, Margaret Matthews, Martha, and Anna, and later, Shirley Crowder. She knew what Temple was looking for: talent, character, and strength.

God hadn't made Martha tall, but she was fast and strong, and like many of the other Tigerbelles, she relied on her faith to get her through tough times, of which she had plenty. Martha was born in the southeast part of Georgia, the pine forest region, where her father was a truck driver for a factory that processed rosin, turpentine, and other pine products. Later the family bounced back and forth between Georgia and South Carolina, with Martha and her mother being the consistent caregivers for her two young brothers. Martha excelled in school and in track, where she regularly beat Lucinda Williams in the statewide meets, and she was invited to the summer program at Tennessee State. She was valedictorian of her high school class, and only one of four out of the class of twenty-four that attended college.

"She was without a doubt the strongest little person that I have ever seen," Temple said. "She was a real fighter, but you'd never hear her complain." Martha knew Mae Faggs as a junior runner before she came to Tennessee State. "My big ambition," Martha said, "was to beat Mae just once, but I never did."

Anna Lois Smith also had her family challenges, moving several times with her father, who was chasing construction work. She was coached by Marian Morgan, who took a special interest in her, encouraging her to go to Tennessee State. Anna was more reluctant than most members of the team. Track was not her first love, and she knew that she would have to put her all into it to succeed. "She was a good student and a hard worker," Temple said of Anna, "but she just didn't have that fire for track all the time. Some were crazy to compete, and others were not. Don't get me wrong, though . . . she was dedicated enough. . . . She just didn't always want it the same way the other girls did."

Anna admitted that her real interest was basketball, and with track, she preferred the long jump over the sprints. She was often caught in the middle of the intense competition between Willye White and Margaret Matthews, the two regularly chasing and setting national records.

Anna's natural talent and work ethic kept her at the elite levels of competition. Her mother and her high school coach encouraged her to grit it out for the education and the experience, and she did, pushing and often beating the other women in practice and in the meets.

Anna would have been a top-tier college basketball player had women's teams even existed at that time, but she used the skill that she had in the form that it took to take her the farthest in her life. In the late 1950s, it was laps around the track and being a Tigerbelle.

Regardless of what was available to women at the time, Temple knew how to work with what he had been given. He gathered the best, and in return, taught and molded them, guiding them in sport and in life. The women on his team were exposed to opportunities they had never imagined.

"Tennessee State is not this good because it is geographically located in some pocket of natural track talent. It is this good because of Ed Temple," wrote Barbara Heilman in *Sports Illustrated*.

Temple was at the prime of his talent and education as a coach. He'd learned what it took, and knew how to teach it, and he stuck to the strategies that were racking up the wins.

Temple had a standard pose in practice: hands on his hips and eyes on his team. He wore slacks and a collared shirt, a cap and glasses to shield his gaze from the sun, and a whistle on a string around his neck. His clipboard and his well-worn stopwatch were always at hand, essential tools of his trade.

His most important tool was his coaching philosophy, which he described as "a mix of my experiences and influences from my middle school and high school coaches." Temple picked up strategies and techniques everywhere he went. "A lot of it was just me," Temple said. "I would never stop looking for new techniques or how to perfect old techniques. I just believed in my way of coaching."

There was overwhelming agreement that while Temple was tough, he was fair and kind. "Coach Temple never raised his voice at any of us. . . . We were treated like young ladies."

Temple didn't have to bluster and dominate; part of his genius was being able to play to his team's strengths. He took advantage of the competition among the teammates, and even encouraged it. Each of them wanted to win, and they ran against their biggest challengers every day. Daily practice was as intense as any competition they would face. "We ran hard against each other," Margaret said. "Going to a meet was the easiest thing for a Tigerbelle. Running in a national championship was easy. The toughest part, for me and the others, was in our practice."

Other coaches noticed the difference with the conditioning of the Tigerbelles. "One day we were at a track meet and another coach suggested to him that he sit at the finish line," Isabelle Daniels remembered about Temple. "But he said, 'No, I am not going to do that. I am going to sit at the starting line.'" The other coach thought the finish line was the right spot, "because if your girl fell out at the finish line you would be there to help her." Temple stayed at the starting line because, he said,

Friends and Rivals: Willye White and Margaret Matthews at practice. Temple Archives

"none of his girls were going to fall out." Daniels continued, "He never had to worry about that because we were in good shape. If we were going to fall out it was going to be at school during practice. We weren't going to fall out during a track meet."

"The time trials at practice were something else," Temple said. "No one would win the 100 two straight days. The teammates were the best of friends—until they got down to the starting line, and friendship went out the window."

Temple often ran the junior runners against the seniors, a strategy that worked in two ways. First, if the junior runners could compete against national and international champions, nothing would faze them when they got to the bigger meets. Secondly, the young girls kept the senior runners from getting complacent. The young runners were hungry, always striving to prove themselves and earn a spot on the team.

Every now and then the time trials took the form of an organized exhibition meet. The team was split into two groups and competed against each other for points and sometimes a few dollars for extra motivation, as if bragging rights weren't enough. It was coined the Blue and White meet, for the school colors. "When kids around campus heard there was going to be a Blue and White meet," Wilma said, "they'd all turn out to watch."

The half-track they practiced on was wrapped around part of the football field, so the students filled the stadium seats knowing they were going to get a show. It was anyone's guess as to who would win any particular event. When crowds gathered in the Tennessee State stands, song would sometimes break out. The students would lean back and forth together in unison singing "A & I" to the tune of a gospel song, "Amen." ("A & I" was often used as a nickname for the school, referring to its formal title, Tennessee Agricultural and Industrial State University.) Sometimes the white kids from across town would come to watch the sports, but it wouldn't cause a problem. The students seemed to understand the reason—the superiority of the performance.

"There are so many white persons who have walked up to me and said, 'Man, I remember coming to TSU and going to those basketball games and seeing the greatest basketball I've ever seen,'" Howard Gentry Jr. said. "We were welcoming; we were not offended by it. It was okay."

Football and basketball remained the priority sports on campus, despite the groundbreaking success of the Tigerbelles. There was a culture built around the two primary sports—cheerleaders dancing on the sidelines, families gathering before the games to share food and drink, stadiums full of spectators that bought tickets.

The lack of respect Temple felt at school was reaching a boiling point, and he believed a good deal of the problem stemmed from jealousy—not *from* him, but *of* him. The national and international achievements reached by Temple's team had yet to be matched by the men's teams in any other sport.

The Tigerbelles had gone to the 1956 Olympics essentially as a team. "We didn't realize at that time," said Howard Gentry Jr., son of the Tennessee State athletic director, "that nobody goes to the Olympics as a team. It's unheard of, and it's never happened again. But for us it was not unusual." Gentry considered the Tigerbelles the beginning of the golden era of sports at Tennessee State. "In 1956 when they went to the Olympics," Gentry said, "my dad was the head football coach, and the football team won the Black national championship." The basketball team also won the national championship each year between 1957 and 1959.

The way that the collegiate basketball tournaments were set up at the time was that the Black colleges and universities would have their own tournament, where the winner would then be invited to compete in the National Association of Intercollegiate Athletics (NAIA) championship with the rest of the schools. "So, you had to win the Black national championship [in order] to qualify to play in the NAIA tournament," Gentry explained. "They only took one Black team. So, they played two tournaments in a row." The physical strain on the team of playing in a full tournament before they met their competitors in the integrated nationals must have been intense, and still, they prevailed, winning both the Black national championship and the NAIA for three years in a row.

"What really is the thread between all of this," Gentry said, "is that everybody looked at Coach Temple and his methods of practicing and his successes and wanted to copy that in order to be successful." Football players began working out on the track, basketball players started running the hill. There was evidence of Tigerbelle strategies in every team on campus, and they all improved as a result.

There is no doubt that the basketball and football teams were right to be proud, and emulating Temple's strategies was part of the reason for their success, but the Tigerbelles were not reaping the benefits of their glory.

Still, the Tigerbelles ran on their "oval ribbon of dirt." There was no groundskeeping team taking care to keep what cinders they had available spread evenly across the dirt. It was Temple and his team smoothing and lining it themselves before the early-morning practices. Temple hitched a roller to the back of his station wagon and dragged it around the track, trying his best to level the tiny cinder pebbles raked over the ground into something that could be safely run on. "He goes down there with a shovel and a rake and works on it," Charlie B. said. "Then the football team comes out with those cleats. 'They've been on it again,' he'll come home and say. One day he went down, and somebody was trotting a horse around it. I've never seen him so mad."

Money in the budget was not increasing at the level it needed to be, but the expectations to maintain the elite level of success remained. "I'll never forget one time I was bringing [Wilma] Rudolph and Ralph Boston back from a meet in Madison Square Garden. I dropped Ralph off at his dorm and someone yelled out, 'Hey, Ralph! How'd you do?' 'Got first.' 'How far'd you jump?' '25 feet, 5 inches.' 'Aw, man, you ain't did nothing!'" Winning first was not enough if he hadn't passed his prior jump, breaking 26 feet.

Temple used his own money to purchase an eight-millimeter camera to help the team work on techniques. He had three major jumpers on his team, and not a lot of time or expertise to share with them. Margaret Matthews, Anna Lois Smith, and Willye White coached each other most of the time, and he knew it would be helpful for them to be able to review the film and make adjustments.

At a meet in Cleveland, Temple set up his camera with a view of the long jump landing pit. Another photographer set his camera up inside the pit, to get an aggressively close angle on the jumpers. The best of the athletes were jumping in the range of 16 feet, and he was just beyond. Willye sprinted down the runway and leapt to 19 feet, twisting in midair "to avoid spiking the man" and badly hurting her ankle. "So, on this film there is a record of the beginning of Willye's fine jump, and then blue sky, just a succession of clouds across the sky as the camera went right on shooting where Ed Temple dropped it." One can only imagine the fury that other cameraman caught from an outraged coach protecting his jumper. The incident prevented Willye from her next two attempts, causing her to come in third that day behind both Margaret and Anna.

Margaret Matthews was having the best year of her career, but she was also fighting a private battle with her coach. In 1957, after the Melbourne Olympics, Margaret secretly married Jesse Wilburn, a fellow Tennessee State student, and football star. The two of them were a major power couple on campus. She had been the first American woman to jump longer than 19 feet, in the same year that Jesse Wilburn ran 19 touchdowns.

The couple went to the courthouse for their wedding, and tried to keep it a secret from everyone, but didn't realize that they printed the marriage announcements in the paper. Temple was furious. He didn't even like for the women on his team to date, thinking that their social lives were simply a distraction from the considerable responsibilities each of them had otherwise. Men were the biggest distraction and could wreak the most havoc. Marrying the star football player in a school where football was king would not usually be considered a big problem, especially in the late 1950s, when marriages generally happened in young people's early twenties, but Temple held Margaret, his captain, and all of the Tigerbelles to a higher standard. "He finally accepted it," Margaret said. "He was really angry with me, but after all of that hullabaloo I became captain of the Tigerbelles [again] in '58."

"I wanted them focused on nothing but school, work and track," Temple said. "If a girl wanted to go out carousing around after I wore them out at practice, she was a pretty tough customer." But though he did his best, he couldn't protect his team from all the temptations and trouble that chased them.

Mr. Ab echoed Temple's philosophy: "Time to play. Time to work. If you can't distinguish between those two, you cannot become great. He stayed on both of those."

Wilma Rudolph and her boyfriend were getting serious. They were leaders of the Clarksville social scene, the football captain with the Olympic medalist and runaway basketball star. The two of them were spectacular together. He was taller than her six feet, a crack athlete, and had a smile that melted her heart.

No one ever talked to her about sex, so how was she supposed to know that a little fun with her boyfriend could end up putting everything at risk? She went to the team doctor with a stomachache, and he broke the news to her gently. She was pregnant.

Wilma was devastated. She thought her athletic career was over, and worse, she was letting everyone down—all of the people that had been cheering her on and lifting her up.

When she finally confessed to her parents, they were kind. Her father said, "Everyone makes mistakes. You hold your head high, and don't be ashamed." Her mother promised to stand by her and help where she could. But her dreams of a college education and more Olympic medals vanished. One of Coach Temple's most serious rules was having no mothers on the team, so Wilma was out. If anyone asked after her, they were told she was either "working on a tumor" in her stomach or sick with "appendicitis."

CHAPTER 8

On the Road

THE COLD WAR TENSIONS BETWEEN THE UNITED STATES AND THE Soviet Union were reaching their peak, and sports was an important part of both the US and Russian PR strategies. Russia was constantly criticizing the United States for racial inequities, and American officials actively sought out people of color to participate to counteract that narrative. But right or wrong, the most important thing was to win. It was considered a critical part of a cultural campaign against communism to prove that female American athletes could compete against the Soviet threat while being "ladies," something they implied the Soviet women could not do.

Temple had finally secured a slightly larger budget for travel in 1958, and the team was able to charter a bus for the trip to Morristown, New Jersey, for Nationals. The upgrade in travel from the caravan of station wagons to a chartered bus was a vast improvement. "We thought we was on a jet or something. Here we have a chartered bus. We done worked up to a chartered bus."

The mood on the bus was festive. The team was confident in their preparations, and ready to test their skill. The athletes took advantage of being out of the cramped old station wagons and sauntered up and down the aisles, keeping up a steady game of Bid-Whist, a card game that is a cross between bridge and spades, along with music, and plenty of chatter. Instead of navigating the roads, Temple was able to spend the time up front near the driver, going over his lists of athletes and their events, weighing their collective advantage against the stats he saw from the other teams and clubs. He placed them by event for the personal advantage of each athlete and also for the greatest advantage of the team. According to the most recent rules, each person could only enter three events, and to achieve the highest number of points for their team, he had to have at least two people in each event. It was a balancing act and a puzzle to piece together.

The 1958 AAU Nationals served also as a qualifier to make the national US team for an international tour of competitions in Russia, Hungary, Poland, and Greece. It would be the first time an American team would compete behind the Iron Curtain since before World War II.

Temple was feeling confident about his team's ability to qualify for the international tour, and for the first time, he considered being able to travel with them. Before leaving Nashville, Temple told Charlie B., "Pack my suitcase; if the team is going to Russia, I'm going, too." Mrs. Temple asked if he had received a letter inviting him to coach, and he said "No," but she packed his bags anyway.

Having a Black man coach a national team would be unprecedented, but her husband had done unprecedented things before, and he would have to keep on busting through those doors every chance he got, for as long as he could. It was the best way he had to fight for the rights of his team, for all of them. He was determined to be with them that time.

Temple brought a full roster of his junior and senior teams along with his assistant, Marian Perkins Morgan, the Georgia coach responsible for bringing half of the girls on the team to Tennessee State. No one could be sure if the help or the luxury travel had any effect, but the team outperformed expectations once again. The finalists in the sprints and the long jump were all Tigerbelles, and eight women were placed on the international team.

"We'd taken first, second, third in the 100, first-second-third in the 200, one, two in the long jump, won the hurdles. So that's when I put eight girls on the US team," Temple said.

Margaret Matthews was a standout at the meet, winning the 100-meter and the long jump and becoming the first American woman to break the 20-foot barrier in the long jump in national competition, crushing Willye White's record set two years before in the Melbourne Olympics. Tennessee State also won the 4x100m relay and their B-team came in second, giving Tennessee State the top eight sprinters in the country, and a new recruit, Shirley Crowder, won the 50-meter hurdles.

The hurdles were a particularly perilous event. They not only required the speed of the sprinters, but also the strength and spring to jump, as well as the intellect and body control to learn the complicated series of movements and to adjust them within a fraction of an inch with complete perfection of timing. The event is a near ultimate test of an individual's athletic prowess and endurance.

Of all the events, the hurdles also provide the most opportunity for disaster. Shirley Crowder competed at an elite level for years before she joined Tennessee State. In her early high school years, she ran with the rival summer program at Tuskegee where she won the AAU junior division in the 50-meter hurdles, setting a national juniors record. She earned a spot for the 1956 Olympic trials, and during the meet her coach asked her to sub in on the relay. While Shirley ran another runner stepped on her with the spikes, causing her to fall and twist her ankle.

The fall left Shirley badly shaken. There was just enough time between events for Shirley to watch her ankle continue to bruise and swell, and to worry. One race stood between this high school sophomore and the Olympic team. If she placed first, second, or third, she'd make it.

Shirley found her lane and prepared to start when an announcer called over the loudspeaker for an ambulance to be brought onto the field. "I was sure he was ordering that ambulance for me," Shirley said. The movement of the ambulance stayed in the back of Shirley's mind, but when the starting gun cracked, she got off to a good start. "I was leading up to the seventh hurdle. Then I did it again; I tripped over the hurdle." Shirley's Olympic dreams fell with her.

Like so many other Tigerbelles, Shirley came from Georgia. She was the youngest child of eleven. Her mother stayed home to care for her family while her father worked for the railroad. Shirley grew tall, running and jumping with her brothers and sisters. "I was driven by the act of competing," Shirley said. "I love competing—whatever it was, I wanted to be in the mix. My brothers were my first teachers."

The family moved to Atlanta by the time Shirley was in high school, where she attended Booker T. Washington High School and dominated the basketball team. "That little, long-legged girl play like a boy," people at the high school said of her. "I didn't know no other way to play," Shirley responded.

Shirley Crowder discovered the hurdles in high school when she was hanging out after classes watching track practice, waiting for her friends. A kid who had graduated a couple of years before was working out on the track and called up to her, "Shirley, what are you doing up there?"

"I don't know," she responded, "just watching."

"Come on, we're going to find you something to do."

He brought her down on the track and showed her how to jump over the hurdles, "the best he knew how," Shirley said. She didn't have the techniques down right, but she got over those hurdles with the height and the speed that she needed to beat almost everyone she ran against. Later, she would work hard to correct those early habits, but she said, "My technique was always off because it was hard for me to change."

Basketball was her first love, but her PE teacher, Emma Reed, was an early Tigerbelle who had attended the 1948 Olympics and encouraged Shirley to consider track. Shirley idolized Reed, who gave her "something to look forward to," and ultimately helped her get to Tuskegee and then to Tennessee State after graduating in 1957. Basketball wasn't available for women past high school, and track, she reasoned, would get her to college.

"I knew from jump street that I was going to college," Shirley said. "My mother had developed this plan that the older children would help her with those coming up." Shirley, the baby of the family with so many older siblings, felt a responsibility to all of them to prove that their efforts to support her had been worthwhile.

Shirley preferred the hurdles from the start, but she didn't have the training she needed, and her form left a lot of room for improvement. She figured it out on her own, her speed and determination alone earning her that AAU record. Even when Shirley arrived at Tennessee State, there wasn't any particular instruction for the hurdles, where the most technical skill was needed. Temple didn't have the hurdles experience, and he always focused on his sprinters, so he pulled in the assistant basketball coach, Richard Mack, who had been a college hurdler, to work with her.

Shirley had trouble adjusting to the rigor, like everyone else had.

"That first summer I wondered if I had made the right decision when Mr. Temple had us running up hills and through cornfields. In Tennessee it's so hot, you'd see the [heat] waves bumping off the ground. He'd have us running out there in midday. Our uniforms would get so wet, we'd just run through the sprinklers and then keep on running." Shirley wouldn't go home, though, "because I knew I had better stuff in me than that."

Shirley was busy creating a space for herself on the Tigerbelle team, and she was also struggling with the academic load. The educational foundation she'd had in high school hadn't quite prepared her for the rigor at Tennessee State.

It wasn't for lack of effort. She remembered being terrified when she received a C in high school, knowing she'd have to tell her mother. "I can't take this home," she told her teacher. "My momma will kill me." The teacher realized she had made a mistake and revised her grade upward, to Shirley's immense relief. "You just saved my life," Shirley told her teacher.

Shirley knew that giving up or failing either academically or on the team was not an option. "I knew I owed it to my parents to stick to it regardless. I knew I owed it to those people that worked with me so hard to stick to it. That's what kept me going. I just kept on going. Temple made it hard some days, but I kept going."

Shirley's struggles only highlighted one of Temple's primary motivations: to educate young Black women so that they could become leaders and uplift their communities. Wilma Rudolph's younger sister Charlene had joined the summer program as a high school student and said of Temple, "He cared about each and every one of his girls individually. He wanted them to be the best. 'Cause nobody really came from a family of any means. [For] many of them, it was the first time to go to school from their families, to get an education. It was real important that he educated young Black women to be strong and give back to their communities."

Charlene benefited from the relationship that had already been built between Wilma and Temple, but she felt honored to be accepted onto the team, even if she had not earned the title of Tigerbelle. "He was just a giving man with a big heart," she said, "but stern. When you love people, you are stern."

The women on the team also helped each other out and held each other accountable. "We really kind of monitor[ed] each other," Margaret said. They were expected to go to the library every night that it was open, and Temple would often drop in to make sure they were there. "If any of us sort of veered toward not going to the library, we would police each other. This is how we became so close. We were family at Tennessee State. We were like sisters."

If the Tigerbelles were like sisters to each other, Temple was universally considered the father figure. Barbara Jones said, "Mrs. Temple and Mr. Temple treated us like they were our mother and father." Isabelle Daniels agreed. "Like I said, Coach Temple was a father to us when we were away from home. He loved his Tigerbelles." Also, as any parent of multiple children knows, Temple knew that his attention needed to be carefully shared among his young charges. He purposefully spent the same amount of time talking to each of them, keeping constant tabs on their mental, physical, and spiritual health.

Performance and safety were two factors that remained paramount in Temple's mind. The reason all of their families had sent them off and allowed them to travel to places most of them had never dreamed of was to have the chance to make a name for themselves and get ahead in life. He promised—and they believed, to a person—that education was the key to that success, and their performance on the track made the education possible.

Temple got copies of each of their grades, and when their report cards were out, he would hold meetings as a group, and with individuals. He used pride as a motivation, announcing their grades aloud to the group, but also as an encouragement.

"He would have us all in the same room, and he would say, 'Report card time," Barbara Jones said. "And he would say, 'Barbara Jones, okay, you received this, this, this, this,' so you [knew] you had to do well. You didn't want everybody to know anything. And if you didn't have good grades, you had to go to the library. He had to see you in the library. C's, he didn't even allow C's. If you received a C, that meant you didn't work

Ed Temple looks over the semester report cards. Temple Archives

hard enough. So, he instilled A's and B's. That was it. My boyfriend and I, after dinner—straight to the library, five to nine. And then at nine to ten, we were in the rec hall, and then at ten o'clock he had to walk me to my dorm. And that's how it was, that was our life."

"If someone needed help with a class," Margaret said, "he would get that for you."

"I told them you can't run, jump, and throw forever," Temple said. "You have to have something in your head." The work-aid scholarships most of the athletes were given did not include the cost of textbooks, so they would keep and pass books down to each other. "The sophomores had to pass theirs down to the freshmen, and the juniors passed theirs down to the sophomores, and so forth. And we gathered books. We didn't get no books like they do in the NC2A."

The time had come for the coach of the national team to be chosen for the upcoming international tour. Temple knew that this was his opportunity to make his pitch. His team worried about having to travel and perform with a coach they didn't know, or who wouldn't necessarily respect them. Temple worried about anyone else being able to give them the level of attention and care that they deserved. It had been just two years since he'd sent six on their own to Melbourne, and he knew he would have been able to help them do just a little bit better. When mere inches could make the difference between first and third place, every bit, every advantage, was critical. This year, he didn't even have Mae Faggs to comfort and corral the team for him.

Temple considered the roster of women that had qualified, and eight of them were his. All of the sprinters, the long jump, hurdles, all of the marquee eventers were his team. There were "about twenty-something girls on the team," Temple said, "but the bulk of them were Tennessee State. In other words, we could have called the United States team Tennessee State's team."

They had earned leverage and power with their performances, and Temple looked to take advantage of it by tracking down his old friend, Frances Kaszubski.

Frances was easy to spot with her short, curly blonde hair, and at six-foot-four, she had a few inches on most of the men, including Temple. That height had helped her earn her own way to the Olympics in the 1940s for the discus, and must have given her an edge competing in a predominantly men's world of athletic administration as well. She was known to be tough, thorough, good at her job, and she loved winners.[1]

The coach of the New York Police Athletic League, Bob Magnum, was considered to be the top choice, with two others behind, but Temple made his case. "I came up here on a chartered bus," he said, "and it's returning to Nashville in the morning. I've brought a mighty good team

---

1. Frances Kaszubski participated in the 1948 Olympics with Mae Faggs and wrote a scathing complaint about the treatment of the women's team, particularly Mae, named derisively by Avery Brundage and others on the Olympic Committee as "the Kaszubski Complaint" before they dismissed the issues as "mental maladjustment."

up here, and if I'm not the coach of that team going to Russia, then everyone on my team is going back with me on that bus."

"She looked at me like I was crazy," Temple said, laughing. "You know, Frances was real tall, lookin' down on me."

There was a big white tent set up in the infield, where the powers that be were making their decision. Frances agreed to make his case, and Temple stood outside, watching as she went in and talked to the men who would decide his fate. A few minutes later, Frances came out and said, "Ed, you're it." Temple was going to be the coach, and she'd be his manager.

While Temple was finally able to travel with his team, and the AAU administration had recognized, albeit reluctantly, what Temple was bringing to the sport, there were still other issues to move past.

The AAU seriously considered leaving the women's team behind and taking only the men, because they worried that the Soviets would embarrass the US women with their supposed superior strength. The Soviet athletes were, by almost any measure, state-sponsored professional athletes, training full-time, year-round, a luxury that was clearly not afforded to American athletes, particularly women, and especially at underfunded educational institutions.

"We didn't have more than two or three track meets a year in this country," Temple said. The eight women from Tennessee State "had to compete against the country of Russia, the USSR National Team."

At the last minute, President Eisenhower's White House weighed in, tipping the scales in the women's favor, believing that sending a team of primarily "colored athletes" would counteract some of the propaganda that Russia was putting out about the racial tensions in America. More cynically, they suggested that if the women failed, it might not reflect on the entire country because they were, after all, only the women, providing another example of the exploitation of women and minority groups on both the athletic fields and in the country, overall.

Even though the AAU agreed to send the teams together, the men's national team still wanted to keep the men's and women's teams separate, feeling confident that the men would outperform the women against the Russians, and the women would only drag the scores down. The Russians, also believing that their women were superior, fought to have the scores tallied together to prove their dominance.

It was a "big argument," Temple said. "The Russians called themselves a national team. We didn't call ourselves a national team at that time. The men didn't want the women. We had the men's USA team, but they didn't want the women to go along because the women weren't as strong."

It was nothing new for the Tigerbelles to be fighting for respect and funding. Temple knew that the best way to prove their worth was with their performance. Times don't lie. Results don't lie. Sooner or later, he had to believe that truth would win out and his team would be seen.

"We weren't supposed to do well; we had no big names on the team. Of course, women's sports was minus zero then. We weren't zero, we were minus zero for attention." Temple knew different. He also knew he could help them perform, and he could help them prepare. They traveled to New York to meet up with the men's team and get the uniforms and gear they needed, and a few of them had to send home for their birth certificates to obtain expedited passports to leave the country for the first time.

"That was my first trip," Temple said, "and I didn't know what to expect, so everything was new to me." He was, however, impressed with the upgrade in travel experience, even from their chartered bus. "When you make the US team," Temple said, "then you travel first-class. First-class hotel, first-class airfare." Simply having new uniforms was something to be excited about. "When you wore a US sweat suit," he said, "that was the greatest thing in the world."

CHAPTER 9

Russia

BEFORE THE PLANE LANDED IN RUSSIA, THE TENSION GREW AMONG THE athletes and coaches. Another coach, Eddie Rosenblum, brought a big American flag and planned to wave it as they disembarked onto the tarmac. When the plane's door opened and a "big Russian soldier with a tommy gun stepped inside," Temple hoped his friend would change his mind. "Everyone suddenly became real quiet. You could have heard a feather float on that plane." Rosenblum's flag now looked even bigger to Temple, and he decided he'd let Rosenblum go first and see if he made it to the bottom of the stairs before he stepped out.

Interpreters were assigned to stay with the US team for the trip and informed them of the restrictions they were mandated to abide by, including a prohibition on photographs in certain places. They were also explicitly prohibited from venturing off on their own.

Normally, when the team traveled Temple tried to find a church to visit on Sundays, their faith being critical, he believed, to their state of mind. "All of the girls had brought their Bibles and set aside a quiet time for study," Temple said.

The Soviet Union was uniformly secular, so Temple, not seeing any churches, asked for and was granted permission to have their own church service. Former Olympian Reverend Bob Richards[1] led the service with the singing of "Onward, Christian Soldiers."

---

1. Bob Richards participated in the 1948, 1952, and 1956 Olympics as a pole-vaulter and a decathlete, winning back-to-back gold medals for the pole vault (in 1952 and 1956).

Onward, Christian Soldiers!
Marching as to war,
With the cross of Jesus
Going on before.

Temple emphasized how vital their strict training was as preparation. The pain they suffered and pushed through prepared them for a moment where all the odds appeared to be against them. It gave them the strength they needed to refuse to back down in the face of a race that everyone believed they would lose. It was their job to prove the doubters wrong.

The women's fight wasn't only against their opponents, but against everyone who said they couldn't win. Against everyone who said that they weren't worthy simply because of the color or gender they were born with. Temple argued that the fight they were facing was also against the doubts in their own minds. He believed that the key to winning was to stay focused on their goals.

A favorite passage was 1 Corinthians 9:24–25: "Do you not know that in a race all the runners run, but only one gets the prize? Run in such a way that you may win. Everyone who competes in the games goes into strict training. They do it to get a crown that will not last, but we do it to get a crown that lasts forever."

The words had power for the women, conjuring the experiences shared by all those who had come before them, and what exactly they were fighting for. A crown that lasts forever.

The Russian athletes were "way out of our league," Temple said, "but we didn't see it that way. We were naive. We didn't know anything about the Russian women, and we didn't care one way or the other. We knew we were the underdogs; we knew that." They had been underestimated before, and if they kept the faith, anything was possible.

Managing an international team meant that Temple was managing athletes for several events that he had no experience with. The women were world-class, and knew what they needed to do to prepare, but they were still young, always cutting up and looking for a little fun. Temple was focused on logistics, safety, security, and spirit, with an eye on international relations, while his team was poking fun at the kitchen staff with their breakfast orders by asking for eggs in ways they thought would not be translatable. It became a running joke to find the most obscure egg preparation, from "sunny side up" to "over easy" and everything in between. Temple was just trying to get them to the track on time, in one piece. "If they brought an egg that wasn't done just so, they'd send it back." Temple said. "It took us a good three hours just to get through breakfast! We saw right then it was time for a little team meeting."

As always, when the team started practicing on the track, many of the outside issues faded away. "We thought it was going to be something of a strain on us because we had heard so much about Russia," Barbara Jones said. "When we got there, we didn't have the right starting blocks, because America was still dealing with inches and yards, and they were dealing with meters. When we got there all of the starting blocks were in meters and we didn't understand. And the Russians would come over and show us. They would ask us, what did we have in yards, and we would tell them, and then they would place those in meters."

The tension between Russia and the Americans was not a problem among the athletes, but it clearly existed. A tight control was kept over their activities. Unless they were competing, or participating in an organized event, the Russian and US athletes were kept separate from each other. Willye White considered the athletes from Russia under the Soviet regime to have similar struggles to her own. "Their flight to freedom was to be a winner so that they could have a better standard of living," Willye said. "They could have a flat or they could have a car, and they could have money. They didn't have to share—five or six people staying in one room. So, their flight was similar to mine. My flight to freedom from Mississippi, from the bias, from segregation, from illiteracy, from all of those things. So, I could relate very well with them, what it was all about."

The Soviet athletes and the women from Tennessee State all ran for more than medals. They ran for their lives. They ran for freedom from oppression. They ran to improve the circumstances for themselves, and also for their families. This motivation led to an intensity that increased not only the stakes, but the drive as well.

During one of the public events in Russia, Willye saw this "big handsome man come up, trying to get a message to his relatives in Philadelphia. He had a folded note in his hand, and he shook hands with one of the athletes," furtively passing the note and pleading that it be given to his family. The man was former athlete, actor, and activist Paul Robeson,[2] who had become blacklisted in the United States after speaking in favor of communist principles during the Cold War. Russia, in turn, welcomed Robeson as a coup for their propaganda war against the evils of capitalism, but in Russia, Robeson faced a different set of challenges and found it difficult to communicate with his family in America. Willye didn't know who he was or how much of a risk Paul Robeson was taking at the time, but she bore witness to an intense political controversy and the event was seared in her mind.

One of the ringleaders of the group of non-Tigerbelles on the US team was Earlene Brown. Earlene was well known by the team already and was nearly unbeatable in the shot put and discus. She had been on the US Olympic team with some of the Tigerbelles in 1956, where she got to know many of the Russian competitors, teaching them to dance the "cha-cha" in the Olympic Village. Earlene came from Los Angeles, where she attracted media attention because of her skill, and because she was always a lot of fun. She was hardly mentioned in a story without being called "jolly." According to Ralph Boston, Earlene's friends called her "Big Mama Do-Right."

As fun as Earlene was, she was equally determined and strong, and her physical traits gave her a distinct advantage. Earlene said, "My mother told me that the first thing she noticed about me when I was born was my hands." She had large hands, a strong grip, and a tall, sturdy frame.

At the Nationals meet in Philadelphia in 1956, Earlene had set AAU records in both the shot put and the discus, but at the Olympic

2. Paul Robeson was a professional football player, bass-baritone singer, theater and movie actor, and activist. Well known for his civil rights activism, Robeson was investigated during the McCarthy era, but his legacy remains with his many performances and recordings, eventually earning him a Lifetime Achievement Grammy Award and a star on the Hollywood Walk of Fame.

Earlene Brown. Temple Archives

trials in DC the following week, Lois Testa broke the shot-put record in the morning round. Earlene was stung by the defeat of her short-lived record, so she skipped lunch, instead going behind a barn and throwing the heavy metal ball over and over again, perfecting her technique until the afternoon round, when she reclaimed her top spot and setting a new American record with a throw of 46 feet, 11 inches. The press went wild.

Earlene was hailed by the media, but her personal life suffered. A newlywed with a five-month-old son, Earlene had to leave her young family behind to travel to Melbourne. Her husband, Henry Brown, who was a strong athlete in his own right, was reduced to being called "Earlene Brown's husband." He stayed home with their infant son listening to the reports of Earlene being the life of the party with Willye White, and dancing to the newest rock 'n' roll music with the Russians and Nigerians.

Earlene's marriage crumbled, but she gained popularity around the world. "There was something warm and easygoing about the big brown

Earlene Brown. Temple Archives

girl in the white horn-rimmed glasses who was as light on her feet as a ballerina," wrote historian Michael Davis.

The Russians were thrilled to welcome her to their country. She marched into the stadium wearing a black Uzbek hat and was hounded for autographs. The AP reported, "Mrs. Earlene Brown was the toast of Moscow." Earlene had spent the two years since Melbourne honing her craft, and told reporters she was throwing nearly 50 feet in practice, a claim so outrageous it was assumed to be a gross exaggeration, until she repeated the feat while training in Moscow.

Lillian Greene was on the team as a distance runner—a category that had just been added to the women's events. It had previously been excluded because of the widespread belief that women weren't capable of running distances, and if they were, it couldn't be good for them. "Because my event was so new," she said, "no one really knew how to train a woman for that distance, so I trained with the white fellows from Oregon."

In anticipation of the trip, Lillian had learned some Russian, so she was taken into people's homes to see how they lived. She knew that seeing people with dark skin was rare in Russia, and they were full of questions. Because Russian propaganda had described racial tensions among Americans as pervasive and intense, they were shocked to see Black and white teammates "running and playing together and laughing and hugging each other. We'd run through the park, and people would stare at us and their mouths would drop open."

Lillian was able to communicate enough to break the ice, and the people responded by showering her with gifts of bread and scarves, Russian hats, and even a violin.

Before competition began, the United States coaches held a press conference. "I was the only Black coach on the US team, and there were about eight coaches there," Temple said. The men's team coaches represented a wide range of powerhouse universities including Stanford, Ohio State, and several other programs, while Temple was the sole representative for the women's team. George Eastman as the head coach of the men's team fielded most of the questions. At first Temple thought the lack of questions was probably due to ambivalence about the female athletes. Toward the end, a question was finally directed to Temple. He sat up straight, waiting for the translation, preparing to promote his team.

Temple said, "All of a sudden, through an interpreter, they said, 'Coach Temple, how many Blacks are on the team?' I knew, but I started counting, and the coach from Ohio State interjected, 'We are one United States team.'"

Immediately, the other coaches jumped in, with Dan Ferris, head of the AAU, saying, "Oh, we don't even know because we are just one family."

Temple was asked one more question: "In your democratic country, are Blacks allowed to marry whites?" After a beat, Temple answered directly, saying that in some states they were, and in some, they weren't. He could have gone on to say that in many states there were more limitations than just marriage, but he was frustrated with the reaction of his colleagues. "I had to go [to Russia] to find out we were all one big happy family!

"When you get on the plane and come back [to the United States] you can't even go to the same hamburger place or sleep in the same hotel," Temple said, pointing out that even though they were considered to be one team, one family, his team was not treated the same way.

On race day a crowd of one hundred thousand gathered to watch. Both the US and Russian teams marched out onto the field. They played the National Anthem for the Americans to a silent, standing crowd, followed by the Russian anthem. "You could have heard a pin drop," Temple said. It was a stark contrast to the anthem being played before an event in the States where the audience shifted, talked, sat or stood, took off their hats, or left them on.

There were ten events for the women. "We might have been in a foreign land," Temple said, "but once the women got on the track, they were right at home. They didn't give up anything, and they had some tough competition." Their competition included Irina and Tamara Press, the formidable Russian sister duo that had defeated the Tennessee State relay team in Melbourne.

Barbara Jones proved herself as the "money runner" that loved to perform to a crowd. It was her first international competition after missing the 1956 Olympic team, and Mae Faggs's advice to get some serious training at Tennessee State had paid off. Barbara came back on the international scene with a vengeance and became the first American woman to beat a Soviet athlete by finishing first in the 100 meters.

Lucinda Williams followed to win the 200 in a close finish, and another all-Tigerbelle crew of Isabelle Daniels, Margaret Matthews, Barbara Jones, and Lucinda Williams won the 4x100m relay. It was a stunning upset, with the Tigerbelles from Tennessee State dominating the sprints. Winning the sprints was exciting enough, but no one expected the US team to produce any wins in areas that required more strength than speed. Earlene Brown defied the odds and lived up to her promise of a 50-foot shot-put distance by throwing 54 feet and 3.18 inches, winning in a huge upset.

The only disappointment came with that most challenging event, the hurdles. Shirley Crowder was disqualified, echoing back to her fall in 1956. She was resolved and determined to use her experience to improve. She'd won at Nationals. She could do it again.

"Here was a school running against a country," Temple said. "And we went over there and beat them. We won the 100, we won the 200, we won the 4x100-meter relay, we won the shot put. Now we wasn't supposed to win nothing. We was just supposed to go along for the ride. Now that opened up their eyes."

1958 Tigerbelles return from Russia From the bottom: Willye White, Margaret Matthews, Lucinda Williams, Anna Lois Smith, Martha Hudson, Isabelle Daniels, Ed Temple. Temple Archives

With the Russian competition behind them, the team competed successfully in Poland, Hungary, and Greece. "We finished the tour winning everywhere," Temple said. It was a whirlwind tour and an indisputable success, but when Temple got back to the States, he wanted to "kiss the Statue of Liberty."

While the Tigerbelles and Earlene Brown dominated their events, the overall score including the men's team was a loss to the Russians. When reporters searched for an answer for the defeat, Temple had one ready. "We have the material, but we don't give it a chance to develop. Our women just need more opportunity," Temple said, noting that the Tigerbelles won their events because "the sprinters had proper training."

The European countries did not understand the reluctance of the United States to properly train their talent, but Red Smith, US syndicated columnist, explained it this way: "In America, we feel that if we ever train up a breed of gals who can outrun the boys, we'll be the losers." It was an admission of the shortsighted view on progress that the Tigerbelles, and all women athletes, would fight for generations.

CHAPTER 10

Wilma and Willye

THE TIGERBELLES CONTINUED TO COMPETE ANY CHANCE THEY GOT, and traveled to Cleveland, Ohio, for the 1959 Outdoor National championship in the summer, a trip well worth their while. The team won with a landslide 123 points versus their nearest challenger, Spartan Girls Athletic Club, with 40 points. According to the *New York Herald Tribune*, "Mrs. Earlene Brown, a 215-pound Los Angeles mother, and Isabelle Daniels, one of Tennessee State's sprint sensations, were double winners today."

Isabelle was at her peak performance, and it was spectacular. She finished first in the 60-meter and 200-meter dashes, and Wilma Rudolph, who had been invited back on the team, won the 100-meter. The team again had first-, second-, and third-place finishes in all of the sprints, with Barbara Jones, Lucinda Williams, and Martha Hudson filling in the other top spots. Shirley Crowder won the 80-meter hurdles, and the relay team dominated again. Margaret Matthews won her last competition in the long jump, followed by teammate Anna Lois Smith in second, and Willye White in third, when she collided with a cameraman who didn't anticipate how far she could jump.

The qualifying members of the team traveled on to Chicago for the Pan American Games, where Lucinda Williams won three gold medals for the 100-meter, the 200-meter, and the 4x100-meter relay, which was, again, a collection of all-Tigerbelle all-stars.

L to R: Willye White, Margaret Matthews, Isabelle Daniels, Shirley Crowder, Lucinda Williams. Temple Archives

The team had become so uniformly strong that there were no standouts. The only thing that was certain was that the winners would be Tigerbelles.

Wilma and Willye both entered Tennessee State as freshmen in the fall of 1959. Temple struggled with the decision to bring Wilma back, staying up nights and talking to Charlie B. about it. He ultimately chose to make an exception to his hard-and-fast rules for Wilma. She was humble, she was a team player, and she was special in so many ways. If anyone deserved an extra chance it was Wilma, and she was unlikely to act in a way to make him regret it.

Wilma gave birth to her daughter, Yolanda, in July. Her father was ill, so her mother wasn't able to care for Yolanda, but Wilma made arrangements with her older sister, Yvonne. Wilma had a new love and a new responsibility. She was determined to succeed for both of them, and while it was excruciatingly painful for her to leave her six-week-old baby, she knew that getting her education and making a name for herself would make the difference in their lives.

Willye White also became a high school graduate and could officially and finally leave Mississippi. "She came out of the same location after me," Barbara Murrell said. "She ran in high school barefooted. I thought she was amazing. She was always independent. I guess you have to adopt that, coming out of places like that, because if you came out shy or something you would never have made it."

Willye was invited to become a student and an official member of the Tennessee State team. It was a tenuous situation from the start. She had run and traveled with the Tigerbelles during the summers from her freshman through senior years of high school, and she felt, with good reason, like a seasoned veteran of the team before she had taken a single class.

"I was ahead of my time at Tennessee State," Willye said. "I liked to date older boys and I ran around with older girls. I knew how to drink whiskey and I loved to dye my hair different colors. I knew that wasn't something that they were used to."

Barbara Murrell, who had her finger on the pulse of social life at Tennessee State, didn't think Willye's behavior was so far from the norm on campus—it was only when you compared it to the other Tigerbelles.

"Well, not being able to ride in a car, that's the thrill, riding in a car," she said. "[Willye] was going against the rules, but she didn't break any society rules. All the other girls were a little bit different. You know, in a group, there's always one that has their own personality, that wants to do it their way. It was probably her mouth that got her into the most trouble," Barbara said.

"Willye's attitude, I'm sure, did not help," Boston said of the contentious relationship between Willye and her coach. "She did have an attitude, yeah, she did. Did I see it up close? Yeah, I saw it a few times. She had that brazen attitude toward Temple."

Temple saw nothing but trouble. "Red didn't want to be a freshman," he said. "She wanted to be a junior or senior. You see, Red had been here for three summers as a high school student, and she figured that meant she was more like a senior than a freshman, and she didn't think she had to go by freshman rules."

Temple also felt that Willye came by her attitude from her early success. "If you're the second best in the world and are still in high school, you are great. And she was great, no doubt about it. But the point was that she was still a freshman, no matter what she'd done." If the rules were different for Willye than they were for any of the other women, there would be problems.

"Even with me, rules were made to be kept, not to be broken," Charlie B. and Ed Temple's daughter Edwina said. Edwina and her brother, Bernard, were expected to uphold the same standards as the team. "He was like that with everyone; there were no favorites. He was fair. If you followed the rules, then everything would be fine."

The rules were clear when Willye came to campus, and they had never changed. Freshmen or sophomores were not allowed to ride in cars. "Your freshman year you didn't ride in nobody's car but mine," Temple said.

The rules were famous around campus, so much so that Ralph Boston knew them by heart. "That was the rule," Boston said. "You don't get in cars, you don't ride in cars, you have a curfew, and you adhere to that. I heard that."

Lucinda Williams listed off the rules by memory. "We had the rules," she said. "Number one, you don't ride in cars. You don't stay off campus after eleven o'clock. You don't be disrespectful. You keep your grades up. You be on time."

"People look at that [as] being kind of harsh, but I had a reason. I didn't want them to be exposed to people that they didn't know because anything could happen. You didn't know people here. They get in a car, somebody take them someplace, something happen to them." Temple shook his head at the thought. It's a fear that any parent can relate to, of any of the horrible stories you've heard of happening to someone in your care.

"See, Mr. Temple wasn't only a track coach, Mr. Temple was a father. He was a guidance counselor, he was a minister; he even helped with your relationships. You know, he was everything you would want a person to be with your child," Barbara Jones said.

"He protected us," Barbara said. "We couldn't get in cars. Our boyfriends, he had a talk with. They knew how far that they could go and if he saw them doing anything wrong, then we could not deal with them. So, he almost had a blacklist for the boys, you know, the guys that we went with. And we are still married to those same guys."

"He said, 'I am the one that had to go down and ask their parents to let these young women go to school,'" Edwina Temple said. "He took that responsibility very seriously. He promised their parents that he would take care of them. And he also said [that] if you don't follow the rules, he'd pack you up and send you home."

Willye was continually breaking one of Temple's biggest rules. "She just wouldn't stay out of those cars," Temple said.

It may seem like an unusual or arbitrary rule to outsiders, but Temple had a good reason for sticking to his principles. Most of the young women that joined his program had never left home before. They were brought to a large, vibrant campus with instant status, and gained a lot of attention from young men with various motives. Temple had looked each of their parents in the eye, promising to look after their daughters as he would his own, and he worried over their vulnerability. "The girls were away from home, and they didn't know people. Somebody could have come in here and put them in their car and then taken them off somewhere. . . . It wasn't the fact of riding in a car, but I just wanted to make sure my girls knew which cars to get into and which cars not to get into." Temple figured that by junior year, the women should have gained enough experience, but freshmen and sophomores were still too young to be going off with the boys.

If rules were broken, Temple would hear about it. "I think he had people who watched us," Isabelle Daniels said. "He knew where we had been, where we were and all of that."

Lucinda agreed. "He had his spies out," she said. "We knew he had spies out and they would tell him, Coach, I saw your girl. And he'd make you run extra laps or something. So, we didn't do anything that he would find out."

"He was everywhere," Barbara Jones said, sneakily shifting her gaze from side to side. "It was like he knew we were going to do something wrong."

It might not have even been appointed spies but simply the fact that Temple's rules were so well-known around campus; if anyone was seen acting out of line, someone would eventually tell him about it. "People would tell on them, okay? Some people would tell on them," Edwina Temple said.

"So, one night [he'd get] a telephone call. And he would say, So how did they leave? And they would say, They sneak out the back door, and then they would go out to the club or wherever they were going to dance," Edwina said.

"The only way we could get out of the dormitory was to put a brick in the back door," Barbara Murrell said, "so you could go down the back steps and not have to come back in the front, and you could ride across town in a car."

When Temple got the call that his team was sneaking out, he knew what to do.

"So, he drove his car, turned the lights out, and when they came down the steps, he turned the lights on." Edwina laughed out loud, recalling the story, imagining the looks on their faces as they were caught like deer in his headlights, scampering back up the outdoor staircase of Hankal Hall, knowing how many extra laps they'd have to run the next day. "They never did it after that—they got busted. You can imagine how scared they must have been after that," Edwina said, but they were all laughing about it years later.

Willye and Wilma's paths were beginning to diverge. Wilma was as focused as she had ever been. Four years can feel like a lifetime to teenage girls, and their lives can swing dramatically in the years between sixteen and twenty. As Willye White was testing her limits, Wilma Rudolph was becoming ensconced in the Tigerbelle fold. Historian Michael D. Davis wrote, "Every year some of the most promising young athletes become track dropouts. The miracle is not that Wilma dropped out of track in 1958 to have a child, but that she returned in 1959."

Wilma's world had changed completely since the 1956 Olympics. She'd been a junior runner then, still in high school. She knew she could do even better when she got back to Tennessee State. She had to. Whenever she was written about in the papers, which was admittedly rare, they always talked about her overcoming childhood polio. But to Wilma, it was just as hard to leave her baby girl behind. If she was able to make it back to the Olympics, and if she earned another medal, that particular pain would be worth it. It could change her life, and also her daughter Yolanda's.

By 1959, Wilma had gone through intense challenges, and she had grown both personally and athletically. Coach Temple had endeared himself to her for life by inviting her back onto his team. He broke his own rule for her and gave her another shot, but she knew there wouldn't be a third or fourth chance. There would be no more breaking rules or cutting corners. Wilma was glad to be back in school, glad to be running, and eager to prove that she was the fastest woman in the world.

"My speed was tremendous after I had the baby," Wilma said. "I was much faster than before. . . . I wanted the Olympic Games badly. Almost four years had passed since Melbourne, and I had gone from a skinny little high school girl to a woman, a mother, and a college student."

Wilma came to Tennessee State with considerable raw talent and speed, but she had few of the skills and techniques that she would need to reach her full potential. "She had to work really hard after having this baby," Temple said. "She had to work awful hard to come back." But she didn't have to do it on her own. The team and her coach were there to help her.

"When Wilma joined us, I remember her being so tall that when she would take her mark, get set, go, instead of her pumping her arms up and down, they would be flapping everywhere," Margaret said. "We helped her, and we helped each other."

Barbara Jones agreed. "Skeeter, her arms were all over the place, her knees."

"When I first saw Wilma, she was long and lanky," Barbara Murrell said. "She didn't really look like a runner, in that everything was moving right. She just walked like a teenager. Like a big teenager. She didn't have the same stride as everybody else."

"Oh, Lord, that skinny little lady," Lucinda said. "At first, we couldn't understand how she could run so fast with her long legs and flailing arms. Bless her heart, she could seem like the laziest person. We would have to stay on her case. We would beat her out of the starting blocks, but by 25 yards she'd done passed us."

The team worked together to help Wilma. "Isabelle Daniels was excellent in the middle, picking up, Margaret Matthews was great for starting, and I was great for the lean at the end," Barbara Jones said. "Skeeter had a form, I think that's why they called her Skeeter, emulating a mosquito, because her arms were all over the place. If you look at early pictures of Wilma running, you would see that. She looked like she was knock-kneed, and her feet were the wrong way. So, we put her on the line, and we tied her arms down so she would have the perfect stride and the perfect form. We had weights on her feet, and then with the weight, the feet came in. So we taught her how to use the ankle weights to keep her feet straight. Now we worked with Wilma."

Temple also helped Wilma perfect the "Tennessee Lean" that the Tigerbelles were known for. Wilma started like everyone else, running straight up and down right to the finish line, but by perfecting her stride she stretched out her legs, taking full advantage of her height with a new, graceful and smooth, "scissoring stride," leaning into the tape across the line. When inches separated first, second, and third place, having the instinct to lean from the waist would often be the difference in a win. "She had to learn to be a gazelle," Davis wrote, "and the learning came hard."

While her teammates helped with her form, Wilma remained concerned about starting out of the blocks. She always talked about her trouble with the starts; it was a source of frustration for her, and she worked hard to smooth it out.

"For one thing," Wilma said, "I had very bad reflexes on starts, and for another thing, my long legs made starts very awkward for me." Her speed coming off the blocks also affected her acceleration, tending to leave her in the position of having to chase from behind. Wilma tried clearing her mind for everything but the starter's gun, and several other techniques, without success, ultimately leaving her with the preference for the longer sprints. "Heck," she said, "I needed 45 feet or so just to get started."

Temple didn't think Wilma's starts were nearly as bad as she did. "For some reason she has always considered herself a slow starter," Temple said. "I have seen some quicker, but I wouldn't classify her as slow. If she'd get through that first 15 yards, she'd really accelerate—then it would just be a matter of how badly she was going to beat you."

"Wilma always thought I could beat her," Barbara Jones said, "and I did. But when we started teaching her how to have the perfect form, and the perfect arm movement, she put so much dirt in my face, I could have slapped her." Barbara laughed. "I said, I didn't want you to do all that, now, just a little bit. But she was that good. She was a gazelle. Her form, if you noticed her form, it's perfect. Going around the corner in the 220, in the 100, the lean. If you watch her in motion, you would see an altogether different person, and you would see the confidence in her face. That's how all of us were, we had that confidence."

Those moments on the track or in the field without a crowd were the moments that made a champion. It was where the focus and challenges for training the body crept into their souls. Temple always told them, "Only the pure in heart survive." Meaning that it was not just the strength of their bodies that mattered. The body was just a mechanism to discipline their souls, which was ultimately the most important in their lives.

"He used to have all of these little statements," Barbara Jones said. "Only the strong survive. That's a strong statement. And I live by that. I live by all of those little statements he used to make."

When their soul would be hurting, when there was pain in their lives, when they felt the injustice in the world, they could learn to overcome that within themselves. By running, and running to win, they would earn true strength. Winning took the ultimate sacrifice, and that kind of achievement was about more than themselves; it was about everyone. Everyone who came before them and everyone since. When they achieve the kind of purity in heart and self-discipline that it took to get that far, then they became a shining example in the world for others to see and follow.

That was what Temple was working for, what each of the Tigerbelles worked for, and that would become the enduring legacy of the Tigerbelles.

CHAPTER 11

Home Away

CHOICES HAD TO BE MADE ON THE TEAM BECAUSE OF BUDGET, BUT scarcity sometimes came with added benefits. Temple only had enough space in the station wagons (which the team still used for most meets) and money in the coffers to travel with a certain number of women. The travel team was always smaller than the team on campus, and being left behind was a constant concern for the athletes.

"We had to run against each other and if we didn't do well in practice, [Temple] wouldn't take us on trips. He left us on campus," Margaret Matthews said. She was left behind her first year on campus when the team traveled to an indoor meet in New York. "One time," Margaret said. "And after they got back, I told Coach Temple, I looked him straight in the face and I said, 'You will never leave me on this campus again when you take the Tigerbelles on a trip.'" Margaret's promise proved true, and once earned, she kept her coveted travel spot until she retired. It was the time trials in practice that determined who would be brought with the team, keeping the intensity level high at practice.

JoAnn Terry knew the pain of being left behind more than any other. One of the few women on the team not from the Deep South, JoAnn was born in Indianapolis, Indiana. She was the fifth of six children, and her mother was often ill, so JoAnn worked on weekends to help support her family. That work didn't stop when she was invited to the Tigerbelle summer program in 1955. JoAnn loved to run, and was faster than nearly everyone she knew, but she didn't have a formal program or club to teach her techniques. When she got to Tennessee State, she was able to see how much she still had to learn. "I didn't know anything about running," JoAnn said. "I was taught things that I never knew, like running in spikes, how to move my arms, my breathing."

After her first summer, JoAnn wasn't offered a work-aid scholarship like many of the others on the team had received, but she had been offered admittance and a spot on the team. So, JoAnn took the opportunity, working extra jobs in Nashville to make it happen. "Too many of the other girls were better than me," JoAnn said. "Only a few girls could be taken to the competitive meets, and I was never chosen." It was not for lack of effort on JoAnn's part. Her schoolwork was taken just as seriously as the work on the track, her days turning into a blur of studies and "seemingly endless afternoons and nights" on the track. She was working just as hard as the others but didn't consider herself a full member of the team. She watched them leave without her for all of the major events, never giving her a chance to compete at the elite level.

By the summer of 1959 Margaret Matthews had graduated, so there was room on the team for another jumper with technical chops. JoAnn started to focus on the hurdles with Shirley Crowder, and four years into her tenure, JoAnn's persistence paid off: She was finally given a work-aid scholarship and the coveted spot on the travel team.

The responsibility was nearly more than she'd bargained for. A student teacher at a Nashville school a few miles off campus, JoAnn was always cutting it close getting back to the track in time for practice. One day the bus was late, and JoAnn panicked. "I was wearing spike heels and started walking toward campus while I was waiting for the bus," JoAnn said. She made it all the way back to campus before the bus ever arrived, covering the city blocks as quickly as she could in her skirt and heels.

Everyone knew that being late was not permitted, and that day was no exception for JoAnn. Temple questioned her, and already exhausted from the rush back to campus, JoAnn did her best to explain.

His only response? "I understand why you're late. Fifty laps after practice."

"I was so mad," JoAnn said. "I ran all fifty laps while Coach Temple kept saying, 'You're looking good.' After I finally got through, I ran out the door, and my muscles cramped so bad that I fell up against the wall and tears started falling."

Assistant Coach Samuel Abernathy, Mr. Ab, said that it was all a matter of Temple's discipline. What could be considered rigidity by some was meant to set strong boundaries and expectations. "Time to play, time to work—you've got to be on time," Mr. Ab said, reciting the rules by memory. "If you're not there when we leave, you will get left. At six o'clock, you'd better be there. He was strict on times. He'd leave me as quick as he'd leave one of those girls. You didn't get to be such a superstar that you couldn't be left."

"He would have us run extra laps for punishment if we were late," Isabelle Daniels said. "But he didn't have too many people being late."

"I want the girls all at once," Temple told *Sports Illustrated*. "Jones come down, warm up, Hudson come, she'd have to warm up. If I got to fool with Hudson, what is Jones going to do? We all got to do the same thing and keep right together." It was one of many reasons why Temple was so famously strict about being on time for practice.

"I make the girls run an extra lap for every minute they're late. Time for practice, they come out, I tell you, T-shirt half on, one shoe off, but they get there."

He has a story for almost each one of them, suffering the torture of the extra laps.

When Wilma and an assistant manager were late by a full half-hour because their alarm clock didn't go off, he gave them thirty laps. "Rudolph, she went around in pretty good style, but it like to kill that girl, Shirby." He didn't like to punish mistakes, but "you let one go, another one is going to come up, and pretty soon everything is going to be disrupted altogether," Temple said.

Barbara Jones bristled at the penalties the most.

She was late for practice one day, coming from a sorority meeting where she was a leader with the Alpha Kappa Alphas on campus. She snuck into the back of practice, looking relieved when she thought she hadn't been noticed, but Temple didn't miss a thing with his team.

"After practice was over and everyone was leaving, I casually told BeeJay to stay awhile after practice," Temple said. "She ran for two extra hours in the heat. I just sat there under a shade tree and let her run until I got tired." Usually that mistake didn't occur more than once. "If one person gets by with that foolishness, then discipline breaks down all down the line."

Barbara may have complained to Charlie B., who may have relayed the complaint to Temple, but Barbara's temper flared often enough to create a running joke between the couple. "Some days she isn't speaking to him," Charlie B. said with a laugh. "She's out there running, but they aren't speaking." Temple didn't seem to care as long as she kept running.

For Temple, the rules and the adherence to the boundaries was all a part of the total training. It wasn't only muscles that needed to grow. It was will, and it was discipline.

Lucinda Williams understood why Temple was tough on them.

"There was never a reason to ask him why because I understood why," Lucinda said. "I realized his goal was to instill in us that will to win. Not only in that race, but in life. It was such a great opportunity to have a group of African American women, Black women, in those days—to be in charge of them and see them flourish and see them accomplish what he knew all along we would accomplish. It was because of his love, and his father-ness. I saw Bernard and Edwina grow up, and Mrs. Temple herself, she was a jewel," Lucinda said.

"Mrs. Temple was something like a surrogate mother to all of us," Margaret said.

Charlie B. cared so much for the young women and knew how hard the adjustment to university life could be, even without the added commitments of the team. She had grown up in a small town, too. "Edward says that I grew up 'ten miles behind the sun,' since my family lived so far out in the country," she said.

"A lot of times when the girls first come, they get a little bit upset with Ed," Charlie B. said. "He sounds rough, but he just wants them to be the best. He treats them like they are his own children, no more, no less."

Wilma's little sister, Charlene, said, "Edwina shared her father with everybody, and Mrs. Temple, she was right there. I don't know what I would have done without her when I lived in Nashville." Wilma was young when she met Coach Temple, but Charlene was even younger. When Wilma and Charlene's father was ill and they were away from home, Temple was a second father to them. "He was someone you could trust," Charlene said, "that would have your best interest at heart. Such integrity. You knew that he was not going to tell you anything wrong. And he listened. He listened to what you had to say. He didn't always agree with you. He's going to steer you in the right direction. You knew you could count on that."

"Although Edward is strict," Charlie B. said, "He has always had a fatherly concern for the girls on his teams. His drive is also balanced with a true caring for them and their overall welfare. We have always taken them into our family."

The young Temple family's days were full, and they were always adding more to their plates. Charlie B. worked full days at the post office while Temple taught classes three mornings a week, leaving Edwina in the care of a neighbor, and Bernard at school.

"I stayed with Mrs. Woodruff from when I was six months old until I went to school because my mother had to work," Edwina said. "They didn't live far. My mother would drop me off, then pick me up at the end of the day."

"I remember one time I had to go somewhere, and Edward kept the children, and Edwina was a handful," Charlie B. said. "When I got back that night, there she was. Up, her diapers all wrinkled up in one big knot and pinned the weirdest way with the rubber pants the wrong side out. I asked Edward if he'd had any problems, and he was just as unruffled as you please and said, 'No, no problems at all.'"

Edwina later called the Tigerbelles "a family business," with many of the women spending time as her babysitter. "We'd make a deal with Wilma," Edwina said of a scheme she cooked up with her brother, Bernard. "We'd let Wilma's boyfriend come over, and we wouldn't tell if she'd let us stay up late." Edwina threw her head back, laughing at the memory. "He would come over and sit and watch TV with us, and we'd get to stay up past our bedtime. I don't remember the boyfriend; I just remember the deal."

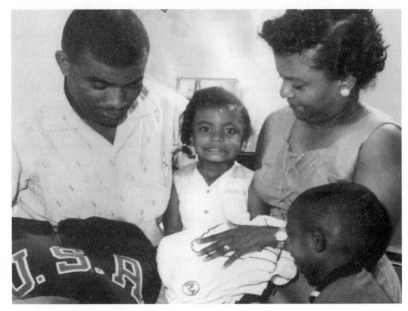

The Temple Family: Edward, Edwina, Charlie B., and Bernard Temple. Temple Archives

Edwina was just as worried about being caught misbehaving as any of the Tigerbelles.

"Growing up as a child, I used to be scared of [my dad] too. My mother was always the mediator. There were no exceptions to the rules, not even for me." If any missteps were made, they all went to Charlie B. to run interference for them against Temple's heavy discipline. "She was the backup," Edwina said, "and they knew that if they went to her, she would help to make it right. You know, if they got in trouble or something, they'd be in there trying to tell her first so she could lighten the load a little bit."

Temple knew what they were up to. "When they'd fall out with me, she'd have them come to the post office. She would sit in the post office and talk to them." Their favorite work-aid assignment was always the post office, because that was her domain. "Mrs. Temple ran the mailroom." Howard Gentry Jr. said. "They said Coach Temple ran it, but Mrs. Temple ran the mailroom."

"Mrs. Temple, she was the mother," Barbara Jones said. "She had all of these young, wonderful, beautiful women with her young husband." The running joke was that Temple was the only man allowed around "so many fast women." But Barbara said, "We thought he was a hundred, because he was so disciplined." Charlie B. was not threatened by the women because she was just as invested in their success as he was. "She worked with us, she cared for us, and she was Mr. Temple's right hand, left hand, right foot, left foot," Barbara said. "That's what made him so great, I think, is because he had a woman who was behind him one hundred percent."

Temple knew well how important his wife was to the team. "She was always involved," he said. "I mean, when they were sick or had a cold, she would carry soup up in the dormitory. She would bake them a cake, and if they had any problems that I couldn't solve, I'd send her up there in the dormitory and she would talk to them. She went up there a lot."

Charlie B. went downtown with the young women to help them shop for winter coats, formal dresses, or support bras, often buying them herself if they didn't have the funds, and to show them the ropes as they ventured downtown. "They didn't make a lot of money either," Edwina said of her parents, "but they pulled it together. Their big store was Sears Roebuck. She would take you to Sears, and put it on her Sears credit card, and pay for it until she had it paid for. If they needed something, they weren't going to have them go someplace and not be dressed like the rest of the girls. It came right out of their own money."

By shopping with the team Charlie B. was protecting more than their feelings or their image. "She would take them downtown because she didn't want them to go there by themselves because it was still segregation, and she didn't want no incident," Temple said. "I didn't want no incident, either."

Charlie B. insisted on washing all the uniforms, to keep them bright white. Taking special care of the uniforms was critical because they were passed down from year to year. By 1960, the team was still using the same uniforms that had been issued to the 1955 team, and they would keep using them for several years more, even though the football and basketball teams had new uniforms every year. "I have washed uniforms and tennis shoes by the hundreds," Charlie B. said.

Samuel Abernathy said, "When I was equipment manager, I did not wash her stuff, because she wanted it to stay white."

"She didn't let the school clean the uniforms because they cleaned the football uniforms, and the men's basketball [uniforms], too," Edwina explained. "One time they did it and it looked so horrible. She didn't want them to go out not looking like young ladies. She wanted them to be [well] dressed."

The laundry on its own was an enormous undertaking. "You've got to remember, we're talking about indoor and outdoor—all three seasons," Edwina said. "You're talking about sweats, running shoes, uniforms, eight to ten people going to meets on any weekend. They used to just have one uniform, then they got two, so they could rotate. When he got home after a meet on Sunday, she started her wash, and she would have them ready to go on Monday or Tuesday. Then she would take them to the post office, and she would take them to the back, and line them up in bags, and everybody would come get their laundry."

On their birthdays, Charlie B. would often bake a cake for them, German chocolate being the one she was known for. "They loved that German chocolate cake," Temple said.

"My mother made the best German chocolate cake," Edwina agreed. "I have the recipe, but it's so complicated. The way she made it, I watched her a thousand times."

"It's hard to explain to someone else because it was so private and so beautiful," Barbara Jones said of her time with the Temple family. "It was just that they were a mother and father to us, and you didn't fear anything. You didn't fear being away from home, you didn't fear being homesick, because Mr. Temple was there. If he saw that you were kind of moody, he'd ask, and he'd give you money to call home."

The family had the team over for dinners on a weekly basis. "Back then there weren't a lot of restaurants or fast-food places they could take you. Everything was cooked at home," Edwina said. "My mom would cook, and outside she would grill, and have potato salad, baked beans, cole slaw, hamburgers, and hot dogs. It wasn't anything very expensive. I didn't think anything about it because it happened so much when I was growing up."

While Charlie B. was busy caring for the team, Temple used the time for one-on-one instruction. "He had an eight-millimeter camera and he would film their practices," Edwina said. "When they came down on the weekend, he would have the projector set up, and they would watch the film. He would tell them what they were doing wrong with their arms, or whatever, so he would have the opportunity to talk with them individually. They would watch together, but he would say, 'Okay, this time we're going to play it back and we're going to watch Barbara, and we're going to watch Wilma on this one, and see what you're doing? This is how you're running.' All the way from coming out of the starting blocks to leaning at the tape. This happened all the time." Edwina remembers the endless clatter of the reels in the projector and watching the silent images move along the screen, but admits that she preferred to run around with her brother while her mother set up dinner on the picnic tables outside.

"Mrs. Temple taught me how to be a woman," Barbara Jones said. "I came there a girl and left a woman. She would say, Come on over to the house. And she would make sure our hair was looking pretty. She made sure our clothes were pressed if we didn't know how to iron."

"She did everything our parents would have done had we been at home," Margaret Matthews said.

Mr. Ab described Charlie B. as the den mother who was always taking care of and looking out for the team. "They were crazy about her," he said.

CHAPTER 12

Foxes, Not Oxes

KEEPING UP THEIR IMAGE WAS A PRIORITY FOR THE TEMPLES, AND FOR the team. Whether the Temples liked it or not, appearances mattered. Due to the disdain the culture had toward female athletes, their appearance was of particular importance, and they took great care to present themselves fully polished in public.

Edward and Charlie B. Temple both believed that the way a person presented themselves to society had a lot to do with the impact they were able to have on the world, and the impact the world would have on them. They expected and encouraged nothing but the highest standards for the women in their care.

"It was like you can't become a team member if you can't become a lady," Barbara Jones said. "Education is first, that's priority. Secondary, track, [and] third, always being a lady. Mrs. Temple instilled that in us. She helped us with our hair; never did you see us anywhere on campus with anything but our hair looking the best. She brought me from my dorm because she noticed that my clothes were still dirty, and things of this sort. See, I didn't have to do all of these things, because . . . Mom always did those things. . . . So, when I got to Tennessee State, Mrs. Temple said, 'Oh, no no no no no no no, we don't send our clothes out to the cleaners, we wash our clothes."

"Our personal appearance and our personal hygiene," Barbara Jones explained, "everything we did was to prepare us for what we were going to encounter in the new world, you see? A world that we knew nothing about." The effort, according to Barbara, took "discipline and consistency."

The Tigerbelles dressed to perfection. Temple Archives

Temple said, "I have tried to promote a good image for women in sports through the years. When we travel, they dress up, and nobody has ever suspected that we are a track team. In fact, the girls have often been mistaken for a choir group."

Margaret Matthews said, "Coach Temple reminded all of us about our character—to be a young lady, to always look nice. He didn't care where we were going, from the dormitory to the cafeteria." The Tigerbelle standards quickly became well known, even outside the campus community. The Tigerbelles were said to be "graceful, beautiful women, not muscle-bound, unattractive athletes"—a distinction that while objectionable to modern sensibilities allowed the team a higher degree of respect in the late 1950s than they would have otherwise been able to garner.

Extra care and time would be taken after practice and competition to towel off, straighten up, brush their hair, and put on some lip gloss. "I had it in my mind," Temple said, "that if we went someplace, I wanted a stranger to wonder, 'What do you young ladies do? Do you sing or are you on a debating team?' I wanted this because at that time, there was a real dilemma over women participating in sports." Temple's responsibility was to clear barriers for his team, and perceptions, although at times unfair, remained a critical impediment.

Temple admitted that he factored in appearance when recruiting his team. He seemed to be fighting an uphill battle against the image of female athletes, and every advantage he could get, he used. He had to counter common beliefs that women who became too muscular would not be able to have children, that they would not be attractive to men— that they would therefore forfeit their ability to perform what so many thought was the chief role of a woman: to be married, have babies, and care for their homes.

"I don't want oxes," Temple said, "I want foxes. I wanted nice-looking girls who took care of themselves who could also run. . . . I was going to prove to the world that you could be feminine and still get the job done."

Mr. Ab agreed. "You had to be ladylike, you see that now. All of them are ladylike. You had to be that." He remembered a time when they would drive ten miles out of the way so that the team could be dressed properly for dinner after a meet.

The focus on their appearance created one more pressure point that the women were forced to bear, something their male counterparts did not have to be concerned with.

"It is pretty difficult being all female, you know," Willye White said. "You are out there on the track and you're in all that dirt and grime and grit, doing the same things the boys are doing. You're not as dainty, because most times your feet hurt, you have sore muscles," Willye said, describing the frustrations they all had. When they ran, they would sweat, and when they sweated, their hair and makeup would be wrecked. It was a plain fact. Willye eventually came to the conclusion that she had to let it go. "So, what you do is your hard work," she said, "and you look ugly out on the track, and after the track meet is over you come back, fix yourself up, and then you're a pretty lady."

Appearance was one part of Temple's philosophy, and one that he felt was crucial to their individual and collective success. Temple's approach has since been criticized as problematic, but as historian Tracey

Salisbury stated, "It is hard to believe that Temple, if he was coaching young African American males, that he would not have expected them to be responsible students first, young men second, and athletes last." He undoubtedly would have required men to also hold themselves up to the highest standards and to be mindful of their public image.

Temple had reason to believe what he did. There was evidence in what he heard from his community, and from the media attention, or lack thereof. Even those who could be considered "friendly" members of the press had opinions. A popular national journalist, A. S. "Doc" Young, wrote in the *Chicago Defender* about Wilma Rudolph, saying she was "probably the first Negro girl athlete to be described as being 'beautiful' in the general-circulating daily press. She proved that a girl didn't require a face by Frankenstein to qualify for the world of track and field."

Wilma Rudolph found help sprucing up her image from the Queens on campus. Barbara Murrell was voted Miss Tennessee State in 1960, an honor that allowed her to be called Queen and live with the prior year's Queen in a plush suite in the dormitory, complete with a private bathroom and television. Wilma endeared herself to Barbara Murrell when she was still in high school, staying on campus for the summer programs while Barbara took extra classes. "One of the sweetest persons that you would ever meet," Barbara said of Wilma. By the time Barbara and her roommate were set up in their suite, Wilma was a regular visitor.

"Wilma would come up and visit me, and she really liked my roommate, and we just became friends. So, we looked out for her like a little sister," Barbara Murrell said. They became close enough for Barbara and her roommate, Jeannine Keane, to invite Wilma to pledge their sorority, Delta Sigma Theta. It was well known that the Tigerbelles were loyal to the rival sorority, Alpha Kappa Alpha, of which Charlie B. was a member, so Barbara worried about the conflict.

"We didn't know how the coach felt about it because his wife was in another sorority, and most of the young ladies running track were in that other sorority. So, we were concerned that the coach and his wife would think we were trying to draw Wilma into our sorority." Charlie B. solved the issue promptly by visiting Barbara personally and thanking her for being so sweet to Wilma. "She said, 'We're just so happy to have you two working with Wilma, and anything we can do to help, just let us know.' Well, that was a relief," Barbara said. "Mrs. Temple was just a lovely lady. She was involved in the young ladies' lives to make sure that anything they needed . . . maybe bake them some food, just to make them feel at home. She was really a wonderful coach's wife."

At the start of January in a new decade, Edward Temple was selected to coach the US women's track and field team for the 1960 Olympics in Rome. It was the first time the national committee had chosen the same coach for four international competitions in a row. The assistant coach selected was Fran Welch of Kansas State Teachers College in Emporia, Kansas. Calls from the newspapermen found Temple at his desk in the post office, and he told them, "I certainly am surprised, but I feel highly honored and am deeply appreciative of the Olympic committee's confidence in me."

Temple had racked up a string of wins leading his sprinters and jumpers in the previous international competitions, starting with the Russian–American games in Moscow in 1958, and followed consecutively by another Russian–American competition in Philadelphia in 1959 and then the 1959 Pan American Games. Temple had proved his mettle to the committee, and the undeniable talent of his team.

Wilma showed the excitement and relief that all of the Tigerbelles must have felt. "Boy, was I overjoyed to hear that," Wilma said. "How lucky can a girl get? My own coach, the one who stuck with me through thick and thin, was going to be the Olympic coach. . . . I knew somebody up there was taking care of me this time around."

The Tigerbelles were seen to be so dominant that they were asked not to participate in the Star Games in DC, when the Chicago Comets (the Chicago Youth Organization) dropped out of the meet. With the Tigerbelles' closest competition out of the games, the remaining participants would have been so far behind that the officials called Temple asking him to withdraw, so "these youngsters wouldn't be too discouraged in their first competition." Temple and the Tigerbelles bowed out, despite their own need to train and record times in official races.

Unfortunately, Temple was often reminded that the admiration of talent didn't always go hand in hand with respect.

Willye White pushed the limits of Temple's rules again and again, and by the spring of 1960 it was finally time for Temple to enforce his three-strikes policy. He called her in to discuss it with her, but she kept going out. He called her grandfather, and she kept going out, and finally, he bought her that Greyhound bus ticket and sent her home.

"It was a hard decision to make," Temple said. "I knew she was great. I knew I was losing a good person, but something had to be done." He ultimately told her, "Now look here, Red. Somebody's got to go, either you or me, and it's not gonna be me, so you're just going to have to go."

Willye had gone too far. "It finally got to the point where Willye had to go," Edwina Temple said. "She challenged him on everything. She'd been on her own, kind of survival mode, she was used to doing whatever she wanted to do, and she just couldn't do that. When everybody else had rules, you had to follow the rules too. He gave her several times, but I just think that she had been on her own too long."

The community was shocked at the move. Not only was Willye an Olympic medalist, but she had also earned national wins every year since. Temple was cutting Willye off his team in the spring of an Olympic year. It was a difficult situation for both of them.

"Willye White was another story," Lucinda Williams said. "A great athlete, a great person, a great woman, but she had some things she wanted to do, and Coach Temple don't take no stuff. As a matter of fact, I think she might have been the only girl who had to leave Tennessee State. Even Margaret [Matthews] with Jesse [Wilburn] made sure she didn't go too far."

Barbara Jones said, "He didn't care how fast you were; you would go home if you did the wrong thing. You would say, Well, I know he's not going to get rid of me. I'm a diva. And all of us were divas. We were fast, but he did not play."

Willye seemed to think that conforming to Temple's rules was compromising. "I was not the kind of athlete that he felt that he was looking for in that I was very independent. . . . I was a maverick. And I wasn't intimidated, I wasn't threatened, you know, and you had to be timid. You know, if he asked a question, if it's something that I didn't understand, I inquired. You don't do that."

Willye was convinced that the decision had been made as more of a personality conflict than any disrespect or breaking of rules on her part. "I had fought hard to get out of Mississippi," Willye said. "And there were things I wanted to see and places that I wanted to go." Willye also believed that there was some jealousy among her teammates, and some unfair rumors had been spread about her.

Being forced to leave the team, this new family that she had chosen, harkened back to her very first betrayal: that of her father denying her at birth. Her father had seen her light skin and gray eyes and said, "She can't be any child of mine." He abandoned Willye and her young mother, still a child herself, who was ill-equipped to raise a child on her own. Willye's father soon admitted that she was in fact his own and took Willye to be raised by his parents. The back-and-forth affected Willye's formative years in such a way that she was forced to depend solely on herself, demanding the independent spirit that could not be confined by Temple's rules and methods.

The decision had been made, and instead of going back to Mississippi, Willye moved to Chicago to train with the Catholic Youth Organization. Her grandfather quit speaking to her, and instead of being a freshman in college, she was on her own. Willye paid a high price for her pride, but she was a survivor, and her will had proven to be unbreakable.

Chicago welcomed Willye with open arms. Mayor Richard J. Daley said to her, "Chicago will give you whatever you need. The only thing I ask of you is that when you're no longer competing, give back to the City of Chicago."

The Tigerbelles had reached their full power by the spring of 1960, but they had lost some of their depth. The AAU Indoor Nationals were held in Chicago on April 16, and local papers named Barbara Jones and Lucinda Williams as favorites, while Wilma Rudolph, Martha Hudson, JoAnn Terry, and Shirley Crowder were noted as ones to watch. Together, the Tigerbelles competed for their sixth straight AAU championship title.

Temple brought eight women for the senior competition and one for the junior. With the recent retirements of his leaders on the team, Temple worried about how ready the small team actually was. "We aren't as strong as a team this year as we were in the past three or four years," Temple told the reporters. "We'll have to make it or break it in the sprints, hurdle competition, and the relays. Numerically, this is about our weakest squad since we won eleven national outdoor and indoor titles." He noted that the sprinters had the speed, but they were lacking in field and distance events.

Track meets were won as a team, and the larger teams often claimed an advantage by having specialists in each of the events. The Tigerbelles won by the versatility of their athletes. Long jumpers could also sprint or run hurdles; sprinters could cover a range from 50 meters to 200 meters, some even covering the 400-meter, a bear of a long race for a sprinter. Over ten events, with only eight competitors, each woman on the Tennessee State team would have to win first, second, or third in every event they participated in to earn enough points for a team win.

Temple's strategy looked like this:

Barbara Jones 100, 400, plus medley relay

Lucinda Williams: 50, 100, 220

Wilma Rudolph: 50, 100, 220

Anna Lois Smith: long jump, 50, medley relay

Shirley Crowder: hurdles, 220, 400 relay

JoAnn Terry: 70-yard hurdles, long jump, high jump

Martha Hudson: 50, 100, 400 relay

Temple not only had his eyes on his own team, but on the other athletes as well, because some of them would end up being on the Olympic team he was assigned to coach. Temple expected his team to do well, but he didn't know who would be coming up behind them.

The Tigerbelles did not disappoint. Together, they won six events and set five American records. Wilma alone was responsible for two of the records, winning all three of her events.

Her moment had arrived.

The qualifying standard for the Olympics was to beat a time set by the third-place finisher from the prior Olympics in each event. In the 100, that translated to 10.9 seconds. Wilma's result and new record was 10.7. Temple was not surprised at her time, simply raising his eyebrows at the result. "Remember," he said, "she did it on a curved run. I know she can do it in a 10.5 on a straight course," noting the difference between the indoor bank curves and the outdoor flat tracks.

Wilma also beat Lucinda Williams in the 200, bumping Lucinda from her reigning position in the event. Her personal performance even merited a few lines in the *New York Times*, although the report was buried deep in the sports section under a page headline about a miniature poodle in a New Jersey dog show.

Now Temple, called "a maker of champions who demands perfection" by the hometown *Nashville Banner*, could see a clear path to Rome for most of his team. His job at that point was to get them ready, keep them healthy, and make sure they stayed safe and out of trouble—a task that could be much harder than it seemed.

When the team arrived home to Nashville, a racial explosion shook their community, putting everything and everyone at risk.

CHAPTER 13

Season of Change

ACROSS TOWN IN NASHVILLE THERE WAS A HIGHLY ACTIVE SPORTS media group. The newspapermen—they were all men—were friendly with the local coaches of the white colleges and high schools, one in particular: Vanderbilt football and track coach, Herc Alley.

Herc had the habit of walking his wife to work in the Romance languages department of Vanderbilt before crossing West End Avenue and meeting his gang of friends at the Elliston Place Soda Shop to catch up on the latest news over a second cup of joe.

Herc, short for Hercules, made his name as a college football star, cheered weekly by thousands of Southeastern Conference (SEC) football fans at the University of Tennessee as their All-American end and captain. When he graduated from playing to coaching, somehow he snagged the most beautiful woman he'd ever seen, a preacher's daughter from Mississippi.

They had three children, two boys and a girl, and lived on campus at Vanderbilt University. Herc considered himself a lucky fellow, being able to play games for a living, even though being a coach meant slightly more pressure and slightly less fun than being a player.

Herc took a smaller role on the football coaching staff in order to run the physical education department, then took over the head coaching position for the men's track team. Though it wasn't the blood sport he knew in football, he admired the purity of a footrace and the versatility of skill required for the various events. He also hated to lose at anything, so he was always scouting the student body for athletes.

That spring, in 1960, Herc had spotted a young man running around the track on his own. "A man came over to me and said he was Coach Alley and asked me my name. I introduced myself, and then he asked me if I'd ever run track in high school." The young man was the future governor of the state of Tennessee and US senator Lamar Alexander. When Lamar said his high school hadn't had a team, Herc asked him to run 100 yards for him at his top speed. "He had a stopwatch and said, '10.1—that's remarkable.' I knew that was fast. . . . I told him I'd never been timed before."

Herc immediately recruited Lamar into the track program and onto his relay team, the fastest he'd yet gathered, that included another young champion, Guy Tallent. "I found out later that he must have been fudging a little bit on the stopwatch," Alexander said, "because I never ran a 10.1 again in my life."

Herc joined up with his buddies Fred Russell and F. M. Williams at the soda shop, along with the regulars, an assortment of coaches, newspapermen, and professors. Mixed into the gossip was more and more chatter about the growing prospects over at Tennessee State with their young coach, Ed Temple.

After the 1960 Indoor National AAU Title win, Russell wrote of the Tigerbelles, "Tennessee A & I State women under Coach Ed Temple promise to surpass their 1956 marks when they dominated the United States team . . . Wilma Rudolph, from Clarksville, with a :10.7 time in the 100, bettered the Olympic International standard of :10.9 this year. Only 19, she could become one of the great women runners of all time." Russell then went on to contemplate how fast human beings could run, noting that Babe Dickerson,[1] the last major American woman who ran on the international scene in the 1930s, would not have been able to qualify.

Fred Russell was one of the only white reporters that kept close tabs on Temple and the Tigerbelles. Dwight Lewis, a Tennessee State student

---

1. Babe Dickerson won two gold medals in the 1932 Olympics (80m hurdles and javelin) before turning to an outstanding career in golf, winning ten major LPGA championships between 1940 and 1954.

who later wrote for *The Tennessean*, noted, "Our sports might be in the paper, but we'd be way in the back."

There was no doubt among the newspapermen's chatter at the Elliston Place Soda Shop that some of the student athletes at Tennessee State would be heading to the Olympics again that year, and no matter how fast the new relay team at Vanderbilt would be, Herc knew they'd never make it past the SEC.

Herc sensed an opportunity.

Just a couple of miles away, there was a team of elite runners that didn't have a proper track to practice on. Herc had a decent track, and his young men could use an up-close look at how international talent performed. An introduction was made, and Herc extended an invitation to the track teams at Tennessee State to practice on the Vanderbilt track.

It seems like an unremarkable and even obvious sharing of resources between the two neighboring universities, but in Nashville in 1960, the situation could not have been more fraught.

In the late winter and early spring of 1960, racial tensions were rising in an otherwise quiet town. The battle played out in downtown stores and restaurants, but it had its roots in the churches and universities, two crucial communities for the mind and soul of the people.

Herc Alley and his wife, Thelma, had been forced to choose sides years before when the church they attended, and where Herc served on the board of stewards, made a choice of their own. The pastor at the Belmont Methodist Church, Dr. John Rustin, hoping to address the inequities of segregation, invited a close friend and scholar from the Black community to join the church.

That same year, the School of Theology at Sewanee in eastern Tennessee had after some considerable controversy agreed to admit qualified Black students, and Vanderbilt followed quietly and without public statement with the admittance of Joseph A. Johnson to the Divinity School at Vanderbilt.[2]

The result was a rift in the church where the beloved pastor was ultimately forced to leave. Herc also resigned his post as steward in protest,

---

2. Johnson earned his PhD at Vanderbilt and was elected bishop in the Christian Methodist Episcopal Church in 1966.

and the family left their community, joining another, more open-minded church.

In contrast, the churches on the other side of Jefferson Street regularly had guests such as C. T. Vivian urging members to stand up for their rights as citizens and as people. "We were human beings," Vivian said. "We have to reach the consciousness of other human beings. To make them understand that every human being should have certain kinds of rights, and that we should have equity in the use of them."

In 1960 Vanderbilt was dealing with a related crisis that threatened to bring down the entire university. Because they were among the first in the South to integrate, the leadership at Vanderbilt considered themselves to be progressive at the time, being ahead of their peer Southern schools such as Duke, Emory, and Tulane, who hadn't even considered the issue. The leadership at Vanderbilt looked forward to a gradual, peaceful transition for the changing landscape. Their goal was to keep things civil and distinguished, and let change be organic and slow-moving. Their best-laid plans were upended, however, with the admittance of a brilliant young man who had studied with Gandhi and had become impatient with the slow arc of change.

Jim Lawson had met Martin Luther King in the spring of 1957, and the two men discussed Lawson's wishes to participate in the "Southern struggle." King encouraged Lawson not to wait, saying that his help was needed urgently. Lawson was advised that Nashville would be the right place to work, and Vanderbilt's Divinity School, the place to study. He applied and was accepted for the fall term of 1959. Lawson spent his nights and weekends working with the Southern chapter of the Fellowship of Reconciliation,[3] and his days as a student.

"When I came to Vanderbilt," Lawson said, "I had no notions about limitations upon my being who I am or who I was then. . . . I loved sports then and wanted to play football and basketball with the Divinity School teams, and I did (I learned later on, of course, that this had some eyebrows lifted)." Lawson was one of the only Black students on the otherwise all-white campus.

---

3. The Fellowship of Reconciliation (FOR) played a crucial role in the civil rights era, continuously advocating for nonviolent advocacy.

Lawson had been participating in workshops on nonviolence throughout the South and was ready to organize in Nashville. The plan was quickly developed to target downtown Nashville, and students from local schools joined him, including John Lewis, Diane Nash, and Marion Barry. One of the early targets was Cain-Sloan department store, where, known or unknown, one of the owners served on the board of trustees at Vanderbilt. The protests started peacefully as planned with over 250 students participating in various locations, and eventually an opposition developed, with local "roughs" in their white T-shirts and slicked hair meeting the students with signs painted with slurs and thrown cigarette butts.

Vanderbilt students were generally dismayed by the unrest. One woman said, "When I saw the photos in the paper of the boys in their blue jeans and their white T-shirts with the sleeves rolled up" antagonizing the protesters in front of Woolworth's, "I was always afraid I was going to see somebody we knew" from her high school.

On Sunday, February 27, 1960, eighty-one students were arrested, and the *Nashville Banner* ran an editorial declaring Lawson the leader of the movement and claiming that he was "inciting anarchy." The *Banner* at the time was run by James Stahlman, another member of the Vanderbilt board of trustees, and an outspoken segregationist.

The board of trustees immediately demanded that Lawson be expelled, and several members of the Divinity School faculty resigned in protest. A months-long battle ensued at the school where the future of the entire university was put at risk. The major financial supporters, the Ford Foundation and the Vanderbilt family, were embarrassed by the scandal that was capturing national attention. It was said that by taking such a stand against progress, Vanderbilt would be forfeiting their status as a major national university and would end up nothing more than a "Southern finishing school."

This was the moment that Herc Alley chose to make a statement of his own and invite the Tigerbelles to campus.

Herc's friend, Fred Russell, was a Vanderbilt graduate and vice president at the *Nashville Banner*, covering sports. Russell had become friendly with Temple, providing most of the local media coverage of the team. Russell made the arrangements between Herc and Temple for the Tigerbelles to use the Vanderbilt track for an hour before the Vanderbilt team had their practice. Time on a smooth track was worth leaving campus for. "It's difficult to run on an uneven surface," Temple said. "We'd get out to practice, and I wouldn't even bring it up. I'd just act like it wasn't even there. Somebody might say, 'Well, you know that surface is uneven.' I'd act like I didn't even hear them. I know it's hard to hit a soft place and then run on a hard stretch. I know it's hard to dodge potholes. But when you've got work to do, you can't get involved in excuses. When we'd get away and run on all of those good tracks, we'd just burn them up."

Vanderbilt's track was no exception.

Temple gathered his team for the two-mile trip across town. "I would make two trips from Tennessee State in my car," he said. "I'd bring about six girls, six or eight, and we'd practice out there about an hour before the men would practice. We were just happy that we could run on a nice smooth track. They had a nice cinder track around Vanderbilt's football stadium, much, much better than the one we had." Temple and Herc got to know each other during those hours. Temple noticed Lamar Alexander running, along with Guy Tallent, and Herc took careful notice of Temple's strategies and techniques and of the immense talent running on his track. He made sure his team noticed it too.

Lamar Alexander said, "The fastest and the best guys at that time did not get to go to the SEC, because that was when Vanderbilt and the other teams were still segregated by race." Lamar said one of the highlights of his time running track at Vanderbilt was watching the Tennessee State athletes practice. "We just sat back and watched," Alexander said. "They were Olympians. Ralph Boston was on that team. And even though Kent Russ won the SEC long jump for Vanderbilt that year, Ralph Boston would come over and practice at Vanderbilt and jumped 2 feet longer than Russ.

"That stuck in my mind, to have the chance to see those several Olympians among the women and few from the men," Alexander said. "Wilma Rudolph was also there at that time. She was amazing."

The Tigerbelles pushed through the gate and saw the smooth and perfectly lined cinder track. The track circled the football field and was surrounded by stands large enough to seat a small army. The infield grass was so green it looked painted and appeared to have been measured blade by blade. It would have been difficult not to imagine how much easier the women's own training would have gone if they'd had access to a facility like that all the time.

The perfectly maintained track was just minutes from where the women toiled away in the muck and the dust. Even though both tracks were in Nashville, one was on the other side of a division that separated the Black part of town from the white. The barrier wasn't an actual wall, but it might as well have been.

The teams practiced side by side long enough to become friendly, joking around together. Ralph Boston, who rarely met a stranger, watched the Vanderbilt relay team practice. He couldn't help but tease his new friend, Lamar Alexander. "Hey, Lamar," Ralph called out to him, "you know why you're on that Vanderbilt relay team?"

"No, why?" Lamar called back.

"It's because they need four guys. Because you are terrible."

To understand how this joke would land, one has to understand Ralph Boston. The friendliest kid who ever leapt through the sky. He spoke with a wide grin, and it was impossible for anyone who received his attention not to respond in kind.

Vanderbilt's success, or lack thereof, was not due to insufficient effort; they simply were not as fast. Herc was tough in his training, too, though he could not possibly be as strict or maintain the level of command Temple had achieved with his Tigerbelles.

The Vanderbilt team used Centennial Park for distance running, across West End Avenue from their more urban campus. The park was and still is a large open space crowned with a full-scale replica of the Parthenon of ancient Greece. "He made something out of not very much," Alexander said of Herc. "He coached amateur athletes and brought the best out of us. He put together some pretty good teams with some average athletes."

Ralph Boston remembers running at Centennial Park, too, "near the Parthenon."

"There is a stretch of nice soft green grass," Boston recalled. "I would take off my shoes and run barefoot through that grass. You could do that, and nobody bothered you. I don't know if you're allowed to do that now. Nobody said a word to you, they just left you alone, and you did your thing." He noted being allowed to run at Centennial Park for a reason; he was well aware that at the time that there were plenty of places he wasn't allowed to go.

Boston was the youngest of nine children and was raised in Laurel, Mississippi. "Growing up in Laurel was like growing up in any small town in Mississippi in the late 1940s and 1950s," Boston said. "You didn't expect much because there wasn't much around set aside for Blacks." He went to school in a small wood building without heating, using books that were passed down from the white children's schools when they were either too worn-out or out-of-date to be wanted anymore.

Everyone in Laurel knew him as Hawkeye. "Before the age of ten," Boston said, "I looked like six o'clock. Skinny and straight up and down. I had a big head and bulging eyes, so large that I couldn't fully close them." His cousin called him Hawkeye because it seemed like he wanted to keep an eye on things, even while he slept.

Ralph Boston. Temple Archives

In high school Boston was a strong student as well as a crack athlete, and had his own ambition to go to college. "Quite honestly, coming out of Mississippi, my first choice was to attend the University of Mississippi," he said. "It made sense for me to want to go there. My family and relatives were taxpayers within the state. It made sense for me to go to a state-supported university which offered the things the traditional Black colleges didn't offer. It didn't make sense to me, why a resident of that state could not attend a state institution. But of course, I couldn't in that time because I was Black."

The University of Mississippi was in the same Southeastern Conference for athletics as Vanderbilt, and the entire conference had yet to be integrated. Instead, Boston came to Tennessee State, much farther from home than he cared to travel. "Understand, I came from Laurel, Mississippi," Boston said. "Nothing happens there but morning, noon, and night."

Boston was terrified to leave home, and his mother, Eulalia Boston, was also overwhelmed by the change. She asked, "Who would have thought my baby's jumping around would amount to this?"

Boston said, "I was scared to death. I thought the old gym was the biggest building in the world."

While the men's team was coached separately, they used the same facilities, and Ralph learned his rank as second to the Tigerbelles as soon as he met Ed Temple.

"I walked out onto the track, and there were hurdles set," Boston said. "And I raised them, because they were too low," as they were set for the women's team. Boston heard a voice behind him say "Ph-shew, old buddy, when you finish, you put them back like you got them." It was Coach Temple, and he wasn't about to let his team's equipment be disrespected by the newcomer. "It wasn't a knock on him," Boston explained. He hadn't yet had the opportunity to earn Temple's notice. He'd have to show some results to earn Temple's respect.

Boston didn't mind. His world was just beginning to expand. "So, when I came to Nashville and made the team and traveled all around and was able to see other things, other cities, other areas, how people lived. That was a lesson to me. That was wonderful."

CHAPTER 14

The Children's Movement

THE YEAR 1960 IN NASHVILLE WAS THE EPICENTER OF THE RISING CIVIL rights movement. Nashville was "a seemingly pleasant city in a border state" between North and South, and also an educational hub called the "Protestant Vatican," because it was home base for several Southern religious groups, their publication divisions, and their seminaries. In less than four square miles there were several major universities.

The schools included Tennessee State, the largest historically Black university in the state; Fisk, a private, historically Black college with a distinguished academic history; Meharry Medical, the historically Black medical school and hospital where Wilma Rudolph had been treated as a child; the American Baptist College, where a young man named John Lewis was a student; Scarritt, a segregated Methodist college; Peabody College, for teachers; and Vanderbilt University with its many divisions, including the Divinity School where Jim Larson had become one of the first Black students accepted.

While the schools were physically close together, there were two distinct parts of town. Fisk, Meharry, American Baptist College, and Tennessee State were on one side of Jefferson Street, and the white world—known to the Black community as Crosstown—started at Charlotte Avenue, just a block away. To move from one side of town to the other required crossing the railroad tracks, often over or under bridges, and was most easily done by bus. The streets had been designed this way specifically to allow domestic help to cross over by direct bus lines to specific parts of town, but to make it more difficult for anyone on foot.

The movement to demand civil rights was noticed by the white power structure in Nashville, but its citizens were under the impression that changes were already occurring peacefully and "in an orderly and civilized way. Yet there was more talk about change than there was change." The movement demanded more than "the right to eat a hamburger where they chose." They wanted to create change in Nashville, and then move their momentum throughout the Deep South, "rooting out segregation in all of its insidious forms."

Jim Lawson led workshops at the First Baptist Church, where students were taught to maintain peace while under attack, often subjected to intense simulations of actions they expected to encounter during protests such as being taunted with slurs, pouring buckets of liquids over their heads, and being physically dragged around.

"You see, the greatness of the nonviolent action is that it says that if you're willing to suffer for what's right, wrong will show itself, and when it does, the people will turn against it because they know it is evil," C. T. Vivian said.

The group chose a target by listening to the women among their ranks. "You men don't know anything about the downtown," one of them said, "You don't shop. You don't know the humiliations that they inflict on us every day." Stores were more than willing to allow Black patrons to shop and spend their money, but they would be forced to use separate bathrooms or none at all, would not be allowed to try on the clothes that they would purchase, and would often be treated like children.

Diane Nash was from Chicago and enjoyed wandering through stores, buying at her leisure and then maybe stopping for lunch, but in Nashville, while she was welcome to spend her money on products, this did not extend to the lunchrooms.

The target was chosen, and the group planned to orchestrate sit-ins at a specific set of restaurants and lunch counters downtown. In February of 1960, 124 Black students visited lunch counters where they were met by "hoodlums pouring coffee on the protesters and trying to extinguish cigarettes on their heads."

It was student-led, and student-powered.

Diane Nash, a student at Fisk, was drawn to the movement after she had gone on a date to the State Fair in Nashville. It was partly seeing the WHITE ONLY and COLORED signs on the restrooms, but it was also because her date, who was from the South, did not appear to be bothered. For Diane, the experience "was so transcending, her anger so immediate and so complete, that she was effectively politicized from that moment on."

Nashville proved to be the ideal choice of training ground for the young fighters. If the city had been more tolerant, it would not have provided enough resistance to test the mettle of the students, but more resistance to the movement might have stopped the protests before they got off the ground. These young men and women were putting everything on the line. They were at the very start of their careers, their lives. They were at the point in time when a single choice or bad decision could impact the rest of their lives.

When it came time for Diane Nash to join the fight, she was terrified. Not only could she lose her position at Fisk, but there was also a serious risk of being put in jail, and of physical violence. Looking around at the group that she had joined, Diane was afraid for all of them. "We are a bunch of children," she said. "We're nice children, bright and idealistic, but we are children, and we are weak. We have no police force, no judges, no cops, no money." The odds seemed stacked against them.

John Lewis felt from a very early age that his people were being exploited and came to Nashville to follow his dream of an education in 1957. "Go to school and end that system," his mother said. Though not far in miles, Lewis traveled a "great distance from the cotton fields of rural Pike County, Alabama," with the "peanut fields and cornfields and preaching to the chickens. I kept my eyes on the prize, stayed focused, worked hard, never gave up, and kept on trying."

Lewis "left home with a $100 bill, more money than I ever held," one suit, a shirt, and "maybe an extra pair of shoes." He found the fight that he was searching for with the movement in Nashville. "The environment in Nashville made me a different person," Lewis said, "made me a better person. If it hadn't been for Jim Lawson and the nonviolent workshops in the city of Nashville, I don't know where I would be today."

The movement needed numbers, and Curtis Murphy joined their ranks right on time. Curtis was a student at Tennessee State, where most of the students had not yet participated. Curtis understood the reason. Most of the other students at Tennessee State had come from backgrounds like his, with serious financial hardship. Most of them simply couldn't afford to put their education at risk. Their families had collectively made significant sacrifices in order to give their children a chance to improve themselves, and it wasn't something they would easily throw away.

The tuition at Tennessee State was $1,000 per year. For the Murphy family, that represented nearly half of the family's annual income. Tennessee State was a shining beacon of opportunity for so many students like Curtis, filled with a vibrant student life, engaging teachers, and a sense of opportunity for change. But the university was also hampered by a severe lack of funding compared to state schools in the North, or white institutions throughout the South.

Curtis's friends thought he had lost his mind when he decided to participate in the protests, telling him he was putting his life at risk. But when Curtis participated in his first workshop, he saw a reason to believe that things could be different—that he could play a part in that change.

The sit-ins were well under way, and soon began to escalate. As many students were recruited to protest for the right to be served, the number of counter-protesters also grew, determined to prohibit them. It wasn't long before the counter-protesters became violent.

Barbara Jones described the violence that was happening, saying, "See, they had put cigarettes, burned cigarettes in the ears, and on the face." Barbara twisted her finger into a spot on her face to show the movement of a crushing cigarette burn. "Things like that, and on the hand, and you had to stand there, you had to sit there. You couldn't move, you couldn't react. You see, that's what they wanted. . . . They came there for the purpose of rioting. So, you had to stay nonviolent."

C. T. Vivian said, "Our motto was, we cannot allow violence to destroy nonviolence."

Curtis achieved hero status on campus on par with the major athletes when he was arrested, and then released from jail. Recruitment then became easy, and he gathered more and more students to the cause.

Because Tennessee State was funded by the state government, the local politicians had fiscal authority and started to pressure the administration to stop the students by threatening expulsion and disciplinary action. Instead, Dr. Walter Davis spoke to the student body at a basketball game. He told the students, "Beware of those who would take you down the primrose path when you have so much still ahead of you." Curtis was certain that the remarks were directed at him as Dr. Davis continued: "Beware of those who want you to do their political work for them. Remember, you're not here for politics, but to study." While humbled for being so publicly chastised, Curtis also understood that it was the school's way of addressing the concern without direct discipline.

The tension was not only between the protesters and the opposition, but within the young and old in the community, the students and their parents, or their teachers and coaches. "That meant when they challenged the laws, they were carrying a dual burden—of violating the laws of Nashville and violating various agreements they had made with their parents as well," wrote David Halberstam in *The Children*.

Barbara Murrell was one of the students who struggled, along with the Tigerbelles and many of her classmates, regarding her personal decision. "I really, coming from Mississippi, wanted to be a part of the sit-ins," she said, but the decision was as complicated for her as it was for many of the others. "I would have missed days to complete my student teaching position, so I had to make a choice. You know, I worked my way through high school, and I had some help from my mother, and I didn't know what would happen if I didn't get a chance to finish. So, I decided that I was going to go on and finish my student teaching and I wasn't going to [be part of a] sit-in. That was a decision that I had to make."

Barbara's painful choice did not prevent her from finding other ways to contribute to the movement. "I did make the decision to do all of the homework for my good friend Lucretia Collins.[1] She was in all the

---

1. Lucretia Collins was arrested in Jackson, Mississippi, for participating in the Freedom Rides on May 24, 1961.

sit-ins. She and Diane Nash and all of those were the leaders of the sit-ins. So, I was completing her assignments and getting them turned in. That was my contribution." The students joined together in support, each doing what they could, and standing behind those that were willing and able to put themselves on the front lines.

As the violence and danger to their children increased, the older generation, led by their ministers, promoted a boycott of the downtown businesses as a way to support them. It was estimated that the cost to shops downtown could be as high as 30 percent of sales. Some of the stores wanted to give in right away, but there were some holdouts, including from one of the major department stores, Cain-Sloan. They were being encouraged by daily reports and opinion pieces in the *Nashville Banner* by its editor and Vanderbilt board member, a hard-line segregationist, James Stahlman.

Once the fight came to the Tennessee State campus, it was heated. "[The] 1960 civil rights [movement] was very much on campus," Edward Temple said.

The world may have been on fire around them, but Temple tried to keep his team focused on what they were there to do. He told them, "We're here to get an education and run track. The things you do are going to open up doors. They're going to open up doors their way by going downtown and sitting at the lunch counters and we're going to support that." The boycott of the downtown stores was holding strong, and none of the Tigerbelles would break it. Still, the women wanted to be involved.

They were natural leaders. They had experience in front of a crowd. They knew how to hold their heads high, be completely composed, and walk together as they had the right to do. The nerves in the air were similar to the pre-race tension they were all familiar with, but the fight they wanted to be a part of carried a darker threat. It seemed absurd that simply walking down a street together could have dangerous outcomes, but it absolutely did. They could get harassed, yelled at, arrested, or much worse. But they understood that unless people spoke up and asked for change, things would stay the same.

"Look, we all had experienced racism," Lucinda Williams said. "Most of us came from the segregated South. We knew what it was like. We also knew why we had bagged lunches and had to go to the bathroom in fields when we traveled. At the end of the day, we knew Mr. Temple had it right: We needed to get our degrees, compete hard, and be young ladies. We were going to get equality through our hard work, we were not going to be denied; we didn't need to protest to accomplish those things."

They each brought their own histories with them, and their own scars were being reopened. Wilma remembered sitting outside the fairgrounds in Clarksville, Tennessee, every year when the annual county fair took place. "We Black kids used to get together and sit on the grass across from the main entrance," Wilma said. "We'd sit there for hours and hours, watching the white people go in and out, dressed in all of their fineries and with their fancy horses."

Wilma was barely in grade school, with the brace still on her leg, and was not allowed to attend the fair. It was the first time she realized that there were two worlds: one for white people, and one for Black. She and her friends would snap off long blades of grass, braiding it, pretending it was a doll's hair, and gossip about the white people walking by. "Lookit that lady's dress," she would say, "or that man's fancy saddle." Then the truth glared at her. "White people treat their horses better than they treated us Black people."

Wilma's mother spent so much time cleaning the homes of people who had all of the helpful time-saving modern appliances that money could buy while the Rudolph family's home had no indoor plumbing. While Tennessee got swelteringly hot in the summer, the winters could be frigid, the temperature often dropping below zero. Spending a winter huddled around a woodstove and running outside to use a frozen outhouse, Wilma saw her mother rise early on Saturday mornings "to serve these people with all the latest conveniences their coffee in bed."

It pained Wilma to see her mother work in this way, knowing how much time and money her mother had also spent focused on Wilma's health. "I remember I was six, maybe, and said to myself, 'There's just something not right about all of this. White folks got all the luxury, and we Black folks got all the dirty work.'"

Wilma questioned her parents about the unfairness of it all, but they told their children that they had to "hold their tongue," and to "accept things because that's just the way it is."

The separate worlds were never clearer to Wilma than when she went to the "white grocery store" with her mother. "White kids could giggle and act silly; Black kids had to keep their mouths shut." They were taunted by the white kids as they walked through town, called racial slurs, and coaxed into fights.

"You get scars deep inside of you that sometimes never heal," Wilma said.

The Tennessean ran a series of articles chronicling the protests. One particularly egregious incident showed John Lewis and James Bevel sitting with their backs to the camera at a Krystal's burger joint. Two young white women in white-skirted uniforms with buttoned aprons and jaunty little caps perched on their heads were busy at the sink, manipulating a metal box with tubes that was intended to fumigate the space with bug spray. In the next photo John Lewis leaned against the glass door from the inside, clutching some papers to his chest and a handkerchief to his running eyes.

The article describes the event as happening at 204 Fifth Avenue in the downtown Krystal's location. The caption said, "Gasping for breath, student demonstrators James Bevel and John Lewis stand inside the insecticide fume-filled lunch counter after the manager turned on a fumigating machine to disrupt their sit-in. The pair remained inside the restaurant for half an hour while it filled up with a dense cloud of non-toxic insect spray. They finally left when asked to do so by Assistant Fire Chief W. D. Gallaher, who was called by the police."

Whatever was considered to be "non-toxic" in 1960 included the chemical components of many currently banned substances.

There was division among all of the communities in Nashville. While intense arguments continued on the Vanderbilt campus and in the white churches, the Black community was divided as well. The older generation encouraged the fight for equality to be waged in the courtroom, but the young students were impatient. They believed that change was happening far too slowly.

While the white "hoodlums" escalated the violence, it was only the Black students that were arrested, including many from Tennessee State. The Tigerbelles were warned by the administration that if they were arrested, they would forfeit their opportunity to compete, and an order from the government was made that any arrested students would be expelled. The stakes could not have been higher for the women. They each had their own personal decision to make.

CHAPTER 15

Their Own Path

IN A JUST WORLD, THE TIGERBELLES WOULD HAVE BEEN ABLE TO STAND up and speak their minds for the sake of righteousness, but time after time the world has not been proven to be just. It wasn't possible in their world to be both an activist and an elite athlete. To even dare to believe it possible was a luxury of youth.

They were running against headwinds as it was. They couldn't afford distractions, much less the kind that could land them in jail, or worse.

It didn't stop Barbara Jones from trying.

"Martin Luther King came to Tennessee State," Barbara said, "and he asked us if we wanted to participate. Because that was a personal choice. My boyfriend told me, you need to not be a part of the sit-in, but at the telephones. Because you don't have the type of temper. Your temper will not allow you to go down there. You will spoil Dr. Martin Luther King's whole program," Barbara said, laughing. She spread her hands in the air, imagining a headline: "Ladies caught beating up . . ." Barbara trailed off, amused at the possibility. She and her boyfriend were both very aware of her ego, and her unwillingness to accept a slight of any kind. She was a champion, and she was not used to standing down.

Barbara still wanted to find a way to participate. "I said, no, I've got to be a part of this." She and a group of people decided to go downtown to scope out the situation. "You see, we didn't have to go off-campus," Barbara said. "Everything was on campus. So, we didn't know anything about Nashville downtown."

They went to a cafeteria style restaurant with a velvet rope blocking off the seating area with a sign that read, WHITES ONLY. Someone in the group asked, "Where do we go to get a hamburger?" and the restaurant worker told them to go outside to the back of the building. "And we went around the back, and we knocked on the door," Barbara said.

Someone in the kitchen answered, "Yeah, what do you want?"

"We want a hamburger," Barbara and her friends replied.

"Now we weren't going to eat it," Barbara said, "because we knew how he prepared that hamburger. But he slapped it in our hands. No napkins. That's how we received the hamburger. So of course, I'm not going to say what we did with that hamburger, but he didn't like his door when he opened it, I'll just say that. Because we weren't going to eat it.

"But this is the first time I had sensed something like this, and I was steaming, because I've never been treated like that," Barbara continued. "So, then we went to the movies. We went to the front. You had to pay in the front, and then go around the side, where it was fire escapes. Four flights high. And you walked up the fire escape. But it was supposed to have been a privilege to go downtown to the movies.

"Well, when we got there, there were benches that you sat on. And you were so high that the picture looked like a little handkerchief down there. So, then we had an idea. Then we understood what Martin Luther King was trying to say. That we were just as equal and privileged as anyone else," Barbara said.

After the movie, Barbara and her friends went next door to the five-and-dime restaurant. "We sat down, the girl was sitting there," said Barbara, mimicking the woman at the restaurant with her arms crossed, head back in defiance. The woman told the group, "We don't serve n******."

Barbara and her friends then went to another spot. Barbara said, "When I sat down, this man came up and said, 'N*****, get out of that seat.' And I just looked forward, and he spat. And I can still feel that sting. Right here," Barbara pointed to a place on her cheek, just below her eye, next to her nose. "Right here. He spat in my face," she said. "But then he grabbed my hair after he spat in my face, and that's when my boyfriend said, 'Sir, she's getting up.'"

Barbara's boyfriend told her, You're leaving, "Because he knew I was about to—I just couldn't take it," she said.

Willye White said that she had been actively discouraged from participating not because of her athletic status, but because of her hot temper. "They were asking for nonviolent people," Willye said. "And I am definitely not going to allow someone to stick a match to me, a cigarette to me, spit on me and sic a dog on me and I'm gonna walk away. And I knew that, and my parents knew that, and everyone who knew me knew that. And they just said, 'We don't need people like you because you will not help the cause.'"

Willye knew that her way to help was by speaking with the press when she gained attention through her accomplishments. "We had the press and we talked to the press and shared with the world what was occurring."

Even Mrs. Temple counseled them to keep their peace. "We advised them to get an education and not use the track team as a political forum," Charlie B. said. The Temples always fell back on the belief that the women would be more effective advocates for their communities from the place of achievement, excellence, and status they had worked so hard to earn.

The team was forced to stand on the sidelines for this race, but their hearts were with their fellow students. They were so young and full of righteous anger. It seemed to the older generation that the young protesters didn't have a sense of the danger they were stirring up, but once they saw their progress, they began to believe that maybe these young students were on to something. Maybe they knew exactly what they were doing and what it would cause and were willing to sacrifice that much. For the generation that had spent their lives trying to stay out of trouble and under the radar, it was terrifying to see all these bright young students with a world of promise ahead of them risking everything.

When their calm, quiet, and peaceful protests were met with such rage and hatred, their youth was taken away, just as their elders had feared. The light of optimism within their eyes shifted to the steely determination to fight on.

The Tigerbelles were forced to focus on their own fight for equality, for the recognition that they deserved. People who so casually dismissed them or refused to acknowledge their achievements knew nothing of these women and who they really were. They didn't know how hard they worked, how much they pushed themselves, and how they'd taken so many courageous steps to be in the place they were.

"But you know what was great about Mr. Temple is that he didn't let us have any fear," Barbara Jones said. "He would tell us, 'All you have to do is the right thing. That's all you have to do. And don't let anyone make you feel any less than what you are. Because you are somebody. And if they don't know it now, but shoo, they'll realize it later.'"

The drive behind those five a.m. wake-up calls and afternoons in the sweltering heat was for recognition, for achievement. In order to prove themselves to the world, they had to behave in such a way as to make them impossible to undermine, and to ignore. The team, and their leaders, collectively agreed to "show them on the track." In his team's eyes, Temple saw the hope of what could be. It was quieter and not as flashy as a protest, but it was true, and in the long run, he believed it would mean the same.

There was at least one man who bridged the gap between the young activists and the quiet fight of the older advocates using the law for change. Z. Alexander Looby was "a revered figure" in the Black community of Nashville. "Sophisticated, erudite, and tough-minded," Mr. Looby was an active and well-established civil rights attorney.

In the early-morning hours of April 19, 1960, twenty-one sticks of dynamite exploded in Mr. Looby's home. Miraculously, almost unbelievably, no one was hurt, but it became the single event that brought the divided community together and created a force that the political powers in Nashville could no longer push to the side. Word spread rapidly and a call to action was set. There would be a march from the Tennessee State campus, starting at the ROTC building and extending over three miles to the steps of the state capitol. The march would take more than an hour, with students and citizens gathering forces along the way.

Lucinda Williams wanted to participate. "We were down there by the old ROTC building," she said. "That's where they were forming up. That's where I met my husband because he was an instructor at the ROTC. We were there and they were getting ready to go downtown. We were all ready to go and Coach Gentry said, 'If you go downtown and you get put in jail, you're going to lose your scholarship.' Being seventeen years old at that time, and the idea of having that working aid being taken away from me, I had to make the choice. I had to make the choice that I'd rather stay there on campus instead of being put in jail because I couldn't afford to go back home. I didn't want to let my family down, the neighbors that I had, the church folk there. I just couldn't take that chance. So, I made that decision."

The Tigerbelles all stayed behind while their peers marched on.

Temple encouraged them, saying, "You can't take that chance to have your opportunity be taken away. In the long run, you will have the opportunity to make that difference in other ways."

Barbara Murrell watched her friends march as well. "It was difficult," she said, of their journey. "I guess from my school downtown to First Avenue, we are thirty-six blocks out. Fisk University is eighteen blocks out. . . . So, our students started off and went by Fisk and picked up a whole lot of other students, and when they got downtown it was this huge number of students."

As always, when the Tennessee State and other students of Nashville were out in the world, they were dressed to perfection, leaving no room for anyone to disparage them. "They were walking in three-inch heels for thirty-six blocks," Barbara Murrell said.

"What was unique about the movement," she continued, "was we were from all over. If I had been in my hometown, then someone in city government could have called my parents and said they wanted me out, so I couldn't have participated. But when you've got students away from home, in college, and here comes a movement. Parents hear about it and they call on the phone and say, I know you're not in that . . . and they'd say, of course not!"

Thousands of people stood outside the capitol building. Folk singer Guy Carawan played his guitar and led the crowd in an adaptation of an old spiritual that was adopted as the song of the movement from that day forward, "We Shall Overcome." Diane Nash stood at the front of the crowd when Nashville mayor Ben West met them on the steps and said, "I appeal to all citizens to end discrimination, to have no bigotry, no bias, no hatred."

Diane Nash pressed the mayor, saying, "Do you mean that to include lunch counters?"

"Little lady," West said, "I stopped segregation years ago at the airport when I first took office, and there has been no trouble since."

Nash responded, "Then, Mayor, do you recommend that the lunch counters be desegregated?"

West answered, "Right, that is absolutely right!"

The crowd erupted in emotional relief, with tearful embraces and ebullient cheers. The students had won. The mayor had ordered the restaurants downtown to serve everyone, and the headline in *The Tennessean* the next day shouted the directive: INTEGRATE COUNTERS—MAYOR.

It was a major win, but it was not expected to solve everything overnight. Howard Gentry Sr., athletic director at Tennessee State, told his son, "Now just because the law says that you can go to these restaurants, and go to school with the white kids, don't think that people are just going to change their attitudes and treat you differently. You're going to have to help them. You're going to have to teach them that you know how to read, you know how to write, you know how to swim, you know how to ride horses, you've been to New York, Washington. You've got to help them to understand that you're no different than they are, because they have grown up being told another story."

Little Howie lived up the street from the Elliston Place Soda Shop where the newspapermen and Herc Alley gathered in the mornings. All he wanted when the lunch counters were ordered to serve him was some ice cream. He walked up to the store and a waitress rushed outside, asking him what he was doing there.

When he asked for some ice cream, she shook her head, refusing him and sending him away in tears. When he told his mother what happened, she wrapped her arms around her son and told him to pray for that waitress, to pray for all of them. "When it comes to discrimination, we were taught that was one of the worst things you could do to someone," Gentry said. "My mom would tell me that I needed to prepare myself to take my rightful place in society when my time came, and you can't do that trading hate for hate."

He went back every day until he finally was given an ice-cream cone to eat outside on the curb, and then eventually, he was allowed to sit at the counter.

While Little Howie prayed for the waitress at the soda shop, the dormitories on the Tennessee State campus were dealing with regular bomb threats. "It was a very difficult time because when you were in it, you didn't know what was going to happen," Barbara Murrell said.

"They were bombing houses. It rained in Nashville every day, it looked like, so we had these big rubber boots that we wore, and the dormitory director would say, 'When you get ready to go to bed every night, take your winter coat and put it over the bottom part of your bed and put your boots right by it,' because every morning at three o'clock we'd get a bomb threat. So, then everybody had to run out of the building. The idea was that you have your boots and your coat right there because it was cold in Nashville. And if you got out there and you didn't have your proper boots and your coat on, you'd really be cold, because they had to come and check the whole building."

The entire dormitory would be emptied out while the fire department combed the hallways for hours on end. Students stood out in the cold losing valuable hours of sleep and study time and making themselves vulnerable to colds and flu.

"That shows you how dangerous it was," Barbara Murrell said, "with Attorney Looby's house being bombed, because the signal was, why wouldn't we think they would bomb the residence hall? So, when the fire alarm goes off, you wouldn't question whether or not there was a bomb, you just got out. Because you know, down the street, they just bombed this man's house, so why wouldn't anybody come here and bomb us."

The upheaval and the cost levied on the students was exactly the point of the threats. The students became suspicious of anyone on campus that wasn't student or faculty, anyone from a different part of town. Living through fear and anxiety night after night, losing sleep and confidence in their own personal safety, caused all of the students to consider their environment differently.

At a point in their lives when the students simply wanted to live their lives, creating a better future for themselves and hopefully also having a little fun, they faced regular threats. "I was Queen," Barbara Murrell said, "and I was ready to run every night."

Most turned to their churches as a refuge from their pain, and as a place to heal. Wilma Rudolph came to that practice young. "My mother used to take us to the Baptist Revival Week." Wilma remembered the tradition as a time when folks all over town would gather with baskets of food spread over blankets and tables, and the men would sneak off into the woods to take nips of whiskey while the women pretended not to notice. The point was to gather the community, and to center around the church.

There was solace to be found in scripture. In Acts 10:34–36, it is written, "Then Peter began to speak: 'I now realize how true it is that God does not show favoritism but accepts from every nation the one who fears him and does what is right. You know the message God sent to the people of Israel, announcing the good news of peace through Jesus Christ, who is Lord of all.'"

"Look, Black people were still drinking from separate water fountains back then," Wilma said. "Why? They couldn't get credit because white-owned stores wouldn't give them any. Why? They couldn't even eat in the same restaurants that white people ate in. . . . But the churches didn't have restrictions. The churches said to Black people, Come, we've got a place for you, with no questions asked."

"We are all strong believers," Lucinda Williams said. "We would go to church on campus. And go to Mass with Barbara [Jones], because she was Catholic. I was the praying one. I would lead the prayers. That was just a part of us."

CHAPTER 16

Blue and White

WITH TRAVEL FOR AWAY MEETS, CHARLIE B. WAS LEFT TO KEEP THINGS in shape at home. "When I was growing up, he was gone just about every weekend and my mother ran the show," Edwina said. "They would leave Thursday or Friday, depending on if they were driving in the vans or station wagons or taking a bus. That would make a difference. And then they would come home on Sunday and the whole cycle would start all over again. I remember him being gone quite a bit."

Charlie B. worked out a strategy to help manage her heavy workload. "She would do everything she needed to do before he would come home so that she was ready to do the laundry," Edwina said. "Make dinner every night. No shortcuts. She would cook ahead on the weekends, a roast or green beans, or do a chicken." Charlie B.'s sister would often come and help her bake and cook, and keep her company, but Edwina said, "She did a lot of it solo."

Two weeks of vacation were required by law, but Charlie B. hadn't seen time off in years, and neither had Temple. He asked President Davis for a few days off, and according to Temple, Davis responded, "But Temple, you've just come back from Russia!"

"I ask for a raise, he say, 'Temple, you're young.' I told him, 'Listen, Mr. President, when I go through the supermarket, that cash register just the same as for a person ninety years old.' I went in once and asked if I could have just two jobs, and I thought he like to have died." Three jobs, a young family, and a team full of responsibilities all weighed on Temple, but the burden would have been easier to bear had he felt respected by his school.

Tennessee State seemed to still consider him "Little Eddie," as if he were still the young student athlete that came to school a decade before. Temple worried about the funding not only for himself and his young family, but also for the team and their needs. They could work and perform all day long, but still had to rely on the school to give them the money they needed for travel and equipment. Every medal, every championship, every world record they obtained, Temple hoped the ask would be easier, but it never seemed to happen.

"In the springtime, he would try to save some of his money for the outdoor meets," Edwina said, "and they would take his money for spring football. They would just take the money out. So, what could he do? Before Christmas break, he would get all of his requisitions in before the semester ended for the spring and have it all approved and the checks already cut because he knew they were going to take his money."

Howard Gentry was the man that made the call on funding decisions. He was the athletic director presiding over a golden age of sports for Tennessee State. He'd been the head football coach until recently, and as the AD, he put all of that energy and drive into the whole sports program. Their football and basketball teams were at the top of their games, regularly sending athletes on to professional careers. There were other sports, too, but nothing quite brought the spotlight like the big two, including the Tigerbelles.

"He was AD in a time where it just was not popular to fund the women's sports, and they got away with not doing it," Howard Gentry Jr. said. "My dad would find ways to put money into the women's programs from the men's programs without having to budget for it, but he was never satisfied that he had done enough. Coach Temple had a right to say that he only had a station wagon and three hundred dollars. That used to hurt my dad so badly because he was telling the truth, and there was nothing he could do about it. And he did all he could. Coach Temple was not exaggerating. They had little or nothing, and he created the fastest women in the world [even] with [that] lack of resources."

For Temple, the sparse funding was a kick in the stomach. He was never able to trust that the nice words and platitudes would turn into the dollars they couldn't make ends meet without. Their funding was always last in line, and even at a school specifically for Black students, they were underrated and undervalued—not because of their race, but for their gender.

It seemed like he faced a fight in every direction. He wasn't only fighting for the funding needed for the team, but for the women themselves. The time they were putting into their training, work study, and schoolwork didn't leave them with much time to earn money for their living expenses, which most of them desperately needed. More than just the physical work and toil, the athletes faced an actual cost of lost earning potential and time away from their classes. Still, the women did their work; they did everything that was asked of them.

"The athlete has had to make all kinds of financial sacrifices to make it to the Nationals and to be away at training camp," Temple said, noting that while "Uncle Sam picks up the tab" for the qualifiers at the international level, simply being away for so long is often a hardship. "Sure, it's an honor to participate in something like this," Temple continued, "but when you get back you can't buy a new dress or a new pair of pants for school."

It wasn't only Tennessee State athletes that faced this issue. The problem was systemic. Team USA was responsible for their own training, while their greatest international competition had the full support of their governments.

"In Europe they take their track and field seriously," Temple said. "It's a well-supported major sport over there, and their facilities are superior to ours." The disparity in support between the nations kept the women from the States, and especially the Tigerbelles, in the underdog position on the international stage. "When you get into this international level of competition, you're really diving into deep water."

Earlene Brown, shot-putter from California, gave up training between meets almost entirely while she went to beauty school and spent long days on her feet, making other women beautiful, to feel better about themselves. She had no choice, as a newly single mother; her own survival and that of her child had to be the priority.

With all the headwinds the Tigerbelles were facing, on campus and off, they kept working. They were very nearly prepared to go out into the world and see where they stood among the best.

A team competition, the Blue and White meet, took place on Tennessee State's campus on Friday, May 20, 1960, earning the focus and praise of Fred Russell in the *Nashville Banner*. A photo was placed in the sports section of the finish of the 200-meter, showing Wilma Rudolph out in front with Lucinda Williams a few feet behind. The caption read: "Tennessee A & I's famed girl track stars, working hard under Coach Ed Temple for berths in this year's Olympic Games in Rome, are competing in a bit of intrasquad competition on the A & I campus. Here is the finish of the 200-meter event Friday with Wilma Rudolph an easy winner over Lucinda Williams (in white) and Shirley Crowder. Wilma's time: 24.7."

In Fred Russell's weekly sports column, Sidelines, he devotes the entire column on May 25 to discussing the team's strengths. This kind of attention was exceedingly rare in the media in general, and particularly for the *Banner*, whose managing editor had been one of the city's most ardent and outspoken segregationists. But Fred Russell had earned the right to cover what he was interested in, and during the spring of 1960, it was the Tigerbelles.

"Wherever United States Olympic track candidates are training, it's unlikely that the personal competition approaches the rivalry among the renowned women runners at Tennessee A & I," Russell wrote. "Ed Temple, A & I coach who also coaches the 1960 women's Olympic track squad, divided his Tigerbelle sprinters into Blue and White teams. Striving to meet Olympic time standards, they really push each other."

"Feeling has become so high, with our freshmen and sophomores competing against the older girls, that I've had to call off our races for a while," Temple said, laughing as he described the ferocity of the competition within the team.

"To me, we were close," Isabelle Daniels said of her teammates. "Some of us still are close. We were close and a family because Mr. Temple taught us that. He said when you go to a track meet, you are real close and you're sisters. But he said when the starter says take your mark, you are on your own. You try to win, but when the race is over, you're all still sisters. The Tigerbelles loved each other."

Willye White took a more cynical view on the intrasquad competition and Temple. "He was a man who brought in the world's greatest talent and pitted it against each other."

That was precisely the type of comment Willye was known for that would drive Temple mad. "I hate for people to make excuses," Temple said. "It's always when they lose—you never hear excuses when they win."

On the day of the Blue and White meet, three sprinters had times of less than 12 seconds for the 100-meter, and the Olympic qualifying standard was 11.8. Russell goes on to note that Lucinda Williams, with the added surname of Adams, had already beat the qualifying time in the 200-meter.

Lucinda, in addition to maintaining her top speeds, had taken her relationship with her boyfriend and ROTC instructor, Floyd Adams, to the next level in a secret wedding. She, like Margaret Matthews Wilburn, had to keep her wedding secret in order to avoid the disappointment of her coach, perhaps thinking that once the marriage had occurred, Temple would have to acquiesce.

Temple didn't have much time to worry about one of his most stable and successful athletes getting married; this was just one small issue compared to the many worries he was facing. One, in particular that was always front of mind was Wilma's health. The prior year she'd had to have her tonsils taken out and had endured a tough recovery, refusing to eat or take her post-surgery medication, reminding everyone of her severe childhood illnesses. Her history of weak ankles was also always a concern.

Time was getting short and the competitions more critical. There was a meet in Cleveland on June 25, 1960, where qualifying times could be officially met for Olympic standards, followed by the AAU Nationals in Corpus Christi, Texas, and the Olympic trials in Abilene, Texas. The runners who made the Olympic team would go straight to a three-week training camp in Emporia, Kansas, then to New York City and on to Rome for the Olympics in mid-August.

The entire summer was a series of obstacles that had to be cleared. The end goal for all of them had always been clear: the winning podium in Rome.

Summer training was as tough as ever. Vivian Reed joined the junior team for the first time that summer and fell to the same struggles as so many other Tigerbelles had. "I felt on some occasions this coach was unmerciful," Vivian said, "that we were training too hard for young ladies. If I went through three weeks and it was this tough, how can I stand it for a year or two, or as long as four years?" She very nearly quit before her chance at Nationals.

Shirley Crowder said, "We were so well prepared that everybody envied us, but they didn't know how hard we had prepared to get there. We would have early-morning practice, six o'clock in the morning. Before breakfast we'd be down in the gym, running laps. We'd be running around in circles until we flopped on the floor. Too tired to get breakfast, maybe go get a milk or a juice, but that was it. Then one o'clock you're outside in the heat, working hard. But those that were competing against us didn't know that. Coach had a plan. Only the pure in heart shall survive."

Ralph Boston always made time to eat at the cafeteria, no matter how tired he was.

Most of the students depended on the cafeteria as their only food source on campus, and on Saturday and Sunday nights, the cafeteria was closed. The students used their ingenuity to solve this problem. "We didn't have any money, back in the day, we were all struggling to get a dollar," Barbara Murrell said. "We had to make sacrifices. When you went to brunch, you would get cheese and bologna and make a sandwich, and you put it in wax paper. So, everybody would have two or three of those coming home, and we would leave it in the window, so it didn't spoil. In the later part of the evening, you would get your iron out, and you would iron the sandwich, and that would be your dinner. And that wax paper would give it a special taste, and it was so good."

"The cafeteria was the one place where we would hang out," Boston said of the Tigerbelles. "Mealtime was set, and you would not miss it. I'd see them in the chow hall," Boston said of the Tigerbelles, although he never practiced alongside the women. "The Tigerbelles had first dibs on the track," he said, "and then we worked our way in as they finished." By the summer, Boston's performance had started to capture the attention and respect of Temple. "He said what he thought," Boston said of his interactions with Temple, "and then he was through."

Boston understood that the Tigerbelles had a higher status on campus than the men's team did. "They were the Tigerbelles and that was it. They were the bigwigs on campus. They were as noted as the football team, and at that time, football was king in the South. . . . They could pretty much have their way. But I can't remember any of them really stepping out of line."

Boston couldn't remember them stepping out of line because they rarely did. And neither would he. "One thing that was paramount in my mind," he said, "was I did not want to go back to Laurel, Mississippi, having flunked out of school."

"Nobody wanted to go back," fellow Mississippian Barbara Murrell agreed. "Once you got out, you did what you needed to do to stay out and send some [money] to make it better back home."

As far as Temple was concerned, the intensive summer training was critical. Not just for strength and endurance, but for the unity and cohesiveness of the team. Wilma Rudolph, Lucinda Williams, Barbara Jones, and Martha Hudson had been running in the summers together for a few years by this point, and their performance reflected their training and their relationships. The four of them were becoming clear favorites for the relay.

The 4x100m relay was the most coveted spot on the team. It depended on the speed of the runner, absolutely, but also on the technical skill. Being able to judge and adjust speed while her teammate was coming at

Ed Temple and Wilma Rudolph in training. Temple Archives

her like a freight train, all while keeping her head down and her hand, ready to take the small metal baton in her grasp and then propel herself to top speed without losing any ground, required a combination of skills that only the most experienced athletes could achieve.

Temple tried them each in all of the positions, and the only position he was sure about was starter. Martha Hudson was the clear choice. She was the fastest of the entire team off the blocks, and reliably consistent. Between Lucinda, Barbara Jones, and Wilma, he wavered back and forth. They were all fast, and no one was yet standing out as anchor.

Each of the relay contenders practiced every variable over and over. "You go through the whole relay routine so many times your head spins," Wilma said. "Something like passing the baton; that takes weeks to perfect, weeks to get down, and even then, it might be off," Wilma explained. "Passing the baton is one of the most important things to running a relay team. If a baton is dropped, it is the passer's fault automatically, no matter what happens . . . because the receiver can't ever see the baton, can't ever see the maneuver of passing it because she's poised straight ahead, concentrating on taking off."

Being able to run at top speed into the 20-meter passing zone looking for the next leg's outstretched hand and knowing it would be there took absolute trust between the runners and immaculate precision. Any error, even the most minute, would result in a loss, or even injury.

Building trust on a team meant time together and complete consistency of treatment.

"Mr. Temple was able to keep us in unity," Barbara said. "As one team."

Part of the team philosophy was to pass the baton metaphorically as well as literally. "If you graduated winning, you didn't help anyone," Barbara said. "Your goal was to help the younger girls behind you get faster than you by the time you left. . . . Temple taught us, 'If you believe that someone can beat you, they will.'"

Looking forward to the Olympics, Temple was keeping as tight a ship as ever.

Fred Russell came back to campus to report on the team's progress. In the June 22, 1960, Sidelines column in the *Nashville Banner*, titled "One Girl, Two Hours, Three Races, Five Watches—And What Time!" he saw Wilma Rudolph as a standout and wrote about her progress. Wilma clocked 11.5, easily clearing the 11.8 qualifying standard and being just two-tenths of a second away from a world-record time. To Russell's surprise, Temple stacked up the sprints within the short period of time to practice endurance. "Why such intensified practice? Coach Temple has a reason for every move he makes," Russell wrote. "At the Olympics in Rome, on the afternoon of September 2, the 100-meters semifinals will be run at 3 p.m. and the finals at 4:20 p.m. If any Australian or Russian is gonna beat Wilma Rudolph, she will have to fly."

The Tennessean also began to notice the women's success and caught up with Temple before their trip to Cleveland. "I want to see what they can do before the AAU National Outdoor meet in Corpus Christi, Texas," Temple told them. He brought a small group of six for Cleveland, presumably those he thought were most likely to make the qualifying times. The lineup was Wilma Rudolph, Barbara Jones, Lucinda Williams, and Martha Hudson for sprints, while JoAnn Terry and Shirley Crowder went for hurdles. It signaled who Temple had his eyes on for the relay—the top contenders.

Shirley Crowder knew that she was good in the hurdles. "I was number one, and I knew everyone was gunning for me," she said. "My technique was not the best in the world, but I had speed."

Shirley also had resources at her fingertips, and those were her two best friends, Martha Hudson and Wilma Rudolph. "Martha had the best starts of anyone I knew," Shirley said. "So we would go down to the track when it wasn't even our time to practice, and we would spend time. One on one side, and one on the other. They would say, 'Keep up, girl, keep up with us,' and I'd be running like heck, trying to keep up with them." Shirley laughed, recalling the story, and shook her head at the memory.

As their travels grew closer, the team worked together and leaned on each other more than ever. Charlie B. was hard at work preparing the team for their journey. She had her hands on everything, from packing her husband's suitcase to bleaching all of the team's T-shirts and socks, and even their sneakers, so they'd look their best on the big stage. She did all that she could before they set off, away from her watchful eyes and protective guidance.

It must have been hard to send them off every year, but particularly when she knew they would be gone for so long. The better they performed, the longer they would be gone. With Edward being long since named as coach, this time he would be gone for the duration, no matter which members of his team qualified to travel on.

Things would be quiet with them gone, her children missing their father and babysitters. There was still plenty of responsibility to keep her busy, caring alone for her young family, and looking out for the team members that stayed behind, but there was also the practice of patience. Waiting for news, waiting for contact, and waiting for their return.

Long-distance calls were expensive, and therefore would be few and far between, and letters would have to cross the country or the Atlantic Ocean to reach her. Ultimately, she wouldn't get that many details until they all came home—or as many details as she might want, anyway. In those long weeks, Charlie B. would comb the newspapers, searching for any hints of their performance, lamenting the sparse media coverage. The women's results were rarely written about in the articles, but after the meets she could usually find a few lines of statistics in the back of the sports sections.

As Charlie B. prepared herself to say good-bye to her husband, and the women she considered family, Temple and his team got ready to travel around the world.

When the bus left Tennessee State, some of them would not return for months.

CHAPTER 17

The 1960 Nationals

COACH TEMPLE STOOD BY THE OPEN DOOR OF THE STREAMLINED PAS-
senger bus with his clipboard out, marking down the runners and the
equipment bags to make sure everyone and everything was loaded
properly. Athletic director Howard Gentry had come through with the
funding for another chartered bus, and the team was grateful to have it.

The ride to Corpus Christi, Texas, was long. Even though they would
spend almost all of their time on the bus, the women dressed up for the
occasion, and Temple was proud of the way they presented themselves—
as always, foxes, not oxes. They never knew when they might have to stop,
and they couldn't afford to go anywhere looking a mess. Even though
their vehicle was an upgrade over the station wagon caravans of the past,
their situation had not changed much. They were still a group of Black
folks on a bus driving right through some of the most hostile territory in
the South, and Temple was in charge of them and their safety.

The ladies in the cafeteria had packed box lunches for the trip, and
the spirits of the team were high. They played music on the radio, a
favorite Nashville station being WVOL, "Where the Music is Swell."
They passed over Elvis or hillbilly country music for Little Richard or
Motown hits.

It wouldn't take long to get past the green rolling hills and thick
forests of middle Tennessee. They drove through Memphis before they
crossed the Mississippi River, after which were hours of flat fields of
cotton, corn, and tobacco, interrupted only by the occasional dusty town

dotted with Confederate flags and monuments. From the Mississippi River to the Red River of Texas, only the crops changed.

Vivian Reed had gotten through the training to earn a spot on the bus, as well as Wilma Rudolph's younger sister, Charlene, and newcomer Edith McGuire. It was a full roster of Tigerbelles that rolled into Corpus Christi, where they were shown to their barracks. Hotels were not an option, due to funding or segregation issues, possibly both.

Olga Connolly, a prior Olympic medalist who often found herself in the news, had arrived and already complained about the conditions of the facilities. She called home to California and told them that in addition to not being provided mattresses, there was "no hot water, poor food, no food for the Negro girl athletes, quarters were humid and infested with insects, and that all in all, conditions were intolerable."

Olga had competed in the 1956 Olympics for her home nation of Czechoslovakia in the discus, against Earlene Brown, winning the gold. In addition to her status as an Olympic medalist, Olga had captured the media attention when she met and fell in love with a fellow Olympian, hammer thrower Harold Connolly, from the United States. The couple soon married, with Olga moving to California with her new husband and earning her US citizenship two weeks before traveling to Texas to compete for a place on the US team, instead of her native Czechoslovakia. The pair of champions made a handsome couple—and great copy. They were serious medal contenders, hoping to compete in the 1960 Olympics together as a married couple.

The junior events did not produce any runaway champions from Tennessee State, with Charlene Rudolph placing fifth in the 50-yard dash and third in the 220, and Edith McGuire placing fourth in the 100 and third in the 75-yard dash. Edith was very young, with plenty of room to grow in future years.

Wilma mothered her little sister, Charlene, just as Mae had cared for her four years before, but Charlene was hampered with a bacterial infection. "I soon discovered that one runner in the family was enough," Charlene said, "but I enjoyed it and had fun. It was such a good learning experience." Charlene went home with the rest of the team that didn't qualify for the Olympics, but her relationship with the Tigerbelles and the Temple family would last a lifetime.

The morning issue of the *Nashville Banner* on race day for the senior competition proclaimed the Tigerbelles as likely favorites. Wilma Rudolph currently held the US records in the 100-meter and 200-meter events, so she was the one everyone was watching, even though she was still seen as a newcomer compared to some of the more experienced runners like Lucinda Williams and Barbara Jones.

The Tigerbelles overlooked the housing issues; they had been trained specifically not to get hung up on facilities at Tennessee State. They donned their fresh race uniforms, fixed each other's hair, and turned themselves out in fine form for race day. The true test had arrived, and it required all of their focus to give their best performances. They each knew how many things had to go right, and how many things could go wrong.

The team boarded the bus provided to them on race day to take them to the track, which was several miles away. The bus was shared with some of their competitors from other schools who happened to be white. The bus driver watched the mixed group walk on to the bus, after which he promptly walked off, unwilling to drive an integrated bus.

"All of us were on this bus," Wilma said, "all the kids who were at the AAU meet, white kids and Black kids on the same bus. Well, the bus driver walked off and refused to drive the bus. They had to get another bus driver to take us around. The new driver didn't seem to like it very much, either, having to drive an integrated bus, but he did it anyway."

The delay cost them precious warm-up time on the track, and the team was forced to sit and ponder the injustice delivered by one hateful and stubborn man. Although they enjoyed many freedoms—the freedom to go to school, to travel, to compete as young women—there remained that final barrier, a wall that could and did rise anywhere, lurking around dark corners or sitting right out in the sunshine, unafraid and unembarrassed.

These were the moments they wished to protest, and also the moments they could choose to let their anger fuel them. They could use it to give strength to their legs and lungs. They could use it to show the world that they could outrun, outshine, and outclass them all. With grace.

Earlene Brown also faced down racism on her way to Corpus Christi. She traveled to Texas with Pam Kurrell and Sharon Shepherd, two white friends and discus throwers from California. They elected to rent a car and drive together instead of taking a flight. "Well, on the road," Earlene said, "we drove and drove, and we got hungry and stopped at a restaurant. We went in, sat down, and grabbed a menu, and a lady came over and said, 'I am sorry, we can't serve you.' And it hit me. I said, 'Oh, my goodness, this is Texas.'"

Her friends were outraged, but Earlene shrugged it off, asking them to order a sandwich for her while she waited in the hot car. Furious on her behalf, they insisted they try to find another place where they could eat together. They finally found another place that allowed them to sit down in the kitchen, which they discovered was filthy, with flies buzzing all around the food. "Heck, I couldn't see why they were so prejudiced when they were serving garbage like that," Earlene said, and they moved on, having lost their appetites altogether.

Barbara Jones finally had her chance to make up for missing the 1956 Olympics, even after her gold medal win in 1952 as a fifteen-year-old. She knew exactly what the Olympics meant, and she was determined to go back. Nerves, pre-race jitters, fear of failure—it all had to be overcome. "If you fear something, that's on you, because you don't have to," Barbara said. "You have everything it takes to be great, and if you allow fear to take over, then you shouldn't even win."

There were several things Temple advised his team to do—and not do—before a race. They tried not to eat two hours before a race, to avoid nausea and keep them light on their feet, and "booze" and cigarettes were strictly prohibited. And there was absolutely no dancing before competition. The Tigerbelles were on the big stage now, and everything had to be done just right.

Temple set up a home base under a tent where he was mired down in timetables and schedules. It took serious concentration to make sure each of the runners was where she needed to be when she needed to be there. When each of them came back from said location, they needed to be reminded to rest and hydrate, telling them to take their shoes off and sip honey tea. It was a constant stream of comings and goings.

Shirley Crowder competed in the 80-meter hurdles. She had her own nerves to beat—the biggest thing to get in her way for her last Olympic try when an ambulance had been moved to the finish line, proving to be a major distraction. "I was nervous every time I came to the starting blocks," Shirley said. "Because if you come up there thinking, I got this, I got this, you look up and somebody has passed you by. I was always nervous." She could only hope that all of her hard work in the prior four years had prepared her for the challenge.

Shirley sailed through the first two heats, winning easily. She beat hurdlers from some of the best clubs in the country, including Mayor Daley's club from Chicago and the New York Police Athletic League, but she would meet the real competition in the finals, when she would run against her teammate JoAnn Terry, and her former Tigerbelle teammate and Olympic medalist, Willye White.

Shirley and JoAnn ran in nearly synchronized jumps to finish first and second with identical times that tied the American record.

The 100-meter final was intense competition primarily among the Tigerbelles. Wilma Rudolph pulled out the win, followed closely by Barbara Jones, Lucinda Williams, and Martha Hudson. The sprint leaders had emerged.

JoAnn Terry also placed in the long jump, along with Anna Lois Smith and Willye White. All three trained by Temple would be continuing to the Olympic trials.

Wilma prepared for the 200-meter, but she was feeling off. It could have been the incident with the bus driver, the shoddy barracks, or the strain or pressure. Whatever the reason, Wilma stood at the start of the race, chatting with Vivian Brown, who she considered her primary competition.

"God, I don't feel it in my bones today," Vivian told Wilma, who agreed with her.

"There was none of the usual pre-race tension and nervousness," Wilma said. "We were both out there with the attitude, 'Let's give it a shot, give it a run, and get it over with.'"

Lucinda was also in the 200-meter final. Wilma and Lucinda both got off to a smooth start, Wilma, as usual, slightly slower out of the blocks. Twenty meters out, Wilma started to pull ahead. Her form was perfect, her legs stretching long, and once she got her stride, there was no one that could catch her—not even Vivian Brown, who had beat her the year before. Lucinda was back in the pack, about even with Lacey O'Neal from Mayor Daley. Twenty seconds later, Wilma was far ahead when her chest hit the tape. Lucinda was a few meters behind in a close finish for third.

Temple watched the officials who appeared to be talking over some detail before they posted the times. It was always nerve-racking when those whispered conferences took place; results could be affected by some minor technicality that was thought to be spotted in the blur of speed.

The scores posted, and next to Wilma's name in the first-place slot was "22.9," followed by "WR," for world record.

Temple thought the track must be short; maybe they were measuring yards instead of meters. "That's what I really thought," Temple said. "There's no way this child could run 22.9. Nobody else had run 23, and hardly 24."

It was the fastest time ever run by a woman, and Wilma had done it.

Wilma went back under the tent and sat down next to Temple.

"Doin' all right, aren't you?" Temple said. It was high praise for the understated coach, and they still had to focus on the 4x100m relay.

The members and order of the relay had been set. It was a collection of the fastest and most reliable on the team. Martha Hudson was the starter. She was quickest off the blocks and her top speed was solid. "She might not always win," Temple said, "but nobody could slack up any because Pee Wee would plow right on by them. She was always good for a place, and many times it was first place."

Barbara Jones ran second. Barbara always ran her best for a crowd and was in top shape. Lucinda Williams took third, a critical leg to round the final corner and hand off to the anchor. Wilma Rudolph had earned her way to anchor the team. She outpaced everyone and finally came into her own full speed at unmatched times. The team had been chosen not only for their speed and skill, but for the way they worked together, and Temple's most important criteria—their purity of heart.

"We eventually realized that the key to being a good relay team is having good judgment as far as your partners are concerned," Wilma said. "You have to know them—their moves, their reactions, their thinking, their reflexes. You have to know them as people. You have to know who is fast, who is a little slow on the handoff, whose reflexes are just a second or two off. Then you compensate for it. All of this takes time, and it works toward precision." The team had been working for years for that level of performance.

Martha fired off the blocks like a bullet and never slowed down. She kept a slight lead and her footing was perfect as she reached to place the baton in Barbara's outstretched hand. Barbara grabbed the baton and took off, widening the lead even more with a clean handoff to Lucinda. Another smooth pass to Wilma allowed her to race to the finish. By the time she broke the tape, none of the other runners were even close enough to reach the trailing ribbons. It was a runaway lead.

At the end of the day, some would continue on, and some would prepare to go home. The competition had been intense. There was so much talent on the track that day that hadn't quite made the cut. All of the competitors must have all worked all summer to prepare for their events, but it wasn't always enough. And it was hard to believe that anyone had worked as hard as the Tigerbelles.

Chapter 18

Trials

THE NEXT STEP ON THE LADDER WAS THE OLYMPIC TRIALS IN ABILENE, Texas. The team said their good-byes to those that wouldn't be moving on, including Wilma's sister, Charlene, Edith McGuire, and Vivian Reed. The three junior runners had seen the scope of national competition, and they had reached a decision point: to dig deeper, or to move on to other pursuits. Two of the three would decide that they were just getting started and find themselves serious contenders in four more years.

Feelings were mixed for those that continued on. They had just cleared the first hurdle, and there were miles to go before they reached their goals. Temple used the time between events to bring his team back into balance, to regain their focus. They had been under an extraordinary amount of pressure, starting with the protests and backlash on their campus and in their city, then compounded by their experience in Corpus Christi, with the repugnant bus driver and general mistreatment. They were forced to constantly refocus and channel their hurt and outrage into forward momentum. They had to stay in shape, stay on track, and keep up the strength they had worked so hard to build.

They were each fighting their own war, their own battle. It might have seemed counterintuitive to the young women, to have to restrict themselves in order to fight for more freedom. That's not what a lot of their peers back home were doing. But the Tigerbelles were different; they had chosen a different path. They had to walk the straight and narrow and do their work, and then, instead of attracting attention by breaking down norms, they would gain notice by their extraordinary achievements. Both routes were valid, but Temple continued to believe and counsel that the kind of fight they could win on the track would serve them better throughout their lives. They were learning to tap into the greatness within themselves, a quality they would be able to carry with them wherever they chose to go.

The Tigerbelles also depended on the love and support of all of those who helped them along the way, and they owed it to all of those people to put their entire effort into it. Each of the women on Temple's team had parents who had scrimped and saved to get them as far as they had, brothers and sisters who gave things up for their support, coaches that pushed them and teammates that pulled them along in weak moments. It was a responsibility that each of them shared, and Temple would not let them forget it.

In Abilene at the trials, the issues were similar, and the results the same. Poor conditions included "dogs, cats, and large-sized bugs in the dormitories," and some even accused the officials of manipulating the heats to favor some athletes over others, penalizing those that had complained about the conditions.

There were 136 athletes competing for 26 spots on the team. There were nine events, where the top three for each would make the team. The fourth-place finisher for the 100-meter sprint would also make the team for the 4x100m relay.

Adding to the Tigerbelles' personal worries, Wilma had come down with a bad cold, her health as vulnerable as ever.

Earlene Brown and reigning gold medalist Olga Connolly continued their intense competition. Olga set a record in the discus, immediately broken by nearly 4.5 feet by Earlene. Earlene blew past Olga's gold medal–winning distance for the shot put by more than 8 inches. Both women qualified for the team and would be going on to Rome, Olga with her new husband, who also qualified again for the hammer throw.

Willye White was setting records herself. Her first jump landed at 20 feet, 4.5 inches, qualifying her instantly for the team. Her relief was immense. According to a *Sports Illustrated* reporter, "[Willye] opened her mouth to render a fair imitation of a west Texas coyote," and said, "I'm on my way." Willye and Temple would have to make peace. Less than a year after Temple had kicked Willye off his team, he'd be coaching her again.

Just as they had the week before in Corpus Christi, the Tigerbelles took the first four spots of the 100-meter race. Wilma won again, followed by Barbara, Martha, and Lucinda, each reaching the qualifying time standard to compete in the Olympic Games. The Tigerbelles competing in the 100-meter in Rome would be Wilma, Barbara, and Martha, with Lucinda being the fourth on the relay. It was a toss-up among the four who would make it, and Martha barely edged Lucinda out.

Wilma also won the 200-meter, setting a new record for the trials, followed by Lucinda, who earned her individual spot for the Games.

Shirley Crowder and JoAnn Terry again tied for first and second place in the 80-meter hurdle, with the same time of 11.4 seconds. Neither met the qualifying standards of 11.2, but Shirley was excused from the requirement by finishing first.

All that extra practice Shirley had put in with her friends had paid off. Shirley said, "When the gun shot for the trials, when they looked up, I was already gone. Because I had prepared for it."

JoAnn would be able to train with the team but would not be able to travel to Rome unless she met the official standards at training camp.

Anna Lois Smith placed third in the long jump, also without meeting the standards for the trip to Rome. She and JoAnn still had some work to do.

At day's end, a record seven women from one program had made the national squad. The Tigerbelles' dominance was secured.

In the men's qualification rounds, Ralph Boston was reaching his peak, with his qualifying jump a mere 2 inches short of Jesse Owens's record from 1936. The men's qualification rounds gathered a crowd of nearly 45,000, and was nationally televised, in a marked contrast to the women's events that sometimes "had more athletes than spectators."

Even though the Olympic team was now comprised of the strongest collection of talented female athletes the United States had ever produced, national expectations of the team were low. They were women, after all, and unlikely to add much to the medal count. The media coverage devoted to the Tigerbelles from Nashville came mostly from Fred Russell at the *Nashville Banner*, with the team being covered nationally in a few dishy articles from *Sports Illustrated* and the *New York Times*. *The Tennessean*, supposedly the more liberal of the two local papers, largely ignored the women's success, making a point to note that Ralph Boston would be the most likely to bring home gold, but there were "seven other Tennessee State athletes competing," followed by a quick mention of Wilma Rudolph breaking the record in the 200-meter.

Whenever quoted, Temple was careful to explain that Wilma would not be where she was on her own. It wasn't to take anything away from Wilma, but to show that none of them would be where they were without the help of the others. "She needs somebody to push her," Temple said, pointing out that all four women on the relay team were running similar times, setting them up to compete against any challenger. "They'll be right there," Temple said.

A *Track and Field News* reporter described the issue of coverage for the women, bluntly stating that even the little space he "devoted to the gals" received criticism from his readers. "Personally, I can't get very excited about girlish athletics," the reporter said. "Maybe it's the old-fashioned streak in me. Or maybe it's that I'm so wrapped up in what the better known, more talented men are doing that there just isn't emotional room for the ladies. Whatever the reasons, I seem to feel about the same as 99 percent of the track fans I know."

Coach Temple and the Tigerbelles joined with the other qualifying women and the group traveled to Emporia, Kansas, for three weeks of training. Temple was now leading the entire US women's team, assisted by Frances Kaszubski as manager and assistant coach Fran Welch of Kansas State Teachers College, who would be providing access to the training facilities.

As the national team leader, Temple's work was clear. "A national coach primarily tries to unify the team, enforce guidelines, work on a few weaknesses, arrange the relays, and keep the athletes in shape by letting them work out with schedules which are prescribed by their own

1960 Olympic Coaching Team: Fran Welch, Ed Temple, Francis Kaszubski. Temple Archives

coaches," Temple said. He had proven the results of the team approach with the Tigerbelles, the collective encouraging the individual to become her best, and he intended to replicate the same success with the larger team. "Creating unity is no small job," Temple said. "You have athletes from different clubs and colleges and coaches representing various training philosophies. They also come from different cultures with all sorts of personalities and attitudes. All of these athletes have been rivals for years, and suddenly they are brought together to make up one big, happy family."

The Tigerbelles appreciated Temple being coach more than anyone. "Just having him there put me in an incredible frame of mind," Wilma said. "I knew I was ready for the Olympics as a runner, no question about that. But I also knew I would be ready mentally no matter what, simply because he was the coach. It was like bringing your second father along to keep you up."

Temple, however, was dealing with tension with his assistant coach. Believing that the main reason Fran Welch was assigned as assistant coach was his access to the facilities, Temple said that Welch took full advantage of being on his home turf. "He ruled the roost on his campus, and it was difficult for me to take full control of the team under those circumstances." Welch seemed to chafe at playing second fiddle to Temple, the younger coach, and didn't seem to be able to accept that Temple had the top spot. "I had all the aces, and he didn't have a single girl on the team," Temple said. "He couldn't do much with my girls, but he sure stirred up enough trouble among the other girls on the team."

Temple hoped that his own Tigerbelles, making up most of the team, would provide a greater influence than his assistant coach. But however dedicated and highly trained his team was, they were still young women, weeks away from their next competition, and they craved the opportunity to let loose and have a little fun. They only had one practice a day, and while the facilities were decent enough, there wasn't a lot of entertainment available.

What the campus in Emporia did have were bikes parked in various locations available for the students and their guests to use. Temple had been adamant from the start that his team should not be using the bikes. One of his primary concerns was keeping them in peak condition for the next few weeks before the Olympics, and cruising all over campus on the big, clunky bikes created any number of potential disasters.

But there they waited, practically begging to be used. And one lazy afternoon, deep into the stay in Kansas, they finally gave in.

The group of high-spirited young women, athletes at the very edge of human strength and speed, were lounging around their rooms, feeling restless. Someone had the idea, and it took hold. They grabbed the bikes for a quick joyride around campus. The carefree ride got away from them, however, and they pedaled outside their range of familiarity with the campus, finding themselves lost and late for practice.

"We wind up in the woods someplace, and we have to pump those bikes for a couple of hours just to find our way back," Wilma said. "The muscles in our legs were sore, we were all tired out, and Coach Temple was furious. We all did some extra running that day as punishment, and we all collapsed into bed that night exhausted. The next morning, we had to help each other out of bed, that's how sore we all were."

Temple's anger and punishment reflected not only this particular transgression, but his need to impress upon the team how little margin for error they had, not only in their physical performances, but also in their total presentation. This meant staying far away from trouble. Temple admonished his team not to give any of their detractors ammunition against them. People looked for reasons to knock them down, and the worst thing they could do was prove them right by misbehaving. Their behavior had to be nothing short of perfect, and acting like wayward children getting lost on their bikes certainly wasn't it.

Although in a sort of holding pattern, the women did seem to enjoy the lighter schedule. Louise Mead Tricard[1] qualified at the trials, and while training with the team in Kansas, she became close to Wilma in particular. "I remember [Wilma] reading her Bible one evening as she sat in bed," said Louise. "It was Ecclesiastes. Time for all seasons."

There is a time for everything,
And a season for every activity under the heavens:
A time to be born and a time to die,
A time to plant and a time to uproot,
A time to kill and a time to heal,
A time to tear down and a time to build,
A time to weep and a time to laugh,

A time to mourn and a time to dance,

A time to scatter stones and a time to gather them,
A time to embrace and a time to refrain from embracing,

A time to search and a time to give up,
A time to keep and a time to throw away,
A time to tear and a time to mend,
A time to be silent and a time to speak,
A time to love and a time to hate,
A time for war and a time for peace.

---

1. Author of *American Women's Track and Field: A History, 1895 through 1980*, Louise Mead Tricard was a lifelong athlete and proponent of women in sports.

What do workers gain from their toil? I have seen the burden
God has laid on the human race. He has made everything
beautiful in its time.

Ecclesiastes 3:1–12

Wilma's teammates also saw her lounging in bed often.

"I guess she would rather sleep than do most anything else," JoAnn
said of Wilma.

"Next to that it's reading," Martha said, "mostly in bed."

The Tigerbelles were all enjoying a brief time for rest. Temple also
tried to maintain their health, with head colds and weak ankles always
nagging as potential problems. "Here's where we really run into two
schools of thought. You have dedicated, hardworking athletes who strive
for excellence. Then you have the immature ones. They say, 'Well, we
made the team. Now we want to have a good time!' Then we've got problems," said Temple.

Temple could have been thinking particularly of Willye. He'd kicked
her off the Tigerbelles team, but he couldn't keep her off the US team
when she'd so easily qualified. He could only hope that those few months
she'd spent on her own in Chicago had forced her to grow up.

The men's team had been set up at Stanford, a true world-class
facility, and the women made the best of it at their outpost in Emporia.
Temple knew the stakes and was prepared, as he always had been, to use
the little support he received. While he'd received more financial and
logistical support than he was able to obtain from Tennessee State, the
US Olympic Committee still had a minimal investment in the women's
team. Temple worried over all of the details and having his team show
in the best possible light. There was no room for error, which meant no
injuries, and no missteps. The spotlight was on them.

Two competitions were held while the team was in Emporia, allowing JoAnn and Anna Lois Smith both to officially qualify. In addition to
the long jump, JoAnn also won the pentathlon, an event not yet included
in the Olympic Games, but to which JoAnn was particularly suited, given
her versatility as an athlete.

After practice. Temple Archives

The team was ready to move on from Kansas, and the Olympic Games, their ultimate goal, was getting closer and closer in their sights. Including Willye, eight women trained at Tennessee State were going together to Rome, and they could hardly wait to get there.

CHAPTER 19

The Image

ONCE THEY LEFT KANSAS, TEMPLE FINALLY SECURED THE UPPER HAND over his assistant coach, Welch. They were off to New York City where they were outfitted with all the necessary uniforms and clothing they would be wearing for official events. The team also began to capture more media attention, and their image was more important than ever.

"They perked up in New York City when they got their uniforms," Temple said. And they also met up with the men's team, including their friend and fellow Tennessee State student, Ralph Boston, and a mouthy young boxer from Kentucky.

"I got off the bus in New York getting ready to get outfitted," Ralph Boston said. "Got off the bus and then I stepped down to the street level. A young man put his hand on my chest. And this, you know, if I lost my mind, I'd never forget this. He put his hand in the middle of my chest and said, 'Ralph Boston, how do you do? How are you doing, man?' And we shook hands. And I said to him, 'Well, who are you, man?' and he said, 'You don't know me now, but you will."

Boston said, "Okay, what's your name?"

He said, "My name is Cassius Marcellus Clay."

Boston said the story is one of his favorites, as he and the man who would later become known as Muhammad Ali and stay close throughout their lives. "Obviously, he was right," Boston said. "We all knew his name."

Even for the team members that had been to the Olympics before, the level of attention that was trained toward them was new, and it wasn't all positive. *The New York Times Magazine* published an article titled "Venus Wasn't a Shot-Putter" by William Barry Furlong:

> At the dawn of the Olympics in ancient Greece, women were not allowed—under pain of death—at the Games, either as spectators or as participants. . . . Among the more discriminating and distressed, it is not the girls' watching that is worrisome; it is their competing. It is felt that by plunging into certain sports, women tend to destroy The Image—that subtle power by which they exercise the tyranny of the weak over the strong.

The author is careful to make exceptions for particular sports that are more favored by the male gaze, such as gymnastics and swimming, before he charges right back to his criticism of the heartier, and sweatier, sports.

"Today," the writer goes on, "when we think of women athletes—if we think of them at all . . . We do not instinctively think of shot-putters and hurlers, sprinters and discus-throwers. Somehow, they do not possess The Image. . . . I, for one, have never met a loveable lady shot-putter."

Clearly, he hadn't had the chance to meet Earlene Brown.

Arriving on the international scene opened the women up to criticism as well as a world of opportunities. Temple chose to focus on the latter.

"It can't be emphasized enough that when you get up into world-class competition, you've got to have everything fall into place like a jigsaw puzzle," Temple said. "Every piece has got to fall into the proper place, and that's when the pure in heart come out. That's when the naturals take over. The other kind can make it in meets here around the States, and they can come on and do pretty good, but when it gets to the big time, everything has got to be perfect—natural ability and techniques all mixed in with your pride, hustle, desire, and good attitudes. That's when you're up in world class. You've got to go first-class—no tourist-class to it.

"On the charter plane we thought it was great," Temple said. "But then we realized we were the only big country that came on a prop plane versus a jet. Russians and French came in on a jet. We came in spitting and sputting," Temple laughed. "Always wanting to be cheap," he said.

The men's team took a separate route, flying through Shannon, Ireland, to Switzerland, where they trained with "a couple of tune-up track meets," Ralph Boston said. Then they took a train to Rome. "I remember seeing the Matterhorn," Boston said. "Oh, look at that," he said, "what is that?" of the view of the Alps.

The Tigerbelles started practicing in Rome right away. Time was ticking, and they didn't have much of it to iron out the kinks from all that travel. The male and female teams were together more often for training, in a reflection of the way most of the other countries operated. "As we trained," Ralph Boston said, "the training track was used by everybody. Not as it was at Tennessee State. It wasn't so at Rome." The head coach of the men's team was Larry Snyder,[1] the same man who had coached Jesse Owens in 1936, and Boston was mere inches away from breaking Jesse Owens's hard-earned record in the long jump.

The Tigerbelles also reunited with Lorraine Dunn and Marcella Daniel, two women on the Tennessee State team that were competing for their native country, Panama.

Temple was spending all of his time trying to manage his heavy load. "You have to realize," Temple said, "we only had two coaches—we had a field event coach and me. And the men had six coaches. We didn't have as many athletes as the men did, but we still had all those events we had to cover, so it kind of kept us busy." He had only one assistant coach for the sixteen athletes, and that particular coach had been undermining his authority from day one, keeping Temple in a tough spot, unable to take full advantage of the national committee resources.

"The women's team has repeatedly been looked on as the second-class team while the men were catered to and received the best of everything," said Temple. "Funny, every time they announce each country's total number of medals, our men's and women's medals were all added up together."

---

1. A former athlete himself, Larry Snyder missed an opportunity to compete in the Olympics after making the 1924 team, due to an airplane crash injury. He then returned to the sport, coaching the Ohio State track and field team for more than thirty years, during which he led a powerhouse program. He was the assistant coach for the 1952 Olympic team and head coach for the 1960 team.

1960 Olympic Team from Tennessee State L to R: Anna Lois Smith, Wilma Rudolph, Ed Temple, Barbara Jones, Ralph Boston, (bottom row) JoAnn Terry, Shirley Crowder, Lucinda Williams, Martha Hudson. Temple Archives

Earlene Brown was a veteran Olympian and had a real chance to add to the medal count herself. Earlene had sway on the team, but not with practice.

"Coaches were always asking me to train the way they wanted me to train. They were always telling me to run laps around the track and do setting-up exercises," Earlene said. "I would run around the track for one lap just to please the coach, but if he wanted two, he would have to run the second one himself." Temple was probably glad to have that battle shifted to his field coach, Fran Welch, as well as the competition between Earlene and Olga Connolly.

One of the biggest factors Temple had to manage remained how intimidated and overwhelmed especially the younger and less experienced women on his team felt on the world stage. "I've never had a girl go into international competition and do well the very first time," Temple said. "I don't care who they were. They are excited, tense, scared, and they don't know what to expect. They hear about the Russians and the Germans. When they see them, our girls are in awe. The Russians and the Germans are good, and there's no doubt about it."

The Russians, however, kept themselves and their athletes isolated from the rest of the teams. "The Russians were separate," Ralph Boston said. "They made it clear they were separate. Somehow, they set up the Village so the Russians were away [from others]." The Soviet athletes were separate from the other nations, but united as a team.

Ralph Boston, who had noticed his own isolation from so many of his friends on the women's team, said that the Russians were "one of the first teams I remember where they had the men and women together. Closely associated, closely related. They kept us separated from the women in the United States. They made us separate."

While looking at their competition, Temple tried to debunk the myth of their superiority. "A runner has to overcome that feeling of awe and get to thinking, 'Well, they've got two arms and two legs, just like I do. I'll get out there, do my thing, and run my race because I'm just as good and [as] well-prepared as they are." Temple maintained that mental focus was as important to success as physical strength.

The Olympic Village itself was a life-changing experience for most of the women. The team walked side by side with people from the far reaches of the globe. They met men and women from vastly different cultures, tasting their food, listening to their music and languages, but the one thing they all had in common was rising to elite ranks in their particular sport. In order to be in the Village, they had to be the best of the best.

Wilma thought that the way Olympic Village was set up in Rome was smaller and more intimate than it had been in Melbourne, and the Italian people often mingled with the athletes, eager to engage. "The atmosphere in the Village was more fun, too," Wilma said. "We could eat anytime we wanted to eat, there was a recreation hall which everybody hung out in, and every night there was a dance."

Ralph Boston said a favorite song was "a kind of waltzy tune like 'Moonlight Serenade.' Something you could dance together." Coach Temple was fine with the waltzing, within reason, but the Tigerbelles were also in high demand for the latest dance moves from the States, which they had perfected with the same precision they brought to the track. "I wouldn't have minded if the girls had done a little light dancing and then gone on to bed," Temple said. "The Russians used some sense about it. They stuck to slow, easy ballroom dancing and shunned rock and roll. . . . I wanted to keep them training on cinders and not dance-hall wood. There was no way they could run on the track in the mornings and dance four hours on hard wooden floors every night and expect those same legs to perform properly."

"We were in popular demand," Wilma reasoned. "We gave them the latest steps we learned straight from *American Bandstand* on television back home. They all thought we were the coolest cats."

Earlene took a leadership role with organizing the fun. She would often lead the dances with her friends, including the boxers Eddie Machen and the young Cassius Clay.

"My girls had to be regular hepcats," Temple said. "Once they started dancing, they wouldn't stop. Everyone wanted to see them jitterbug. I told them if those boys want to jitterbug, they can do it for each other." The women must have laughed at his fussing, especially because the jitterbug had been out of date for years by then.

The more the women defied his wishes, dancing the night away, the more frustrated he became. Temple wasn't having it. "I just told them we didn't come up there to dance. They wasn't getting no medal for dancing. We came over there to run. After you was running, you could get up there and dance all you wanta. But we ain't going up there dancing during the time that we're running and going through the various heats and everything, because we didn't come over there to do any dancing."

Temple laid down the law, instituting a "dancing ban" that caused so much talk among the Village it was picked up in the newspapers. Some of the women still protested, along with their admirers. "Now Red decided my dancing ban was unnecessary," Temple said of Willye "Red" White, "because dancing 'relieved tension.' I told her that they don't give medals for 'Queen of dancing.'"

Blowing off steam, releasing nervous energy, or just having fun, Willye more than anyone wanted to rebel against Temple's rules. She'd already had enough of them.

When the team wasn't dancing, they used their free time to tour around Rome. They tried their best to use the Italian language, but as any traveler knows, speaking in a new language presents its own challenges. They were issued Italian–American dictionaries by the US Olympic Committee, but Wilma said that sometimes they would give up, simply pointing to a phrase in the book. "Eventually, we started learning key phrases ourselves, but I think the Italian people got a kick out of us," Wilma said.

Temple described Rome as "wild and confusing," and was more concerned with the disorganization of the facilities and events. Their schedules were given to them in Italian, and practice and event times varied among the players, creating a complicated mess. Transportation wasn't always easy either. Temple said, "Cab drivers were no help; you'd ask for information, and they'd just shrug and raise their hands over their shoulders."

They took care to practice with the Italian starters, practicing their "ready, set"—or "aposti, via," in Italian—so there would be no confusion.

But even Temple, with his schedule difficulties, still found time to sit on a bench after practice, taking in the scenes at the Village. One day he met a charming young athlete.

"He came out and sat beside me, and he said, 'I'm Cassius Clay,'" Temple said.

"Well, I'm Ed Temple."

"I'm from Louisville," Clay, later known as Muhammad Ali, told him.

"I'm from Nashville," Temple responded. "And that's where the conversation started. Well, he hadn't boxed or anything yet; he was at the Olympics, just like we were. I just sat there and listened to him, and he just talked and talked and talked. I didn't have nothing else to do 'cause we had just finished practice. I was just sitting there, saying to myself, He must be crazy because he hasn't even boxed yet. So, I didn't have nothing else to do but just sit there and listen."

Most of the women on the team spent time with Clay in the Olympic Village. He made his way around so actively, he was hard to miss. Shirley laughed when he was mentioned, saying that back then, he was the "same that he was when the world got to know him, braggadocious. But he was a good guy."

Lucinda also loved to tease him. She'd tell him, "Fool, go someplace and sit down!" She recalled, "He was always talking about being 'the greatest.' Well, bless his heart, six weeks later he was beating everybody up. He showed he really *was* the greatest. He really was something."

Temple tried to get tickets to a match to see what all the fuss was about, but the event was sold out. Temple stood to the side, at the athletes' entrance, where Clay was hanging around before the match. "Cassius was talking, talking, talking, and my dad and one of the other coaches were standing there because they couldn't get in," Edwina Temple said. "And he said, 'Here,' and he gave them a bag and said, 'Get in line here.' Like he was one of the trainers." Clay was not going to let his new friends miss out on an opportunity to see his performance. "And my dad picked up the

Cassius Clay (Muhammed Ali) with Ed Temple. Temple Archives

194

bag and just walked on in there like everybody else, just part of the crowd. That's how he got to see the match, at the Olympics."

Ralph Boston said that after he competed and won a gold medal, Clay walked around the Village wearing it, even being said to adjust to sleeping on his back so he wouldn't have to take the medal off his neck overnight. "But I was more caught up in the things that I thought would make you go gaga," Boston said. "Like Bing Crosby walking through the Olympic Village."

The team made friends with the other athletes, despite the language barriers. "I don't know too much [about] the Russians," Temple said, "but they were friends with the Chinese and the French and all that. They can always smile and shake hands.

"In this kind of competition, you have forces working against each other, such as communists vs. capitalists, small countries vs. large countries, rich vs. poor—besides the usual men vs. women and Black vs. white hang-ups," Temple said. He commented that polo players that had enough money to ship a fleet of horses across the ocean, and swimmers who grew up practicing in country clubs, revealed a vast cultural divide. "I mean, you ain't gonna find no poor fellow riding no horse. He might ride a mule, but you're not going to find him on a finely trained horse."

Political issues were also heating up. Earlene had particular issues with the political theater that the athletes were supposed to play a part in. "I was depressed at Rome," Earlene said. "We had a lot of politics going on that year—what I call politics. When you say Russia and the United States have to go to a tea and that it's compulsory to go—to me, this is politics." Earlene preferred to be friends naturally, and she didn't want to bring the problems between the States and Russia into the Games. She already knew many of the Russian athletes from their trip to Moscow in 1958, and didn't think being paraded in front of the cameras would really help anyone but the propaganda machines. Earlene put her foot down and refused to attend. "I was ready to go home without competing," she said. "All they had to do was give me my ticket."

Ralph Boston agreed that Earlene Brown was no one to be messed with. "There would have been some trouble if you were confronting Earlene Brown."

Earlene's boycott was noticed, but the Tigerbelle team complied with Avery Brundage[2] and the International Olympic Committee's wishes, dressing up and smiling in a line for a photo.

Willye White wasn't happy with the mandate, either. "Avery Brundage was such a dictator," she said. "If you [did] anything out of the ordinary, then [you'd] be banned and disbarred from track and field. Avery Brundage was also the person who banned Jesse Owens from competing after the 1936 Games. Avery Brundage wanted Jesse to run all over Europe and places like that, and he didn't. He wanted to come home. So, they said, 'If you go home, then you'll never run track again.' And he didn't."

Managing blowups like the Russian tea party in the press was Temple's least favorite task. He was notoriously press-shy and avoided the cameras altogether unless he saw an advantage to his team. "Anything to help the program," he'd say. Temple was said to have a "controlled stammer," and his self-consciousness "haunts his pictures," but his "devotion to his girls" would get him in a photo or on a podium.

Temple preferred to leave the publicity to the PR man from Tennessee State, Earl Clanton III. The team gathered up on the steps of the practice track one afternoon for Clanton to get a photograph of the entire Tennessee State delegation at the Olympics. "Somehow they put together some money and got Clanton to Rome," Ralph Boston said. Clanton tried his best to compete with the slew of international photographers for the shots of Boston, Temple, and the Tigerbelles, each becoming increasingly popular with the international press.

It all added up to exactly the pile of distractions Temple had described.

He could only hope that his team was prepared to handle it.

---

2. Avery Brundage was the only American to lead the International Olympic Committee, holding the position for twenty years as the culmination of a controversial career in sports administration. As the head of the US Olympic Committee and a member of the IOC, Brundage notably fought the 1936 Olympic boycott after the rise of the Nazi regime in Germany, and did little for the rest of his career to counteract accusations of a wide range of highly problematic behavior.

CHAPTER 20

Showtime

THE MEDIA ATTENTION, WHILE GROWING, WAS NOT ALWAYS AS FLAT-
tering or fair as Temple hoped. To the veteran writers, women in competition seemed to be such a novel idea that they were often awkward and
patronizing in their coverage.

JoAnn Terry was motivated by her hometown paper, the *Indianapolis
Star*, writing that she would most likely find herself "back in the kitchen"
after the Games. At least they could have said "back in the classroom,"
JoAnn quipped, letting the derision serve only as fuel.

Ed Temple manages the media. Temple Archives

197

The lack of press attention paid to the Tigerbelles prior to the Olympics had caused some tangible harm to the team. Few in the American and European press took the Tigerbelles seriously, and the lack of notice caused the Olympic Committee to discount the records the team had achieved, believing them to be mistaken or fabricated. If a woman from the United States had been able to run as quickly as claimed, the Committee reasoned, would they not have written more about it?

As a result, Wilma, in particular, was seeded much lower than she should have been for her time in the 200-meter, placing her in lower heats than she deserved. They didn't believe her 22.9-second time, because "a girl never ran 23," and they decided to "table" the issue. "That's a nice way of saying no," Temple said. A lower seed forced Wilma to have to compete against more of the front-runners in the earlier heats, making it even more difficult for her to reach the finals than it was for the other top-seeded athletes.

"I wasn't expecting to win anything," Wilma said, "but I really wanted to win something." She told her mother before she left home that she hoped to bring at least one medal back. Wilma knew better than anyone how tough the competition could be at the highest level, and how many other factors could get in the way. It's also possible that some part of Wilma may have wondered the same thing the Olympic Committee had: If she'd done anything that spectacular, wouldn't more have been said about it?

A newsletter was circulated around the Village that had Wilma listed on the sixth page of contenders for her event, ranking far below the top athletes despite her record-breaking times. It rattled her, she admitted, but overall, Wilma felt stronger than she ever had. Temple even told her that he had dreamed three nights in a row that she'd won all three of her races, and she believed him when he told her she could do it.

A new kind of media coverage was added to the mix in 1960, and that was television. For the first time the Olympic Games would be broadcast into people's homes with images on their black-and-white screens. CBS agreed to air twenty hours of coverage over the course of the Games, and images of the Tigerbelles were splashed all over the world. Network television stars in the States were almost uniformly white, so these images were the first time Black children had seen people that looked like them on the screen.

The world saw the Tigerbelles at the same moment that the Tigerbelles saw the world looking back at them and cheering them on when they walked into Stadio Olimpico for the Opening Ceremony of the 1960 Olympic Games.

The team marched with thousands of athletes representing eighty-three nations in the late afternoon heat, from the Olympic Village to the Stadio Olimpico.

Some of the American athletes complained about the requirement that the US teams had to wear their navy blazers and wool skirts, the women marching in their red leather pumps in temperatures over 100 degrees, but the Tigerbelles proudly wore their uniforms, including beret, nylon stockings, red purse, and white gloves.

"Nothing compares to putting on the USA uniform and marching into that stadium," Lucinda Williams said. "That's why every day now I still wake up and thank the Lord. To come from the means I did and not know your destiny and to have it end up like it did, I was very lucky."

The team walked behind Rafer Johnson, the first Black man to bear the flag for the United States team. He held the flag high as they marched to the National Anthem. "Chills running up your back," Shirley said, when asked how she felt that day. "Eyes wide. And you're just strutting and you're thinking about your country, that you are representing your country. And your chest stuck up. That is a feeling that you do not forget."

The US delegation was met with a thunderous applause by the crowd that included European royalty and Hollywood movie stars like Elizabeth Taylor, Eddie Fisher, and Bing Crosby. It was the largest Games yet, with twice as many tickets sold as four years before in Melbourne.

"For the first time I knew what it meant to be an American," Shirley said, "and I was proud."

Ralph Boston said, "I'd never seen that many people in my whole life as we walked into that stadium. Oh, look at all those folks. Wow."

The enormity of the competition was sinking in for all of the contestants. "The pressure of the Olympics is phenomenal," Temple said. "A lot of athletes crack up under the strain because you not only have to perform well, but you have to deal with the emotional strain of knowing the whole world is looking at you."

Wilma was counting on the support from her family back home. They were her "built-in rooting section," and all of her many brothers and sisters were keeping close tabs on the news from Rome. "They all keep up with Skeeter and are just as proud of her as I am," Wilma's mother said. "They say, though, that nobody'll believe 'em when they say Skeeter's their sister." Wilma called home and told her father she was "having a good time over there. But she says she don't know what those folks are saying. Says the only time they can get together on anything is at them dances. They all must do that something alike."

However far away Wilma was from her family, she knew that Charles, Margaretta, Yvonne, Cecil, Odis, Merynelle, Charlene, Wesley, Roosevelt, Elizabeth, Vendexter, Eudora, George, Gus, Henry, Leone, Eddie Jr., Buford, Eva Mae, and her parents each kept her in their nightly prayers.

The events of the XVII Olympiad in Rome began.

JoAnn Terry and Shirley Crowder were the US team qualifiers for the hurdles. They were up against leaders from Germany, Britain, and one of the famous Press sisters,[1] Irina, from Russia, that seemed to dominate nearly every event they entered. JoAnn and Shirley knew they would be facing challengers with faster times, but getting onto the track gave everyone a shot. JoAnn ran in the third heat, a great run at 11.4, coming in just behind the third-place spot for the same time. She would not get another try. Shirley followed in the sixth heat, coming in slightly slower, at 12.3, and still finishing fourth with a clean race on the world stage, in and of itself a personal triumph.

"Victories are not only the numbers that you see on the scoreboard, or the results entered in the final column," Shirley said, "but for most it is

---

1. Irina and Tamara Press were Soviet athletes that dominated their events, setting twenty-six world records between 1959 and 1960. Irina was known for versatility, running and jumping as well as throwing, while Tamara tended to concentrate on discus and shot put.

an inner feeling of personal achievement. I did not win a gold medal, but I made the Olympic team. That's the highest I could go at that time. And I had achieved my personal best, and that was it for me. And I enjoyed it."

Shirley's triumph was in getting there, and in running a fast, clean race. She didn't let her nerves overcome her and trip her up. She competed against world-class athletes in one of the toughest tests of speed, skill, and strength, and she held her own.

"There is no sin in losing," Shirley said. "I think the greatest sin would be not to try."

Earlene Brown, called "a Los Angeles housewife" by the *New York Times*, earned a bronze medal in the shot put. Tamara Press, of Russia, won gold with an Olympic record.

Despite the disruption in Willye's season caused by leaving Tennessee State, Willye believed in herself and her ability to repeat or better her 1956 silver medal. "I was ready for Rome. I kept on training and was overtrained. I was overconfident, too, and this is as bad as no confidence. In Rome, I was the first one to jump and I had no excitement and no butterflies—and that was bad." Willye went from being the naive country girl shocking everyone with a silver-medal win in Melbourne to a twelfth-place finish in Rome. "If someone had walked up to me in 1960 and said, 'You won't win a gold medal in Rome,' I would have shot him," Willye said.

"It's corporate America who pushes gold, gold, gold, gold, gold," Willye said. "You must win gold, but the sadness of it . . . the pressure that society puts on our athletes to be winners. You know, what about doing your best? What about giving 100 percent? There's always someone that's better, but the question you ask yourself [is], did you give your best? If the answer is yes, then you are a winner. But no, the American way is to win at all costs, and it is costing the lives of our young people."

Anna Lois Smith was disqualified, without a clean jump.

JoAnn and Anna were consoled by rumored romances, Anna with long jumper Bo Roberson, a close friend of Ralph Boston's, and JoAnn with 200-meter sprinter Lester Carney. Photos appeared of the Tigerbelles walking arm in arm with their dates in papers all over the world, with reporters speculating and printing more gossip about the love lives of the athletes than coverage of their actual events, their performances being almost an afterthought.

"For them, it was great to make the team! I don't think they had any thoughts about medaling," Boston said, noting that other countries were staying far away from all the extracurricular distractions. "The athletes from the Iron Curtain countries, you knew they were ready."

The sprinters, however, knew they had a chance to win. Wilma Rudolph, Barbara Jones, Lucinda Williams, and Martha Hudson stayed focused on their upcoming events. Of the four, Martha was the only newcomer to the Olympics, and she was levelheaded enough to be able to lean on her teammates to help navigate the circus. Martha tucked her Bible into the bag she carried with her and was often seen reading a particular passage in stressful moments.

The day before the first heat of the 100-meter was hot, as many of the days in Rome had been. Temple arranged for a light practice, so instead of going to the practice field, the team found a nice, grassy lot behind the stadium with sprinklers spraying cool water over the field. It didn't take long for the team to fall into their old habits of cooling off under the sprinklers, and Temple didn't mind; they deserved to blow off a little steam. Jump after jump landed them with soaking uniforms and happy faces, and Wilma took one last jump, landing in a hole behind a sprinkler head.

"I stepped right into the hole," Wilma said, "turned my ankle, and heard it pop."

Trainers, coaches, and all of her teammates ran to Wilma's side as she lay in tears on the ground. They all knew how fragile her health was. They all knew how any little thing could get in the way of all of the excruciating effort that had brought them to this moment.

Wilma was sure that it was done. Her moment was gone. The trainer helped her up, and Wilma saw that her ankle was already bruised and swollen. "The trainer took one look and made this horrible face," Wilma said.

Temple and the trainer taped her up, iced her down, and carried her back to the Olympic Village to rest and heal. Wilma was left with her foot elevated and didn't move until the morning. Wilma wasn't just

Wilma Rudolph practices starts with Ralph Boston. Temple Archives

putting her individual qualifications in the 100- and 200-meter races in jeopardy, but also the 4x100m relay, where her three teammates were counting on her.

Amid rampant rumors of Wilma being out for the Games with a broken ankle, Wilma woke the next morning and held her breath as her foot touched the floor, testing the weight on her ankle. It held. It would take a lot of tape and pushing through the pain, but she could compete. She was ready to run.

The heats for the 100-meter were set up by time, and since Wilma's record performance had not been believed in either of her wins, "they put her in the bottom." Temple said. There were four heats before the finals, and in each, only the first four would continue.

Temple had three runners in the opening 100-meter sprints, but he hovered over Wilma and rode with her on the bus to the stadium, assuring her that she could do what she came to Rome to do. The trust that had been built between the two of them carried through this challenge, but when it came time to walk into the stadium, Wilma had to go it alone.

"When I got to the tunnel with the other runners, a strange calm came over me," Wilma said. "I was nervous in a sense, yes; but I also got a chance to look at the other runners I would be going up against, and I felt, deep inside, that I could beat any of them." Wilma stayed calm, refusing as always to burn any energy with pre-race jitters. She sat on a bench, elevating her legs, and waited.

Stadio Olimpico held up to eighty thousand spectators, and from Wilma's vantage point, every seat appeared full. When she walked into view, the crowd erupted, chanting her name, "Vil-ma . . . Vil-ma . . ." Wilma stayed focused on her preparations, readying her footing in the blocks until the call was made. The gun cracked, and Wilma ran. It was a clean race and an easy win. She had three more heats to pass through before the finals.

In the first round Wilma equaled the Olympic record of 11.5 seconds, the fastest time of all of the heat winners. Not even a bruised and battered ankle could slow Wilma down.

Barbara Jones finished second in her heat with 11.8, and Martha fourth in hers, advancing to the second round with a time of 12.2.

All three Tigerbelles advanced to the next round.

"When Wilma began running the trials," Temple said, "I realized she was going to be someone to reckon with, and when she ran the semis, I thought to myself, 'This child can win this thing. She can go all the way!'"

CHAPTER 21

Up for Gold

WITH EACH RACE, WILMA'S SPEED AND CONFIDENCE GREW. THE FOURTH and last heat before the finals was so fast that Wilma set the world record, only to be devastated by the officials striking the record due to the wind exceeding the acceptable range in her favor. "Now any runner alive knows that when you're out there on the track you aren't even aware that the wind is blowing, so how could a two-mile-an-hour wind help you any?" Wilma said.

By the final in the 100-meter, only Wilma had passed through the heats for Team USA. Barbara Jones made it to the semifinals, but came in at fourth place, barely missing the list of the six finalists.

Betty Cuthbert, the triple gold medal winner from the 1956 Olympics, had run fourth in the last heat of the second round, failing to qualify for the semifinals. But the competition was no less fierce.

The lineup for the 100-meter women's finals included Maria Itkina from Russia, Giuseppina Leone of Italy, Catherine Capdevielle from France, and Jennifer Smart and Dorothy Hyman from Great Britain.

Wilma handled the pressure the way she often did: She went into such a calm state that she fell asleep. Temple rushed around trying to find her, and was stunned to locate her sleeping on the rubdown table in the locker room. Temple, using a significant amount of energy trying to remain calm himself, told her that it was time to get ready, but Wilma took her time, putting one shoe on at a time, stretching and yawning, seeming to Temple to move in slow motion.

"By this time, I was really nervous," Temple said. "You see, this was my first Olympics."

Temple hustled Wilma to the tunnel where the tension was high as the finalists waited together to walk into the Stadio Olimpico for the first sprint final. Wilma didn't chat with the other runners, which had been her habit, instead imagining herself like a boxer, gearing up for a fight and looking her opponents in the eye.

"When we got out on the track," Wilma said, "I followed my same routine: one practice start, then slowly walking around with my hands on my hips, near the starting blocks. No rushing, no jumping, no running around; conserve the energy for when it really matters. I was concentrating deeply."

Temple watched through the fence from the practice field, ready to "swear off the Olympics forever." The runners were called to their mark and Temple said, "Rudolph carefully wiped some cinders off of her fingers and placed them just so on the track. She fiddled and fiddled around." By the time the starter called "*Via!*," the Italian call to "Get set," Temple knew she was ready. "On 'Go' it was never a matter of if she would win, but by how far she'd win it."

Wilma came off the blocks in second or third position, and her speed started kicking in.

"When I reached fifty meters," Wilma said, "I saw that I had them all, and I was just beginning to turn it on. By seventy meters, I knew the race was mine—nobody was going to catch me."

Allison Danzig for the *New York Times* noted Wilma's slower start, but recognized her outstanding performance, writing, "Streaking in front at the 40-meter mark after a bad start the 20-year-old Tigerbelle from Tennessee State ran away from her rivals to win the sprint by a big margin. She is the first American gold medalist in this event since Helen Stephens in 1936."

"I wasn't expecting it," Temple said. "I would have been happy if she was just making the finals. I had no idea what she was going to accomplish. But I saw it on the big scoreboard. People started hollering that Wilma Rudolph won the 100 meters." The stands went crazy. It was a spectacular win. "I was pulling out my cigar now," Temple said. "Frances

Kaszubski was walking like somebody about eight feet tall, talking about 'her babies.'"

Wilma won by several yards, a rare occurrence in the short sprint, where mere tenths of a second separated the winners and the back of the pack. Wilma repeated her time of 11 seconds flat, announced as a world-record time, but again, the record was not counted because the wind exceeded the acceptable 2-meters-per-second speed at 2.752, or 0.475 miles per hour, with the accepted speed of 0.4474 miles per hour, a nearly imperceptible difference outside of highly tuned instruments.

A few yards from the 100-meter finish line Ralph Boston was in his own event finals for the long jump. Jesse Owens watched both from the stands, but his main focus was on Boston, who seemed poised to overcome Owens's long-standing Olympic record.

Boston saw Wilma cross the finish line for her win, then turn toward him to walk back. Boston was close enough to call out to her over the roar of the crowd, and said, "Hey, way to go, babes!"

Wilma called back to ask Boston how he was doing in his event, and he told her, "I'm leading."

Wilma Rudolph at the finish line. Temple Archives

Wilma then jogged to the other side of the stadium, meeting Earlene Brown with a celebratory hug and a victory dance to the delight of the crowd that cheered them on.

Wilma then hid from the reporters under the umbrellas set up for the athletes near the starting line until Barbara Jones met her with a towel and comb to help her get photo-ready for the onslaught of the press and the medal ceremony. Barbara, the self-proclaimed diva and youngest Olympic gold medalist, was watching Wilma's star rise beyond her own dreams, but still she looked out for Wilma like a sister.

Wilma stepped up on the podium with Dorothy Hyman of Britain and Giuseppina Leone of Italy on the second and third steps below her. Wilma bent at the waist for Avery Brundage to drape the medal around her neck, then stood as "The Star-Spangled Banner" played for her.

Ralph Boston finished his own event nearby with six jumps, reaching his farthest, 26 feet and 7.75 inches, on the third try, flying past Jesse Owens's record while Owens looked on, and was heard to say, "There goes another old friend." After his jumps, already back in his sweatpants, Boston watched his friend and fellow US team member, Bo Roberson, take his last jump. It was a great one. Boston wasn't sure who had reached the farthest yet, but already pounded his buddy on the back for the beautiful jump.

In the end, Boston had it. The two came first and second, winning gold and silver for the United States.

A second Tennessee State student would be coming home with gold. No matter what happened for the rest of the Games, Wilma Rudolph and Ralph Boston were champions. The crowd was so exuberant that after his medal ceremony, Boston had to be "smuggled" out of the stadium, but he still thought he could have done better. "I could have jumped farther," Boston said, "but I just couldn't get my steps right. I keep working on them and keep working on them. If I get them right one day, I'll go farther."

Anna Lois Smith was there to greet Boston and her beau, Bo Roberson, when they got back to the Village, congratulating the two medalists.

Wilma's gold medal brought the hot intensity of the spotlight while her teammates stayed behind, struggling to break out. Wilma didn't seem to crave the spotlight; she simply wanted to win. She also wanted everyone she loved to win as well. Wilma didn't seem to accept the glory in and of itself because as soon as her race was done, her concerns went back to her friends.

During the past couple of years, Wilma had become close to Ray Norton, a star on the international scene in track and field for years. During the Olympics, their friendship appeared to turn into something more. Newspapers covered the relationship breathlessly, spotlighting photos of the two of them with their arms around each other and constantly asking for quotes on the status of their relationship.

An old questionnaire that Wilma had filled out for the 1956 Olympics had resurfaced where she had answered two questions: What was her greatest ambition, and who was her favorite athlete? For the first she'd answered that she wanted to win an Olympic gold medal, and for the second, she had answered "Ray Norton." The "newsies" gleefully reported that she had captured both.

Ray stood by while Wilma spoke to reporters after her first win, and she glanced up at him while she answered a flurry of questions. Wilma lamented her slow start, behind the two leaders, that was easily overcome before the halfway point. Ray Norton had fallen short in his expected win for the 100-meter. Despite being the overwhelming front-runner heading into the Games, he had barely qualified for the finals and finished in an embarrassing last place. It was almost as if Wilma wanted to diminish her win so she wouldn't show up her childhood idol, and new boyfriend, as well as her teammates that hadn't gotten as far.

Some even credited Ray Norton with Wilma's motivation to win, saying "Wilma said she did it for Ray." Wilma said, "I was heartsick when Ray was beaten in the men's 100-meter finals. I knew the best way to cheer him up was to win myself—and win good." Immediately asked about their relationship, Wilma answered, "Ray and I have been close friends for two years now. We are together anytime we get the chance. He gives me encouragement and confidence; I try to console him when he is in the dumps."

Temple also noticed the relationship and commented, "We josh them a lot about it. I told him if they get married, I hope all the kids are girls." He couldn't help but imagine the pair producing a whole team of little Tigerbelles. Another unnamed friend said, "It's a great match. If she gets ornery and decides to run away, she's got the only guy who can catch her." However, it would be tough even for Ray, because his top time was not even a full second faster than Wilma's; no one's was.

Wilma left the stadium after her win with her arm hooked around Norton's and his straw hat on her head.

The interest in the pair grew more critical when Norton lost his second medal try in the 200-meter, again finishing last in the finals. A meeting was called by the US Olympic Committee on the topic, among other gripes about the conduct of the athletes.

The complaint was that the US team had been "going too much for wine, women, and song," since they had been in Rome. The track and field team, especially the men, were singled out and were accused of "cruising around Rome night spots in the wee hours of the morning."

Other opinions were that it was about national pride, and that the "insinuations of high-living and late hours have hung heavily on the minds of the men's team," and that Norton "denied vehemently" the charge of a raucous nightlife.

The Committee ultimately determined that the rumors were unfounded, but said the team couldn't afford "even to give the appearance of wrongdoing." It was an admonishment Temple had given to his team all along, and the wider US team was just discovering. Kenneth "Tug" Wilson, the president of the US Olympic Committee, continued to complain about the unfair treatment of his team. "We resent the implications made by uninformed individuals that our athletes have failed to live up to their responsibilities," Wilson said in a statement. "We have complete confidence in our US athletes as competitors and in their conduct as ladies and gentlemen." Wilson explained that the athletes had been swapping uniforms with other teams, and when those athletes from other countries wore the US team uniforms out on the town, they would be mistaken for US team members. He added that more than half of the athletes had completed their events and should be allowed to celebrate their achievements without interfering with athletes who still had competitions on the line.

Norton himself didn't have a good explanation for his performance. "It was just like in the 100," he said. "I was so tense and tied up I couldn't run. I guess it's because I'm trying too hard. Nothing is wrong with me physically. I feel all right. I'm just tied up in a knot inside."

But Jesse Owens, writing his own column on the Games, thought he knew what was to blame. Owens watched the race carefully, also viewing a filmed replay, and concluded that Norton's form was off—indicating a sore or pulled muscle. When Owens confronted Norton about it, Norton wouldn't confirm or deny Owens's theory. Owens admonished the star, saying, "Ray, sometimes you can hurt yourself by having too much guts."

After Ray Norton's loss of the 200, the one who was there to try to console him was Wilma. She met him outside the stadium and said, "Don't worry, honey, you did all right."

"I did awful," Norton responded. "I just can't explain it. I just don't know what's the matter." Norton threw his shoes against the wall and sat on a bench, holding his head in his hands. Wilma sat next to him, her arm around his shoulders.

When they got up to leave, Wilma said, "You're forgetting your shoes, honey. You'd better get your shoes."

Ray responded, "I don't want the shoes. I never want to see them again."

Wilma was showered with congratulations for her win in the 100, her room filled with flowers and telegrams, the first one being a congratulations from Betty Cuthbert, who Wilma had watched win three golds from the stands in Melbourne. Now, in 1960, it was Wilma's year to try, and she already had one around her neck.

An official congratulations was printed in the *Nashville Banner* for Wilma and Ralph Boston, the newly hailed hometown heroes, stating, "It was for each a personal achievement, calling on reserves of strength, and skill, and fighting heart—the qualities of challenge historically implicit to the Olympiad: but no less do these reflect credit on their school, their state, and their nation. They have honored all three."

A reporter for the *Knoxville News Sentinel* wrote that "Wilma Rudolph is a Tennessean better known in Moscow than in her native state," but with her win she was about to become known the world over.

In the Village, Wilma was hounded by reporters and photographers "pounding on doors" to get her attention, but she and Temple wanted the Tennessee State photographer, Earl Clanton, to have the first official photo. They waited for him as long as they could, then the rush of the international press "stampeded" in. Wilma thought between the AP, the UPI, the International Press, and all of the individual entities there, there must have been a thousand photos taken. When the crowd cleared out and Temple asked Clanton if he had gotten his photo, he just shook his head. His camera had jammed up and he hadn't gotten a single shot.

Lucinda and Wilma both qualified for the semifinals in the 200-meter on Monday. Wilma won her heat with an Olympic record–breaking time of 23.2. Lucinda placed second in her heat, with 24 seconds flat.

Sunday was a day off between the first round of the 200 and the semifinals. Temple, worried about her ankle, urged Wilma to take it easy, promising that once she was done with the 200, she could enjoy the celebrations. There was little time to rest before the 200-meter, which, being run on the curve of the track, could put more strain on her ankle. But everyone knew the 200 was Wilma's best event, and Lucinda would be close on her heels.

Earl Clanton's public relations campaign for Tennessee State involved more than just photographs. He posted an article in the *Nashville Banner* about Lucinda Williams and Wilma Rudolph's antics over the weekend as they prepared for the 200-meter semifinals.

"Leave it to American ingenuity to outsmart some of the regulations in the Olympic Village," Clanton wrote. "Rudolph, the new Olympic 100-meter champion, and teammate Lucinda Williams are keeping tabs on their sprint opposition through a hastily devised 'spy system.'" Clanton went on to describe how Lucinda and Wilma had befriended the coach for the West Indies team, American Mal Whitfield, asking him to report on the practices of their Australian and British competitors, who practiced at the same time as the West Indies team.

The day of the finals was the worst weather yet of the Olympics. The bright skies and sweltering 100-degree heat had broken to a pelting rain. But, as Ralph Boston told Willye White, "When it rains on one, it rains on all." Temple's brutal training approach continued to pay off. When you want to perform in the heat, you practice in the heat, and if you want to perform in the rain, run in the rain.

In the morning semifinals, Lucinda gave her best run, but came up short, finishing fifth in her heat. She would not be competing in the afternoon final. Wilma, however, won her heat as she had every other heat in the Games, and was the only team member who was able to reach first place for a single event. She had a chance to repeat the feat that afternoon, doubling her already historic victory.

Wilma was most intimidated by Jutta Heine, a tall blonde from West Germany. Wilma knew that her own height was an advantage, and with Heine, that advantage was gone. "She had won all of her preliminary heats, just as I had," Wilma said, "and she was just as tall as I was. I watched her run a heat and noticed that she had a stride just as long as I had, and yes, she was a good runner."

Wilma had become a media darling overnight, and as she stepped up to her mark for her favorite event, the eyes of the world were on her. Everyone had an opinion about her, most accurately reflected by the views of those that reported the news each day, the newspapermen.

Raymond Johnson, columnist for *The Tennessean*, had finally turned his attention toward Wilma and offered a window into the newsroom culture by writing, "Today when a gangling 20-year-old Negro girl from Nashville's Tennessee State paws into the starting blocks in Rome's Olympic Stadium, there's a whole new world awaiting her 200 meters away, where only that almost invisible string separates her from immortality."

As easy as Wilma might make it seem, she was still running against headwinds, both literal and metaphorical. The wind and rain were not the only factors. Wilma had been placed in the most challenging starting lane. "Worst lane in the 200," Temple said, "lane one, because it's a quick curve. Best in the 200 are lanes seven through nine. But they had to be ready for any lane."

"A little rain meant nothing to me," Wilma said. She pumped herself up by telling herself, "There's nobody alive who can beat you in the 200. Go get it."

Wilma was able to make the race look easy after all, finishing several strides ahead of Jutta Heine and Dorothy Hyman. A strong wind that preceded a coming storm slowed Wilma's time to 24 seconds flat. "I meant to run faster," Wilma said, "but somehow when the race started, I just couldn't get going any harder." The headwinds and the soaked, soft track could not have helped, but Temple thought her time would have been better if she'd had more of a challenge, a knock on her competition, continuing to believe that Wilma had "limitless potential." Temple said, "We don't know how fast she can really go. She never has been really tested, since she came into her real form."

"She has perfect control of her body," Jesse Owens said, himself a triple gold winner in the 1936 Olympics and seeing a path for Wilma to accomplish the same feat. "Wilma could be one of the greatest women sprinters of all time." She might not have needed the qualifier of "women."

Ted Smits with the Associated Press called Wilma the "Tennessee Tornado," and wrote, "She runs with complete grace and almost as fast as the leading men sprinters of the world. In fact, her winning time in the 100 of 11.0, aided by only a slight wind, was faster than all but three of the men in yesterday's 31-man decathlon field." Smits then hit on what appeared to be Wilma's greatest strength: her ability to stay calm and loose. "Unlike some of the American men who have cracked under the terrific pressure," Smit wrote, "Miss Rudolph remains poised despite the glare of attention. Some of the Russian team said that they considered her the greatest athlete, man or woman, in these games."

Temple agreed that this could be her secret weapon. He said, "There's not a nerve in her body. She's almost lazy. She often goes to sleep between semifinal and final runs. She can go to sleep on the rubbing table." Off the track, she never seems to be in a hurry. "We yell for her to hurry up, but she just drags along, with never a quick and jerky motion. Then she gets over those starting blocks and—boom—all that harnessed energy explodes into blinding speed."

Wilma was the first American woman to ever win the 200-meter in the Olympics. She was also the first woman to win two gold medals since 1932, when Babe Dickerson won gold in both the hurdles and the javelin. To sweep the sprints with a perfect winning performance in each heat had never been done.

"She won that going away," Temple said. "She felt bad for her team-mates. She was determined to get them a medal."

Fans and autograph seekers swarmed Wilma after her second win, and Temple arranged for six of the Tigerbelles, all in uniform, to help remove her from the crowd and get safely back to the Village ahead of a vicious threatening storm that followed Wilma's performance by a mere half an hour. "I got six of the girls to form a flying wedge around her and rush her to the Village," Temple said. "She would have stayed out there, signing autographs and catching her death of cold. That's just the way she is. She is too nice for her own good."

The collective speed of the group in a real-world setting off the track made their power even more evident, as they effortlessly took off at top speed, leaving the crowds gaping after them as they sprinted to the safety of the Village.

CHAPTER 22

The Relay

WILMA RUDOLPH, BARBARA JONES, LUCINDA WILLIAMS, AND MARTHA Hudson showed up ready to practice at nine a.m. sharp on Tuesday morning, the day before the heats for the 4x100m relay. Wilma had total confidence in her relay team, saying that her three teammates "can run with any three on any other team," and she was determined to help them get the gold medals she knew they deserved.

Barbara told her team, "If Wilma can win a gold medal, we can too." Wilma agreed, and said, "Get me the baton."

The relay was the most anticipated event of the Olympic Games for a reason: There were a thousand ways in which it could go wrong.

The men's relay team served as a reminder of how hard it was to get everything right. The four-man team finished first in the finals, in a close finish pulled off by the anchor, David Sime, but in a dramatic turn of events the medal was not awarded to the US team because Ray Norton ran through the passing lane before the baton was secured, causing a disqualification of the entire run. The US men's team was out, and the medal was awarded instead to the second-place finishers, the Germans.

"I can't do anything right," Norton said. "First I run too slow, then I run too fast." Norton believed that his career was over, a tough way to bow out for an otherwise excellent competitor.[1] Wilma felt his heartache.

---

1. After the Olympic Games, Norton was drafted to the San Francisco 49ers and played two seasons for the team.

"Ray can't fool me, I can tell," Wilma said. "He tries to play it cool, but I know. He is dying inside."

The women were determined not to make a mistake. To win, they needed flawless execution. The Tigerbelles had been running at a disadvantage through their entire careers, but in the relay, there was a critical advantage they looked to exploit. It was the trust that they had built with each other for years. As Lucinda Williams said after the 1956 Olympics in Melbourne, they knew what they needed to do. They had trained for this moment, and they were prepared.

To complete a relay at the speed required to win at this elite level, each member of the team had to have complete confidence in the others. They had to know each other intimately; their strengths, weaknesses, moves, reactions, who was slow or fast on the takeoff, who might be a second or two off on the reflexes. Then collectively, they needed to compensate for each other, to achieve the highest level of precision together.

To climb to top speed in a passing lane, with an outstretched hand behind, one runner had to believe beyond a shadow of a doubt that her teammate would get that baton into her hand without slowing, without ever looking back, without missing a step or losing a beat.

When the four Tigerbelles hit the track on Thursday, they brought all of their work, everything they had achieved to that point, and all that they had learned and experienced together, with them.

"Everyone always asks me what does it take to get gold," Temple said. "It takes fortune and preparation."

The four women on the track were representing the United States, Tennessee State, their hometowns, their friends and family, and their communities as a whole. They finally had the opportunity to show the world what a real team was. What a group of young Black women from the Jim Crow South could do. Women who had been told their whole lives that there were places they couldn't go and things that they couldn't do were about to show everyone that no, there weren't. They were capable of anything.

Their competitors for the qualifying heat were from the Soviet Union, Australia, and Poland, as well as their two friends from Tennessee State, Lorraine Dunn and Marcella Daniel, competing for Panama.

Martha Hudson ran first. Pee Wee always had the fastest starts, and that day was no exception. Martha leapt off the blocks and pumped her legs hard, passing the baton to Barbara with a slight lead.

Temple's only concern about Barbara was her anticipation getting ahead of her, causing her to run ahead of the baton. "I kept saying over and over, 'I ain't going to leave, I ain't going to leave until I have that stick,'" Barbara said.

Barbara held herself back until the baton was solid in her hand and then took off, passing to Lucinda in a clean handoff, neck and neck with the Russian team. Lucinda poured everything she had into her leg and gained the lead before she passed to Wilma, the fastest woman in the world.

"I just gave her the stick and said, 'Get goin,' gal,'" Lucinda said.

Wilma cruised to the finish with a flawless team win. Their final time was 44.4 seconds, an Olympic and a world record.

To put that level of speed into perspective, sportswriter Michael Davis wrote, "What does 44.4 seconds mean? It means that a little girl not five feet tall was covering ground at the rate of 30 feet every second, less time than it takes to clap hands. That's covering ground."

"We did it, we did it!" Martha and Barbara kept saying over and over. "We got there first and let old Skeeter relax."

"The Tennessee Tigerbelles—Pee Wee, Skeeter, BeeJay, and Lucinda—did proud by Uncle Sam," Joan Marble Cook wrote for UPI. "They ran faster than any four girls have ever run before in a 400-meter relay race."

The next day, for the finals, the Tigerbelles were the team to beat. They went in with the confidence that their record-breaking performance the day before had earned them.

Years of preparation were culminating in this one moment. There was less than a minute between them and the finish line when they would discover what all of their effort had achieved.

The runners took their places around the track. The crowd grew quiet, and friends and family watched, crowded around black-and-white televisions, holding their breath in anticipation.

Televisions were turned on all over the world, and in Tennessee, neighbors gathered in each other's homes, glued to the images on the screen and rooting for their hometown heroes. Guests gathered in the Gentry household, and in the Queen's suite in Hankal Hall, Barbara Murrell and her sorority sisters crowded around the television screen "We had the TV in the room," Barbara said, "and of course we had everybody hanging from the ceiling, trying to see Wilma run."

When the starting gun fired Martha Hudson was quick off the blocks, her consistency at her top skill proven. "Martha got out well," Temple said. "On a staggered start, it's hard to tell who's winning." Pee Wee's lightning reflexes launched her out of the blocks and she pumped her legs hard, not letting her height hold her back. In a clear reflection of her hero, Mae Faggs, Martha finished her strong run with a clean pass to Barbara.

"Barbara was tough on the straights," Temple said. "It looked like they were in the top three." Barbara's strengths were the straight run, and she fought hard, showing her skill as the money runner performing for the crowd. "If you got her in front of cheering crowds," Temple said, "she'd make the rest of the runners blow a gasket. I mean, all pistols would be sparking."

Barbara used every stride to prove her status as one of the world's best. She earned her first gold at the age of fifteen, and she had pushed for eight years for the chance to earn a second. BeeJay seemed even with the lead when she passed to Lucinda, beating two of the competitors that had qualified ahead of her in the 100-meter.

Barbara and Lucinda, the two most experienced runners on the relay, had the added pressure of two handoffs each, both receiving and passing the baton. The pass between the two veterans was flawless, and Lucinda powered up her sprint.

Lucinda ran the curve—her specialty, since she was so strong in the 200-meter curved sprint—and improved on the lead. "As I approached Wilma," Lucinda said, "I knew she wasn't taking off." It was the final handoff. The critical last moment with enormous potential for error. The transfer of the baton had to take place within the specified passing zone, or the team would not only lose their lead, but they would be disqualified, exactly as the men's team had been.

As Lucinda charged up to the passing zone, Wilma hesitated, as if she wasn't expecting Lucinda to come in so fast. The worst-case scenario was beginning to play out. "The handoff was not as smooth as it should have been," Lucinda said. "Wilma did not judge my speed. I knew that was my last chance to get a medal, so I was coming in with everything I possibly could. I ran up her back and we had a bobble in that exchange."

Everything had come down to this moment. This one mistake could upend years of effort and haunt them for the rest of their lives. A trip, a drop, a step too far. The potential hazards were endless.

"Lucinda went to pass, and she missed Wilma's hand," Temple said. "Lucinda tried it again and by that time we were moving through that zone pretty good." The pair was flying closer and closer to the line across the track that indicated the end of the zone, while the other runners passed and rushed by them on either side.

Passing at that speed required an incredibly precise choreography. Having to coordinate a second attempt, to communicate the solution to the mistake in the time it takes to snap your fingers between two people moving at superhuman speed, one with their back turned and hand stretched behind, was undoubtedly an impossible task.

"My heart sank to my feet," Temple said. "That one bobble gave Germany and Australia enough time to pull ahead and put us in third place."

Wilma slowed, losing two strides and precious time, and Lucinda had to "hit her a second time." Somehow the two stayed close enough, and perhaps by instinct or intuition, on the second try the baton stuck. Wilma had a firm grasp barely within the 20-meter passing zone. Raising her voice over the roar of the crowds, "I yelled at her to go," Lucinda said, assuring Wilma that the baton was secure, "and finally she took off, and

4x100m relay handoff between Lucinda Williams and Wilma Rudolph. Special Collections and Archives—Tennessee State University

it was like all the whirlwinds had broke loose." Lucinda slowed her run and watched Wilma fly.

"I knew that once she got that baton, no matter who was ahead of her, she was going to catch them," Lucinda said. "It was frightening, but we had confidence enough that we knew we were going to do it."

The hours, days, months, and years of practice had proved their worth, allowing the strength of their connection to adapt to anything that threatened them. Martha, Barbara, and Lucinda had each outperformed themselves, and it was left to Wilma to come from behind again.

"When she got that stick it was awesome," Temple said. "It was almost like seeing Carl Lewis get it now. Zoom, gone. I knew this was going to be a race. By the way she jumped on them so quick, I couldn't believe it myself, what I was looking at."

With a standing start instead of climbing out of the blocks, Wilma accelerated to her top speed almost immediately. She passed Jutta Heine and the Australian anchor in the first 15 yards. "She was so determined I don't believe anyone could have stopped her," Temple said. "That child, the first 75 yards, it was just awesome. She chewed them up. She chewed them up like they were standing still. They looked like they were in slow motion, she jumped on them so fast."

Wilma stretched her legs out long, gliding across the track for the final strides, leaning forward and breaking the tape across her chest. The Tigerbelles' 4x100-meter relay team won the gold. There was no doubt who the best team was, and each of them had done what they needed to do to get them there.

The crowds in the stands "bordered on hysterics," Temple said. Everyone was cheering for the Tigerbelles. "Everybody ran their best," Wilma said, "and we won it going away."

Wilma won her third gold medal. And she won the final gold for her team.

Nearly one hundred photographers chased after Wilma while she ran to catch up with her team, her sisters. They wrapped their arms around each other, yelling and cheering their collective victory.

In living rooms around the world, everyone saw what these four women from Tennessee State were capable of.

At the Gentry house in Nashville, packed with friends and neighbors, everyone went crazy. "There was a lot of excitement in my house," Howard said. "They likened it to Joe Louis winning the heavyweight title. People were dancing in the streets. Especially in the 4x100m, when they came from behind. It was bedlam."

Barbara Murrell and her sorority sisters, students all over campus at Tennessee State, families across Nashville and throughout the world, cheered the new national heroes.

"When I saw Wilma run, it made me believe that I could run too," said Loretta Claiborne, who was inspired to overcome her own personal challenges to become an Olympic medalist herself many times over in the Special Olympic Games.

"We are four African American girls representing the whole United States of America, being able to stand on that podium and to see our flag going up," Lucinda said.

It was a moment that changed the lives of not only those four women, but everyone who witnessed it. No matter what limitations or constraints were designed to hold them back, these women ran forward. They weren't only the fastest women in the world, they were also the best team. It took four women to circle the track, to pass the baton one to the other, and they did it with speed, grace, and agility that had never before been seen. They had proven their worth. They were Tigerbelles.

"They went up there and had a good time after they won," Temple said. The team celebrated all night at the favorite hot spot in Rome, Bricktop's, where they rubbed elbows with European royalty and American movie stars who hailed the American heroes, pounding their backs with congratulations and showering them with champagne.

Gold Medalists L to R: Wilma Rudolph, Lucinda Williams, Barbara Jones, Martha Hudson. Temple Archives

CHAPTER 23

Homecoming

TEMPLE LET OUT HIS FIRST FULL BREATH OF THE OLYMPICS, AND PROB-
ably for the year. "I'm breathing easy now for the first time in two weeks.
We've got what we came here for," Temple said. "But the greatest strain
has been on Rudolph. This was her tenth race of the Olympics. Four
100-meter heats, three in the 200, and these two relays. She won all of
them. The remarkable thing is that she's stayed so sound and ever sharp."

Wilma was the reigning queen of the Olympics and the fastest
woman in the world, but only the Tigerbelles seemed to realize that she
couldn't have gotten as far as she had on her own. "She's had tremendous
competition, the three fastest girls in the country," Temple said. "Take
Jones. She ran a world record 10.3 hundred yards at Randall's Island in
1958. . . . Jones would sometimes beat Rudolph, Williams beat Rudolph,
even Hudson was competition right up to the last 25 yards when her little legs give out. Every time trial we had was like a track meet. Rudolph
ran the hundred meters in 11.1 in a time trial because of that competition. Without it she wouldn't have won no three gold medals." Wilma
got most of the attention, but Temple wanted to be clear that *all* of his
runners were great, and that they had each helped the others become
even better.

The chaos that ensued after the Tigerbelles' historic victory was enormous. Everyone wanted a piece of them. Fifteen separate nations invited
Wilma and the Tigerbelles to hold exhibition competitions. Temple
knew that the additional attention would be good for their recognition
and image in the world, but he worried about the cost.

Jesse Owens faced similar demands after his dramatic performance in the 1936 Olympics, but he had refused to participate, opting instead to go straight home. Brundage and the US Olympic Committee were indignant at the audacity of this young man's refusal and banned him from participating in future Games.

Temple didn't choose the same path, always careful to avoid controversy. He agreed to a tour including Athens, London, Amsterdam, Cologne, Wuppertal, Frankfurt, and Berlin. "That's as far as we can go," Temple said. "Wilma has to get back to school by September 25."

Wilma's willingness to give so much of herself was starting to wear her down. She was accommodating to a fault, spending hours signing autographs and greeting fans, leaving her exhausted and drained after all that her body had gone through. Over the course of her time in Rome, Wilma had lost twelve pounds, weight she didn't need to lose.

Wilma wanted nothing more than to go home, to celebrate with her family and her daughter, the people who meant the most to her. She felt as if her victories weren't even real if she couldn't share them at home. But she and the other Tigerbelles were forced to stay, to keep performing.

"I can't go anywhere," Wilma said. "I can't do anything. I'm afraid to go out in the morning. They recognize me everywhere, whether I'm wearing a dress or my sweatshirt. If I'm walking through the Olympic Village, if I'm going to eat, even if I'm just sitting in a group at the men's quarters, people want autographs and pictures."

Wilma said that the photographers were the most frustrating to deal with, pushing her to stand holding her medals for hundreds of shots, moving this way and that way for different angles and light.

"We've been running and training all the time since July," Wilma said. "It's all over, but I still can't get any rest." Wilma couldn't leave the Olympic Village without creating a scene. "Even tables were overturned in the dining hall by people trying to get to her," Temple said. She was hailed as the "Queen of the Olympics" by the Russians, called the "Black Pearl" and the "Black Gazelle." Wilma did have some fun with it, teasing Cassius Clay that if he ever lost his one medal, she'd give him one of hers.

Temple was exhausted, too, but they'd accomplished what they had set out to do, and more.

The world record committee—the ones who didn't believe that Wilma's record set in the 200 over the summer could have possibly been real—were forced to admit that they had been wrong.

"They claimed the clocks were wrong," Temple said, "that a girl couldn't possibly run the 200 under 23 seconds." But she'd done it, with everyone watching.

"Wilma was the spark plug of the team," Temple continued, "but all of the girls were determined because of the fact that women's track has been looked down on for so long." Finally, everyone saw them for who they were and what they could do. They didn't mind that not only were they seen as great, they were also seen as glamourous and beautiful champions.

Temple knew that going forward the competition would become even tougher, year after year. Their competitors would be chasing them, more determined than ever to reclaim their prior status. They would not make the mistake of underestimating the Tennessee Tigerbelles again.

The overall performance of the United States team had been less impressive than the Tigerbelles' own. Avery Brundage was heard claiming that "soft living" was the fault of the poor performances, and the *New York Times* sports editor, Arthur Daley, maintained his claim that women didn't belong in the Games, serving only as distractions to the men.

But both men had missed the mark. The women had proven that they were the strength of the team, and their inclusion was the only reason the United States had fared as well as it had.

Brundage's complaints exposed a major inconsistency in the way that athletes in the United States were treated. While Americans were expected to win, they were given very little support in order to do so. Athletes were expected to bear the entire cost of training and development until they reached the highest level, and even then, the support was only administrative.

Michael Davis wrote, "With a single voice the great mass of American people cheer the great victories of track stars in the Olympics. . . . They are 'our girls.' But let their performance be less than hoped for, and a shrill, fickle chorus of American press and public can be heard saying 'girls are cream puffs, the girls won't train.'"

Arthur Daley showed his own perspective by echoing the earlier article printed in his paper, "Venus Wasn't a Shot-Putter," about the feminine "image." Daley wrote that the Romans had made a mistake in this Olympiad and should have taken the advice of the Greeks. "High on Olympus, the gods conferred and finally Zeus, the king of the gods, laid down one rigid rule. It was to be irrevocable. It was this: no dames.

"Unfortunately, the weakness of man's nature overcame his good sense. Women first were admitted as spectators and then as competitors. Now they clutter up the joint and feminine frills have begun to debase this temple of masculinity."

Daley and many of the other "newspapermen" followed an old and tired tradition of men blaming women for their own shortcomings.

During their grueling tour of repeat performances across Europe, the Tigerbelles proved again and again that they were unbeatable. As the calendar turned to fall, the weather became cold and rainy, and the constant travel started to take a toll on their bodies. One or the other was often sick, Temple calling in doctors and encouraging his athletes to eat, even though the food that was available was usually not what they were accustomed to. Their flight might arrive on the same day as a meet, where with very little sleep they raced against their closest competitors from the Olympics, who were rested and ready for revenge.

"We kept running, and we kept winning," Temple wrote to Charlie B., "I don't know how." Temple's assistant coach, Fran Welch, was furious not to be invited along, once again expecting that he deserved the honor and glory despite not having brought a single athlete to the team. Instead, Frances Kaszubski, the AAU representative that had cared for the team since the Olympic trials, stayed on as manager through the tour.

Frances could see the strain on the team and panicked over each performance. "Ed, we're going to lose this one," she'd say to Temple. "What are we going to do?"

Temple gathered his team and told them, "We've got nothing to gain, and everything to lose. But you are champions." Time after time the Tigerbelles proved him right, and Temple worked hard to get them home, fighting off more demands for their time.

"The girls were tired," Edwina Temple said. "They were ready to see their families, and it was time for school to start. [My dad] was tired, he wanted to go home. I think they would have kept them. Back-to-back, each time it was a race for the girls. In some places it rained, it got wet, it got cold. It was a very hard time. People didn't understand. Everybody wanted to see you and touch you, but they didn't understand, they'd been gone since June."

The Tigerbelles' relay team and their coach returned to Nashville as conquering heroes to the fanfare they deserved, met at the airport by a crowd that included Mayor Ben West and Governor Buford Ellington, as well as Walter Davis, the president of Tennessee State, and Howard Gentry, the athletic director. Charlie B. Temple, overlooked in all of the excitement, had to flag someone down for the ride to the airport that she had been promised. Finally, the family was reunited, and the victories celebrated in full.

"She was just Wilma Rudolph to us, but then she came back from Rome and she was the fastest woman in the world. We were just so excited for her," Barbara Murrell said of the entire Tennessee State community.

Ralph Boston and Barbara Jones shared the back of a convertible for a homecoming parade down Jefferson Street. Boston brought some candy to throw to the children. "BeeJay didn't ask," Boston said, laughing, "she just reached into my candy bag and started throwing candy out of it. I didn't say anything, because this is Barbara Jones. She had won her first gold medal when she was just a pup."

At a "cheering, rafter-packed student rally" in Kean Hall on campus, president Walter Davis said, "This Olympic victory is a symbol of the quality of the work we're doing here in the classroom and out." Martha Hudson spoke in front of the gathered assembly and made a crack about her diminutive size, saying, "I doubt if ever so much depended on so little."

Wilma told a reporter for *The Tennessean*, "I feel I've accomplished something that represents a challenge within me. It's wonderful. It takes hard practice and endurance and a man like Coach Temple behind you all the way."

Homecoming: Lucinda Williams holds the hand of Edwina Temple with Charlie B. and Ed Temple. Temple Archives

Clarksville, Tennessee, had its own celebration that at Wilma's insistence was the town's first integrated event. The streets were filled and the banquet bursting with all her friends and family, along with town dignitaries, both Black and white.

Judge William Hudson stood in front of more than 1,100 guests gathered around tables for dinner, clearly moved by the occasion. "If I can overcome my emotions," he said, "I'll make you a little speech. Wilma has competed with the world and brought home three gold medals. If you want to get good music out of a piano, you have to play both the white keys and the black keys."

Wilma, the shy child who'd once hidden behind Mae Faggs's shoulder, stood and responded with a speech of her own. "I shall always use my physical talents to the glory of God, the best interests of my nation, and the honor of womanhood. I give you my humble thanks for the opportunity to serve."

Wilma was finally able to enjoy some much-deserved rest at home with her family before the honors and accolades continued.

Barbara Murrell and her sorority sisters were prepared to help Wilma be celebrated in style. The national president of Delta Sigma Theta,

Jeanne Noble, was a professor at New York University and connected to the inaugural celebration for newly elected president John F. Kennedy. The Tennessee State band was asked to play in the inaugural parade, and Wilma Rudolph rode on one of the floats. Wilma was celebrated the world over, but the celebrations for an amateur athlete did not include any compensation. After the parade, Wilma was invited to meet the new young president, and Barbara Murrell and her sorority sisters had to make sure she had the proper clothing for her events.

"There must have been about thirty of us in the sorority," Barbara said, "so when a soror got a box from home, they would have to bring the box in the room with us. So if they got anything from home—a dress, a suit, a coat, or whatever—they would have to bring it by the room to see if Wilma could wear it. And we couldn't believe that she could wear anybody's clothes. She was so thin, and tall, so even the short dresses looked good on her."

A friend of Barbara's from Knoxville received a fox jacket that Wilma wore to the White House. "If you see her sitting on the chair with JFK, you will see that jacket," Barbara said. Everyone saw the photos and the news clips of Wilma meeting the president, and Barbara's friend's mother called her daughter and said, "I saw Wilma on television, and she had this beautiful jacket; it kind of looked like yours." Barbara and her friends never told the truth, but "we just fell out laughing because that *was* the jacket."

According to legend, President Kennedy also fell on the floor that day, being so distracted by Wilma that he missed the rocking chair as he tried to sit down to visit with Wilma and her family. Wilma charmed the president just as she had the rest of the world, and the meeting went much longer than planned. Wilma worried out loud that they might miss their flight home, and President Kennedy just laughed, saying, "Wilma, I'm the president. I can hold the plane."

Wilma was continually asked to go places, to meet people, and to represent her school, her community, and her country. She did it all with complete grace, but it came at a cost, with very little reward.

Wilma participated in a game show called *To Tell the Truth*, where each of the participants pretended to be her, and a celebrity panel featuring Johnny Carson and Betty White tried to guess which woman was the real Wilma Rudolph. Johnny Carson excused himself because he had already met her, and Betty White guessed correctly, based "simply on a hunch," she said. Wilma and her two impersonators were each awarded $500 for their participation, but Wilma, who so clearly could have used the money, was required to hand hers over to the Amateur Athletic Union.

"She's done more for her country than what the United States could pay her for," Temple said.

In today's world, Wilma and all of her teammates would have been flooded with endorsement opportunities, paid speaking engagements, and lucrative job offers. But Wilma had to borrow clothes for the events she was required to attend, and through much of the country, she couldn't stay in the same hotels or eat at the same restaurants with many of the people she traveled with.

Looking back later, Edward Temple said to Edwina, "We just came around too early, didn't we?"

It's true that Temple and the Tigerbelles were ahead of their time.

They were trailblazers. They were legends.

Chapter 24

Legacy

The celebrations were grand, but very little changed once the parties had died down.

"All the patting on the back," Temple said, "but no extra money. Still on work-aid. No raise in salary. It was the worst feeling I ever had. I just knew I would get a raise, but no," Temple shook his head. "Not one cent raise. Oh, that really hurt."

The pain was all the more pronounced because Temple had been heavily recruited to lead a delegation to Ghana representing the United States, promoting track and field. It was rumored to be a lucrative, life-changing opportunity, but Temple ultimately passed on the deal, because if he left Tennessee State, he didn't think the program would continue, and he couldn't leave his runners, and the new recruits coming up, without a team.

While they would continue to face many more years of setbacks and discrimination, the Tigerbelles and Mr. Temple carved a path through their example of excellence for women's sports that is widely believed to be the most important influence to the establishment of Title IX, which states, "No person in the United States shall, on the basis of sex, be excluded from participation in, be denied the benefits of, or be subjected to discrimination under any education program or activity receiving Federal financial assistance." Title IX disrupted the sports system and to this day continues to impact women's ability to participate in sports on every level by helping to provide the funding and resources for female collegiate athletes.

The legacy of the Tigerbelles is more than just participating in sports; it's also the expectation of excellence that team members should achieve in every aspect of their lives. Not only were they expected to be individually excellent as scholars, competitors, and community leaders, they were also expected to help each other, and their communities, to achieve excellence as well. They were taught to show up for each other, to support each other in everything they might need, and to continue to lift up others who came behind them.

This combination of expecting the best in themselves and teaching others created a community of uplifting change that has continued for decades. The Tigerbelles achieved an unprecedented graduation rate of 100 percent among their Olympians, and after completing their education, often including one or more postgraduate degrees, the women uniformly maintained a commitment to uplifting their communities by leading nonprofit organizations, coaching, teaching, and sharing their experiences and the lessons they'd learned to benefit the next generations. They passed the baton again and again.

According to **Howard Gentry Jr.**, aka, Little Howie, who considers one of the greatest honors of a very accomplished life to have been asked to hold the door open during the Tigerbelles' indoor track practice, "The legacy of the Tigerbelles is not just about their accomplishments, but how they reached back and helped others that came along after them. Every one of these women became community leaders, teaching, promoting, and encouraging countless young people in the decades that followed. In their later years they were respected as much for their contributions to society as the medals that they had won."

Barbara Curry Murrell continued to work with Wilma, accompanying her to New York on a trip where they met Alex Haley, who interviewed Wilma for a story, and Lena Horne at the NAACP gala where Wilma would be honored. Later Wilma said of Barbara, "I learned from Curry how to be a lady." Barbara also continued her support of the civil rights movement, helping to lead a protest of the graduation ceremonies because their friend and fellow student, Lucretia Collins, was being held in jail in Mississippi after being arrested for her participation in the Freedom Rides.

The Tennessee State Tigerbelles look over their trophies. Special Collections and Archives—Tennessee State University

"The sorority sisters said we are going to boycott graduation if they can't get her out of jail, because we might not ever see her again," Barbara said. "And we talked to the president about how concerned we were. He thought we were serious, and we were, but at the last minute, when they started playing the piano, we were standing out in front of the gym. We were all out there in our caps and gowns, and just waiting. I guess we had faith that something was going to happen, and the other students were supporting us and not going in. So, all of the sudden we heard the sirens coming in, and it was state troopers, and they stopped right in front of the gym, and they let our sister out of the car."

Apparently, a deal had been made at the request of President Davis between the governors of Tennessee and Mississippi. One patrol car from Mississippi drove her to the Tennessee state line where she transferred cars and was brought directly to the graduation. "So, I had her robe, and when we saw her get out, we ran and hugged her and gave her her robe and we walked in and had commencement."

In 2022 when Diane Nash was awarded the Medal of Freedom by President Biden, a photo was shown of her being released from jail into the custody of the dean of men at Tennessee State. "It showed the lawyers up there, including Looby and others, working with the judge to get them out, and the dean of men who was the one standing up there, waiting for Diane Nash to come back, and many years later, I married that man."

Barbara Murrell stayed in Nashville, working with the university, and eventually becoming the first female vice president at any Board of Regents University in the state of Tennessee for her alma mater.

Herc Alley, director of physical education at Vanderbilt University, continued to run the track and field program for the remainder of his career, where he encouraged the athletics program to integrate. He was eventually able to cheer on Perry Wallace, a Vanderbilt student and basketball player who became the first Black athlete to play any sport in the entire Southeastern Conference, before he passed away in 1971. Finally, the door had been opened.

Fred Russell, reporter for the *Nashville Banner*, remained friends with Edward Temple, and played an instrumental role in helping Temple to finally obtain scholarships and a new track for the Tigerbelles.

Howard Gentry Jr. said, "When my dad passed, I was athletics director at TSU. It was Valentine's Day. He told me to always make decisions that were best for the university when it comes to athletics, and then he told me to take care of the women." Gentry asked him again what he meant, "and he said it again; he said, take care of the women. My dad went to his grave regretting one thing, and that is that he couldn't do more for the Tigerbelles. He did everything he could, but it wasn't enough. In his last hours on this earth, that's how important this was to him.

"I just hope that I could do a little bit during my time to make up for what my father couldn't do, or what he wasn't allowed to do."

Today, when Howard Gentry often enjoys the Elliston Place Soda Shop, he is greeted by his friend, the owner, as one of the city leaders he has become.

Earlene Brown made it to the Olympics again in 1964, but the bronze she won in 1960 remained her only Olympic medal. After the 1964 Olympics, Brown retired from field events and started a successful career in roller games, where she was known as the "Brown Bomber" for the New York City roller derby team.

"Sports is the greatest thing for any individual to have," Earlene said. "Without sports I would have been nothing. I don't see where life would have had any meaning. I must be on this earth for a reason, because God has blessed me. He's given me the opportunity to see the world, something even most rich folks are not going to see."

Mae Faggs Starr was the first American woman to attend three consecutive Olympic Games for the United States. Temple and all of the Tigerbelles consider Mae to have been the mother of the Tigerbelles, and many believe that if she hadn't come to Tennessee State, the Tigerbelles would not have been the team that they were.

Isabelle Daniels Holston retired from her athletic career after her graduation in 1959, just shy of the 1960 Olympics, after winning gold in the 1959 Pan American games as a part of the 4x100m relay. Isabelle went on to have an outstanding thirty-seven-year teaching and coaching career, winning state titles and being inducted into several halls of fame. She married Rev. Dr. Sidney R. Holston, who cofounded Church Twinning International, pairing US churches with those in several African nations, including Ghana, for missions outreach.

Margaret Matthews Wilburn and her husband Jesse Wilburn became parents to two boys, one a Washington Redskins player who participated in a Super Bowl–winning team. After earning her degree at Tennessee State, she earned her master's from Memphis State University, and was fifteen hours short of a doctorate. She became a teacher and eventually a school principal, continuing to educate and encourage young people to achieve their best.

When asked to describe herself, Margaret said she is a person "with a lot of character. A person who has a lot of respect for everyone, a person who loves the Lord. I would give you the hat off my head if it was raining and you needed to stay dry yourself."

JoAnn Terry Grissom made the Olympic team again in 1964, winning gold for the 80m hurdles at the 1963 Pan American Games in Sao Paulo. After graduating from TSU, JoAnn moved back to her home state of Indiana, where she became a physical education teacher and continued to train for national competitions. Along with getting married and having two children, JoAnn continued her work as a teacher and guidance counselor until her retirement. She also served as an official for the 1984 Olympics and the 1987 Pan American Games. JoAnn ran well into her adulthood, notably setting a record at age forty-five in discus, with a distance of 106 feet, 5 inches, in the over-forty category, also earning marks in shot, javelin, and long and high jumps. JoAnn took full advantage of her opportunities to see the world, after which she came home and shared her experiences, helping to shape future generations by showing them new possibilities.

"I have had a remarkable life," JoAnn said. "I went from nothing to something based on a lot of very hard work. I do get angry and frustrated sometimes about how I was treated in the past, but I'm over it now. I know what I accomplished, and no one can take that away from me. I got an education. I competed in the Olympics and much, much, much more. And I have also been able to give back a great deal to my home, Indianapolis, particularly to the children. I am very proud."

Willye B. White continued to chafe at the rules laid down by Temple and her banishment from the team. "I didn't have obstacles," Willye said, "I had boulders that were thrown in my path." She went back to Chicago after the Olympics in Rome and graduated from Chicago State University in 1976. "Coach Temple wanted to control every aspect of your life and I was too much of a free spirit for that," she said in an interview years later.

"I had no regrets about leaving TSU," Willye said. "I had a great career; check the record books. I was the first woman from Mississippi to compete in the Olympic Games and to win an Olympic medal. I was the first American woman to win a medal in the long jump at the Olympics, and I was the first American to compete in five consecutive Olympic Games, from 1956 to 1972. I was also the first American athlete to win the highest sportsmanship award in the world. I was truly blessed with such a great career."

Willye won nine consecutive AAU outdoor championships and achieved a career-best long jump of 21 feet and 6 inches, holding the title as America's best female long jumper for nearly twenty years. She participated as a coach or a runner in international programs for the rest of her career, including with Coach Temple, whom she came to respect a great deal later in life. He coached her on two subsequent Olympic teams, including the 1964 team, where she and two other Tigerbelles (Edith McGuire and Wyomia Tyus) were part of the 4x100m relay team that earned silver. She remained lifelong friends with many of the other Tigerbelles. She died in 2007, and the day of her memorial service in Chicago was named "Willye White Day" by Mayor Richard M. Daley.

"Had I not been in athletics, my life would have been totally different," Willye said. "It would have been different in a negative way, because through athletics, you're exposed to all that constitutes life: pain, fear, joy, disappointment, success, and failure. Those are the elements that make up life. And just because I made a mistake over here, it doesn't mean that that's the end of the world. And all you have to do is just go back to the practice arena or look in—within yourself.

"If I see a child doing something wrong, I'm always giving advice. I just don't want to see people make the same mistakes that I made. But, as I said, I took all my negatives and made positives out of them."

Willye's hometown put up a billboard in her honor saying, "Welcome to Greenwood, Mississippi: Home of Five-Time Olympian, Willye White." Willye saw it and felt that she could finally be welcomed back home. "I really feel proud of Mississippi because they have really tried to show me that what occurred forty years ago, you know, it was just the times."

Willye White was inducted into eleven different halls of fame. *Sports Illustrated* named her one of the top 100 women athletes of the twentieth century, and the state that she ran from for most of her life named a stretch of US Highway 49 in her honor that ends in her hometown in the Mississippi Delta.

Ralph Boston was asked if Jesse Owens was upset with him about his broken record, and Boston replied, "No, man. He's a cool cat!" Boston knows of what he speaks. After the 1960 Olympics, Ralph "Hawkeye" Boston participated in both the 1964 and 1968 Olympics, medaling in each, earning what he called a "complete set" of one gold, one silver, and one bronze medal. He also became the first man to jump 27 feet.

During his Olympic career Boston coached at Tennessee State, later putting his personal charm to work, becoming a sportscaster at ESPN, a CBS Sports commentator, and then part owner of a local television station in Knoxville, Tennessee, where he also served as assistant dean of students at the University of Tennessee. Boston remained lifelong friends with the young boxer, Cassius Clay, who had the habit of showing up to the Tennessee State campus in his new Cadillac, looking for Wilma.

Shirley Crowder Meadows stood tall in 2015, legs still long and strong, but aided by a walker as she recovered from knee surgery. She stepped up to a lectern and spoke to a group of students gathered for the Calvin Monk Awards assembly. She had them laughing with stories from her Olympic days and struggles with Coach Temple, then shared her hard-earned words of wisdom. She had spent the past fifty-five years raising a family and teaching students, striving to help those who came behind her to live better lives and share their own gifts with the world.

Shirley was All-American in the 80-meter hurdles seven times between 1955 and 1960, making US National teams in 1958, 1959, and 1960. She stayed close to the Tigerbelles, particularly Wilma and Martha, for life. She moved to Atlanta after graduation, where she worked as a teacher, coach, and mentor for thirty-five years, promoting athletics in schools, and where she remains a valued role model and an active Tennessee State University alumna. After she retired from track and had a family, Shirley played semipro basketball for the Atlanta Tomboys. She was an Olympic flag bearer in the 1996 Olympic Games in Atlanta.

In an interview, Shirley said: "Today I keep moving. . . . I would urge others with challenges to not give up. Get God on your side and keep moving."

Martha Hudson Pennyman moved back to her home state of Georgia after graduating from TSU, where she became an elementary school teacher and coached girls' track and basketball until her retirement thirty years later. In 1996 she spoke to a group of young people, telling them, "I remember when I was very young, I dreamed of going to the Olympics and winning a gold medal, so I worked hard to do that. You, too, can work hard to achieve the best you can. . . . Remember that a quitter never wins, and a winner never quits. . . . May we always remember the power and glory of this moment and the light it brought into our lives."

Barbara Jones Slater said, "When I graduated, Wilma beat me, and when Wilma graduated, Edith McGuire and Wyomia Tyus, it was their time. That's why from 1952 to 1984 you had nothing but winners going to the Olympics from Tennessee State University, thanks to Mr. Temple."

Barbara earned a lifetime total of 335 medals. After graduating from TSU and earning a master's degree from Georgia State, she married a fellow student and the couple returned to Chicago, where they had two daughters, and she became a physical education teacher. She mentored and taught children for thirty-five years and was also a contributor for the Jackie Robinson Foundation. In 2007, President Obama presented her with the Presidential Lifetime Achievement Award.

Barbara said that Temple "prepared us for life because everything I do, I go to a lot of his rules and regulations. That has made me the best mother, the best wife—I have been married for fifty-five years to the same man I met at Tennessee State.

"I have emulated him in so many ways," Barbara said of Temple. "And I laugh, because what I resented when I was a track runner, I now emphasize as a coach. You know, love in one hand and discipline in the other."

After speaking to a group of schoolchildren, Barbara said, "My theme to them was to never let a challenge allow you to quit. I let them know that I wouldn't have this opportunity if I had quit. It is so important to me that kids know who they are and listen to the people that love [them]."

Lucinda Williams Adams retired from running after the 1960 Olympics, but she served as a chaperone during the 1963 Olympic Team European Tour. She later became a physical education teacher and supervisor of athletics for the Dayton, Ohio, public schools and served as an adjunct faculty member at the University of Dayton, continuing to inspire young women. Lucinda contributed to the US Olympic Committee through the Champions in Life program.

When speaking to young women, Lucinda Williams often brings her medal. "I take it out of the case, and I let them put their hands on it. But I try to stress that while I'm proud of it, and I certainly treasure it, I do not worship it. The thing that matters most is . . . being the best at whatever they do, whether they are an athlete or not. I tell them the real gold is inside you.

"When I look back, I see a lot of time spent practicing and training and getting prepared for track competitions," Lucinda said, "the long hours spent studying, working, and traveling, but there was never a moment when I regretted my choices. I sacrificed a lot, but it was worth it. The Olympics, the other events, the traveling, the races won and lost, meeting all those different people in different places, representing my country—the truth of the matter is, it was the most thrilling time of my life."

Wilma Rudolph's stardom continued throughout her life. She worked hard to use her fame to help change hearts and minds for the future. Wilma published her autobiography in 1974 that served as inspiration for the movie *Wilma*, released in 1975.

Wilma ran her last race in 1961 in a dual meet against Russia in Palo Alto, California. Winning easily, she was rewarded with a standing ovation and stayed after to sign autographs for over an hour. When she finally sat down to take off her shoes, one last little boy came over with a pencil and a piece of paper. Much to the child's delight, she signed her spikes and gave them to him instead.

Another pair of Wilma's track shoes has been on display at the Smithsonian National Museum of African American History and Culture.

Wilma never lost her generous spirit. "If she had two dresses, she'd give you one," Temple said. She had a soft spot for a sad story, "at her own peril," Temple said, "because she knew what it was to suffer."

Wilma's sister Charlene said, "She was the most giving person that you ever wanted to meet. She would give her all to complete strangers.

She never told them no. She loved everybody. She would be the same person walking down Jefferson Street . . . as she would meeting President Kennedy or kings and queens, or ambassadors, or anyone else. She opened up the doors for women's sports, period. I ain't talking just about track and field."

"In my opinion, she gave more to her country than they ever gave back to her," Temple said. "Wilma Rudolph was the greatest athlete of her time . . . period. And she was ahead of her time in nearly every way possible in 1960. If Wilma Rudolph was racing today, she would have been rich and famous beyond her wildest dreams. She, I suppose, more than any other runner, opened up the modern door of track for women."

Edward Temple served as head track coach at Tennessee State University for forty-four years, from 1950 to 1994. When he finally retired, his close friend and assistant coach, Samuel Abernathy, said, "He was starting to get tired. Coaching is a lot of work, people don't realize. He'd been doing it since the early 1950s. That's a long time."

"If there's anybody in America who has ever achieved success at the highest level in the area of track and field, it is Temple," said Dwight Lewis, historian and TSU alumnus. "His Tennessee State Tigerbelles opened the door for women, not only in track and field, but in all sports."

"I also feel there wouldn't be as many of these doors swinging open for women today if we hadn't packed tons of those brown-bag lunches and driven those tedious miles in old, beat-up station wagons," Temple said.

Between 1956 and 1994, forty Tigerbelles made Olympic teams, winning seventeen gold, eight silver, and seven bronze medals in international competitions. "People still ask me what you have to do to win gold medals," Temple said. "I just answer that you have to be good, and fortunate—and you've got to know how to use that fortune."

Of the forty Olympians Temple coached, thirty-nine received an undergraduate degree, twenty-eight received a master's degree, and six earned a PhD.

One of Temple's Olympic champions, Chandra Cheeseborough, took over the coaching of the Tigerbelles in 1994, continuing Temple's legacy and coaching the team to eleven more titles, and counting.

"I think the school could have done more for him," Charlene Rudolph said. "And remember, this was a man who was world-renowned and could have gone anyplace after the 1960 Olympics, but he was loyal to Tennessee State. That's the kind of person he was, and he felt that if he stayed, then he could make a difference."

When asked in 2015 about his coaching years, Edward Temple said the thing he was most proud of was that "All of my Olympians graduated. Every single one.

"I was proud when those girls got their degrees," Temple said. "An education is something that no one can take from you. I never promised my girls medals, but I did promise them an education if they were willing to work hard for it. That was my promise to them."

"I miss him dearly," Margaret Matthews said. "All of us do. He set a standard that I don't think can be matched, ever, for women's track and field."

The true love of his life, his wife, Charlie B., said, "We've had many hardships to face, but when I do have to face these things, Edward's still the one I want to face them with—and after thirty years I'm still in love with him."

When Wilma Rudolph passed away in 1995, an Olympic flag was draped across her casket. After the funeral it was given to her beloved coach. He kept it draped on a rocking chair in his office until his own death in 2016, when it was then draped over his casket. Both of their lives had been defined by their success at the Olympics and the accomplishments they both shared. More than that, they shared a deep mutual respect and understanding.

"They would sit and talk for hours," Edwina Temple said.

In an interview late in life, Edward Temple said, "In the end, it turned out all right. I have no regrets. All I ever wanted to do was run, and if I had to make a bunch of girls run around the track to do that, then so be it. I never dreamed it would turn out the way it did."

Author's Note

When Carolyn Alley heard the Tigerbelles were coming to practice at Vanderbilt, she ran to the track to see them. It was just a couple of hundred yards from the Alley family's cottage on campus, and she didn't want to miss a minute.

Carolyn was Vanderbilt coach Herc Alley's daughter. "They were so beautiful," Carolyn told me. "So strong, and so fast." Carolyn had trouble being quiet and still. She never thought it was fair that her brothers got to play all of the sports while she got in trouble when she came home with skinned knees, her short, cropped hair standing on end.

Watching the Tigerbelles run faster than all of the boys, including her older brother Bob, opened up a whole new world for Carolyn. She saw women doing things she wasn't allowed to do, and then she wondered, what else was possible?

Eleven years later, Herc, Carolyn's father, passed away, just as Vanderbilt was slowly integrating. The Alley family watched as the Tigerbelles continued their success on the international stage and supported their ongoing challenges with the facilities whenever they could. Carolyn's older brother Bob was by then starting his own family. His first two children were runners, good ones, and his third was not. That's me. I preferred books and make-believe to hours on the track.

As any child of the 1970s will understand, when your older siblings are doing an activity, you have to do it, too, however poorly. We were running in a summer league, and I was always bringing up the rear, until one day there was a meet and my father, Bob Alley, came to watch. I was better than usual that day, and I came in third place in the 50-yard dash, earning my first yellow ribbon. There were probably only five or six people in the race, but I felt like I had actually accomplished something.

On the drive home Dad said, "Good job out there, Aime. You were so fast; you could have been a Tigerbelle." Of course, everyone laughed, knowing it was a gross exaggeration, but still, it puffed my chest out. It was the highest praise. The Tigerbelles were the fastest women in the world.

The Tennessee State Tigerbelles under Edward Temple's leadership continued to run, to win, and to inspire countless young women to work harder, to be the best that they could be. Each generation had new superstars and new challenges to face, and continued to struggle for the respect and attention they deserved. As historian Tracey Salisbury wrote, "Despite their tremendous individual and team athletic and academic successes, squad after squad of TSU Tigerbelle teams were virtually ignored."

Temple kept charging forward, promoting his program and women's sports. Every year more women followed, and eventually, more sports were available to young girls. Whether or not individual athletes achieved national attention, the Tigerbelles ran on, repeating and improving on their record-breaking performances.

My daughter participated in sports throughout elementary and high school. Women all across the country take their daughters to soccer and basketball games, to volleyball, ice hockey, field hockey, lacrosse, and any other sport they can dream of, without a second thought.

When my daughter was eleven and not connecting with the book she had chosen in the school library to write a report on, I gave her Ed Temple's *Only the Pure in Heart Survive*. She was blown away by his story and produced a report about the Tigerbelles that was highlighted among her classmates. A new generation was being inspired by the Tigerbelles and the triumph over adversity that they represented.

This book is my tribute to the early Tigerbelles, the women who fought so hard so that the girls that came up behind them would have an easier path.

They were trailblazers. And they have my gratitude.

Acknowledgments

FOR NEARLY A DECADE COUNTLESS PEOPLE HAVE GRACIOUSLY ADDED their knowledge and experience to this project to help it make its way into the world. To each of you I will be eternally grateful.

To Edward Temple, the lifelong coach, who invested everything into his belief that the women he worked with would change the world: I am so honored to have met you, so grateful you graced me with your time. To Ralph Boston, a masterful storyteller who had me laughing and crying in the same afternoon. The world is brighter because of both of your lives. To Samuel Abernathy, Mr. Ab, who also did not live to see this story in print, it was an honor to meet you and your daughter, Eloise Alexis. Your valuable support of the Tigerbelles throughout the years is reflected in how much they adored you.

To the legendary Tigerbelles, for your tireless generosity in sharing your stories over the years. Every exasperating reporter who held a tape recorder near your face after a race, or in your home, or out at an event, helped to collect parts of your story that when woven together create a portrait of power, grace, and determination which will continue to inspire generations to come.

Special thanks to Dwight Lewis. Your lifelong work in chronicling the history of your community has made a lasting impact, and your love and care is clear. Plus, you are my absolute favorite Swett's lunch companion. To Tracey Salisbury, for your detailed scholarship, your tremendously kind spirit, and your willingness to both carry and pass the baton. To Chandra Cheeseborough, for carrying on the Tigerbelles tradition, and sharing some time with me. To Loretta Claiborne, for illustrating how many young girls' lives have been impacted by seeing the Tigerbelles on the screen. To Howard Gentry Jr., for your contributions to the community, your candor, your company, and your detailed memories. To Barbara

Murrell, for so generously sharing your experiences, from the glamour of the Queen's suite to your lifelong pursuit of equity, I am honored to know you. My deepest gratitude to Edwina Temple, for opening your doors, and your archives, and for sharing your extraordinary life.

Thank you to Paige Pitts and New Hope Academy, for gathering and sharing your immensely valuable archives; Coach Temple greatly admired and supported your work, and it's wonderful of you to participate in his legacy this way. Thank you to Guessippina Bonner for your valuable and careful reading to be sure the story matched your knowledge and experience from the era. Many thanks as well to Sharon Smith at the TSU Special Collections Archive, for your care and knowledge, and to the Nashville Public Library Special Collections; the University of Tennessee Hodges Library Special Collections; and to the research support staff at the Library of Congress.

To my aunt, Carolyn Simpson, who so vividly described watching practice at Vanderbilt: I wish you could have seen this come to life. To my father, Bob Alley, who mined his memory for hours at a time as I pestered him for details; and my daughter, Catherine Card, whose interest in the Tigerbelles at eleven years old cemented in me the need to share the story. Thanks to Christie Hauck, Andrew Maraniss, and Bo Roberts, for their support and dedication to preserving and promoting the Tigerbelles legacy, and to Betty Jane Maples Taylor and Guy Tallent for sharing their Vanderbilt memories.

To Deborah Norkin, thank you for your constant encouragement and liberal use of red lines; to E. B. Bartels, for the early guidance; and my sister, Emma, for being a steadfast champion.

To my agent, Leticia Gomez, and editor at Lyons Press, Rick Rinehart, thank you for believing in the story and giving it a chance, and to the whole team at Globe Pequot, especially Melissa Hayes, for her heroic copy editing; Jason Rossi, for publicity; and production editor Meredith Dias. To all my friends for lending your ears and advice over the years, especially Amanda Dobbins, Holly Schmidt, Amanda Lewis, Debbie Ames, and Abbe Kopf. To Catherine and Wesley, for thinking the project is cool enough to let me disappear from time to time, and to Scott, for your constant and lifelong support.

Notes

I was fortunate enough to obtain permissions to quote extensively from the following sources to create the oral history format, allowing the principal figures to tell their own stories through interviews they participated in throughout their lives, some concurrent, and others reflective.

Only the Pure in Heart Survive, Ed Temple and B'Lou Carter: Temple

Wilma: The Story of Wilma Rudolph, Wilma Rudolph: Wilma

A Will to Win, Dwight Lewis and Susan Thomas: L&T

Dwight Lewis Interview Archives—Interviews with Barbara Jones, Samuel Abernathy, Isabelle Daniels, Charlene Rudolph, Margaret Matthews, Ralph Boston, John Lewis, C. T. Vivian, Lucinda Williams: Lewis Int.

History Makers—Archived interviews with Willye B. White: HM

New Hope Academy Archives—Oral History Interview Series with Edward Temple, Barbara Jones, Edith McGuire: NHA

TSU Special Collections Archives

Two other special oral history collections include:

Visionary Project—Fisk University–sponsored projects collecting an oral history with Edward Temple, interviewed by Kenneth Thompson: VP

Calvin "Monk" Jones Lecture Series, featuring Shirley Crowder Meadows: MS

Personal interviews will be noted with the last name of the interviewee followed by "pers int." Other sources that were extremely helpful will be noted by last name and listed in the bibliography. Periodicals and other sources will be noted by name and listed in the bibliography.

Chapter 1

"I was on campus": Gentry Jr., pers int. "Dr. Davis knew" "he saw something in him" "dyed-in-the-wool" "If Leroy was": L&T. "We got on" "We had three-quarters" "We were ready": NHA. "Is he worth fooling with?": Temple. "The first thing": NHA. "wanted to give": L&T. "That year, we" "Running a 440": Temple. "They killed us": NHA. "natural talent" "Mae Faggs was": L&T. "cream puffs": Davis. "They just didn't understand": Salisbury. "So, when I woke": NHA. "The US Team": Davis. "When I was standing": "Mae Faggs Faces Last Season of Competition," *TN A & I University Bulletin* (September 1956). "Tuskegee offered" "We almost lost": NHA. "The track was": VP. "We were lucky": NHA. "I was already": Richard Goldstein, *New York Times* (February 11, 2000). "To build this": Temple. "It was a great": NHA. "Really, we just": L&T. "Look like a" "She was the": NHA. "We had to" "We were flying": NHA. "On the day": Lewis Int. "unload from cramped": TSU historian Bobby L. Lovett via Van West. "We had never": NHA. "couldn't wear": VP. "we'd have to": Lewis Int.

CHAPTER 2

"We went from": VP. "Every girl I" "When I call": NHA. "Coach Temple brought" "That first summer": Lewis Int. "She had to be": NHA. "I would sit" "Okay, someday": Wilma. "My doctor told": TSU Special Collections Archives. "You didn't even" "I don't know": Wilma. "I went to visit" "It was rough": NHA. "old pro": Temple. "Mae Faggs was": Lewis Int. "We couldn't afford": Temple. "We'd travel around" "Sunday best": *Palm Beach Post* (August 12, 2016). "You know your" Lewis Int. "It was not easy": *Dayton Daily News* (February 22, 2021). "We didn't have": Lewis Int.

CHAPTER 3

"gas, restrooms": Temple. "We had our" "We knew if" "He had us": Lewis Int. "stop being mistaken": Davis. "I was wild": HM. "because he'd have": *Mississippi Sun Herald* (May 7, 2019). "Why is this girl" Boston pers int. "The only thing": HM. "go to college": Salisbury. "But see": HM. "nearly fainted": Wilma. "The boat is": Tricard. "I'd never eaten": HM. "one of the all-time" "High-strung": Davis. "That year I" "we were starting": Murrell pers int. "I actually went": NHA. "My first jump": HM. "Mae Faggs particularly": Temple. "I was just all": Davis. "Skeeter, baby": Wilma. "Now look": Temple. "I looked up" "As we came": Davis. "Coming down that" "I'll always believe": Temple. "The reporters called me": *Northwest Indiana Times* (September 30, 2022). "She taught me": NHA. "The thing for": Davis. "When I was running": NHA. "Bring Wilma downtown" "Wilma, you lose": Wilma. "You take care" "I think we" "Always remember": Lewis Int.

CHAPTER 4

"It was only": Wilma. "I thought I would never": HM. "unsettling": *Palm Beach Post*. "We didn't know" "Who would have" "teary-eyed" "When I got": Lewis Int. "her feet hit the cinders" Salisbury. "I came out": Tricard. "thought the whole world": Salisbury. "Where Blacks": HM. "I just ate" "I do think" "Actually, if people": Wilma. "I was nervous" "That's history" "Well, you did": Lewis Int. "If I bent": Lynn Seely, *Runner's World* (February 20, 1992). "You've got four": Wilma. "goading her rivals": Hines. "I didn't want": Davis. "I really didn't" "She was a member" "I have always": Lewis Int. "I read the": Salisbury. "Let me share" "I didn't know": HM. "he would have been": Wilma. "Skeeter was upset": Davis. "Mae was the": Van West. "When Mae spoke": Lewis Int. "which was doing": Temple. "Wilma wasn't happy": Salisbury. "That's when we": Lewis Int. "I did have": Wilma. "*Greetings from*" "*The fabulous six*": L&T. "I think you've": Wilma. "You see, Mae": NHA. "They broke the": Lewis Int.

CHAPTER 5

"We had an opportunity": *The Malc Show* int. with Lucinda Williams (March 26, 2019). "I was still": HM. "One of the things": Maraniss video. "Put her on the" "who never missed": Lewis Int. "Okay, what's next" "Always follow": Salisbury. "And when I got there": NHA. "Mr. Temple was" "We thought he": Lewis Int. "It took her": Temple. "We were no longer" "You learned how": NHA. "You can't eat applause" "It doesn't matter": Temple. "Well, it was": Salisbury. "During her childhood": *Palm Beach Post* (August 12, 2016). "When you came": Temple. "I already got": NHA. "At first, everybody": Temple. "One day we": MS. "It's so hard": Temple. "Oh yeah, I resented" "rough training": NHA. "We ran hills" HM. "Going to the" Boston pers int. "I want them" "How much pride": Temple.

CHAPTER 6

"We were confident": NHA. "Here comes Barbara": Lewis Int. "Oh, but you": NHA. "Shut up and": Temple. "It was so hot": HM. "The sun was": VP. "Nobody is gonna": HM. "You just have": Temple. "I remember seeing": Boston pers int. "I remember them": Lewis Int. "When the track": Gentry Jr. pers int. "We had to run": VP. "They would fly by": Gentry Jr. pers int. "There's a sail jump": HM. "Everybody can't": L&T. "separate the weak": Salisbury. "pure hearts": Temple.

CHAPTER 7

"I am really" "Why, you are": Davis. "Pee Wee is": Lewis Int. "Pee Wee!" Boston pers int. "one of the best" "She was without": Temple. "My big ambition": Davis. "She was a good": Salisbury. "Tennessee State": *Sports Illustrated* (November 14, 1960). "a mix of my": Salisbury. "Coach Temple" "We ran hard" "One day we": Lewis Int. "The time trials": Temple. "Temple often ran": *Sports Illustrated* (November 14, 1960). "When kids around": Wilma. "A & I": Alley pers int. "There are so many" "We didn't realize" "So, you had" "What really is": Gentry Jr. pers int. "oval ribbon" "He goes down" "So, on this film": *Sports Illustrated* (November 14, 1960). "I'll never forget": Temple. "He finally accepted": Lewis Int. "I wanted them focused": Salisbury. "Time to play": Lewis Int. "Everyone makes mistakes": Wilma.

CHAPTER 8

"We thought we was": VP. "Pack my suitcase": Temple. "We'd taken first": VP. "I was sure": Davis. "I was driven by" "That little, long-legged" "Come on" "I knew from jump street" "That first summer": MS. "He cared about" "We really kind of" "Mrs. Temple" "Like I said": Lewis Int. "He would have": NHA. "If someone needed": Lewis Int. "I told them you can't": Temple pers int. "about twenty-something": VP. Kaszubski note: *Sport in American History*, Cat Arail (August 26, 2016). "I came up here": Temple. "She looked at me": Tricard. "We didn't have" "big argument": VP. "We weren't supposed to" "That was my": Temple pers int. "When you make" "When you wore": VP.

CHAPTER 9

"Everyone suddenly became" "All of the girls": Temple. "way out of our": VP. "sunny side up": Temple. "We thought it was": NHA. "Their flight to freedom" "big handsome man": HM. "Big Mama" Boston pers int. "My mother told me" "Earlene Brown's husband": Davis. "Because my event" "running and playing": Tricard. "I was the only Black coach": VP. "In your democratic country": Temple. "You could have heard": VP. "We might have been": Temple. "Here was a school": VP. "We finished the tour": Temple. "We have the material": Tricard. "In America": L&T.

CHAPTER 10

"Mrs. Earlene Brown": *New York Herald Tribune* (June 29, 1959). "She came out of the" Murrell pers int. "I was ahead of my time": Salisbury. "Well, not being able": Murrell pers int. "Willye's attitude": Boston pers int. "She wanted to be a junior" "If you're the second": L&T. "Even with me": Edwina Temple pers int. "Your freshman year": L&T. "That was the rule": Boston pers int. "We had the rules": Lewis Int. "People look at" "See, Mr. Temple": NHA. "He said, 'I am the one'": Edwina Temple pers int. "She just wouldn't stay out": Salisbury. "The girls were away from home": L&T. "I think he had people" "He had his spies": Lewis Int. "He was everywhere": NHA. "People would tell on them": Edwina Temple pers int. "The only way we could get": Murrell pers int. "So, he drove his car": Edwina Temple pers int. "Every year some of the most": Davis. "My speed was tremendous": Wilma. "She had to work": NHA. "When Wilma joined": Lewis Int. "We helped her": NHA. "When I first saw Wilma": Murrell pers int. "Oh, Lord, that skinny": Maraniss. "Isabelle Daniels was": NHA. "She had to learn": Davis. "For one thing" "I needed forty-five": Wilma. "For some reason": Temple. "Wilma always thought" "He used to have all these": NHA.

CHAPTER 11

"We had to run against": Lewis Int. "I didn't know anything": L&T. "Too many of the other girls": Salisbury. "seemingly endless" "I was wearing spike heels": L&T. "Time to play" "He would have us run": Lewis Int. "I want the girls" "Rudolph, she went": *Sports Illustrated* (November 14, 1960). "After practice": Temple. "Some days she isn't speaking": *Sports Illustrated* (November 14, 1960). "It was because" "Mrs. Temple": Lewis Int. "Edward says that I": Temple. "A lot of times when the girls": L&T. "Edwina shared her father": Lewis Int. "Although Edward is strict": Temple. "I stayed with Mrs. Woodruff": Edwina Temple pers int. "I remember one time": Temple. "We'd make a deal" "Growing up": Edwina Temple pers int. "When they'd fall out": NHA. "Mrs. Temple ran the mailroom": Gentry Jr. pers int. "Mrs. Temple, she was the mother": NHA. "She was always involved": Temple pers int. "They didn't make": Edwina Temple pers int. "She would take them": NHA. "I have washed": Temple. "When I was equipment": Lewis Int. "She didn't let the school": Edwina Temple pers int. "They loved that German chocolate": Temple pers int. "My mother made the best": Edwina Temple pers int. "It's hard to explain": NHA. "Back then" "He had an eight-millimeter camera": Edwina Temple pers int. "Mrs. Temple taught me": NHA. "She did everything" "They were crazy about her": Lewis Int.

CHAPTER 12

"It was like you" "Our personal appearance": NHA. "I have tried to": Temple. "Coach Temple reminded all of us": Lewis Int. "graceful, beautiful women": Van West. "I had it in my mind" "I don't want oxes": L&T. "You had to be ladylike": Lewis Int. "It is pretty difficult": Davis. "It is hard to believe": Salisbury. "probably the first": Earl S. Clanton III, *Chicago Defender* via Van West. "Wilma would come up": Murrell pers int. "I certainly am surprised": *Nashville Banner* (January 4, 1960). "Boy, was I overjoyed": Wilma. "these youngsters": *Nashville Banner* (January 18, 1960). "It was a hard decision": Salisbury. "It finally got to the point": Edwina Temple pers int. "Willye White was another" "He didn't care how fast": Lewis Int. "I was not the kind of athlete" "She can't be any" "Chicago will give": HM. "We'll have to make it": *Nashville Banner* (April 15, 1960). "she did it on a curved": *Nashville Banner* (April 18, 1960). "Wilma also beat": *New York Times* (April 17, 1960). "a maker of champions": *Nashville Banner* (April 18, 1960).

CHAPTER 13

"A man came over": Bill Traughber, *Nashville Retrospect* (December 2020). "Tennessee A & I State women": *Nashville Banner* (April 12, 1960). "Our sports might be": Dwight Lewis pers int. "We were human beings": Lewis Int. "When I came to Vanderbilt": Johnson. "When I saw the photos": Taylor pers int. "inciting anarchy" "Southern finishing school": Johnson. "It's difficult to run": Temple. "I would make two trips": Temple pers int. "The fastest and the best": *Commodore History Corner* (April 4, 2007). "Hey, Lamar": Boston pers int. "He made something": *Commodore History Corner* (April 4, 2007). "near the Parthenon": Boston pers int. "Growing up in Laurel": L&T. "Before the age of ten": Boston pers int. "Quite honestly,": L&T. "Understand, I came from": Boston pers int. "Who would have thought" "I was scared": L&T. "I walked out onto the track": Lewis Int. "So, when I came to Nashville": Boston pers int.

CHAPTER 14

"a seemingly pleasant" "Protestant Vatican" "in an orderly" "rooting out segregation": Halberstam. "You see, the greatness": Lewis Int. "You men don't know" "hoodlums pouring coffee" "was so transcending" "We are a bunch of children": Halberstam. "Go to school" "left home with a $100 bill": Lewis Int. "See, they had put": NHA. "Our motto was": Lewis Int. "Beware of those" "That meant when they challenged": Halberstam. "I really, coming from Mississippi" "I did make": Murrell pers int. "[The] 1960 civil rights" "We're here to get an education": NHA. "Look, we all had experienced": Salisbury. "We Black kids" "Lookit that lady's dress" "There's just something not right" "You get scars": Wilma. "Gasping for breath": *The Tennessean* (November 10, 1960).

CHAPTER 15

"Martin Luther King": NHA. "They were asking for nonviolent" "We had the press": HM. "We advised them to": Salisbury. "But you know what was great" "show them on the track": NHA. "Sophisticated, erudite": Halberstam. "We were down there by the old ROTC" "You can't take that": Lewis Int. "They were walking": Murrell pers int. "I appeal to all": Halberstam. "Now just because the law says": Gentry Jr. pers int. "They were bombing houses": Murrell pers int. "Look, Black people were still": Wilma. "We are all strong believers": Lewis Int.

CHAPTER 16

"When I was growing up": Edwina Temple pers int. "But Temple, you've just come back": *Sports Illustrated* (November 14, 1960). "In the springtime": Edwina Temple pers int. "He was AD in a time": Gentry Jr. pers int. "The athlete has had to make all kinds" "In Europe they take": Temple. "Tennessee A & I's famed girl": *Nashville Banner* (May 21, 1960). "To me, we were close": Lewis Int. "He was a man who brought": HM. "I hate for people": Temple. "I felt on some occasions": Salisbury. "We were so well prepared": MS. "We didn't have any money": Murrell pers int. "The cafeteria was the one place": Boston pers int. "He said what he thought": Lewis Int. "They were the Tigerbelles" "One thing that was paramount": Boston pers int. "Nobody wanted to go back": Barbara Murrell pers int. "You go through the whole relay": Wilma. "Mr. Temple was able": Lewis Int. "If you graduated winning": NHA. "Why such intensified": *Nashville Banner* (June 22, 1960). "I want to see what they can do": *The Tennessean* (June 22, 1960). "I was number one": MS.

CHAPTER 17

"no hot water": *Nashville Banner* (July 9, 1960). "I soon discovered": Lewis Int. "All of us were on this bus": Wilma. "Well, on the road": Davis. "If you fear something": NHA. "I was nervous every time": MS. "God, I don't feel it": Wilma. "That's what I really thought": Tricard. "Doin' all right": Wilma. "She might not always win": Temple. "We eventually realized": Wilma.

CHAPTER 18

"dogs, cats, and large-sized bugs" "opened her mouth": *Sports Illustrated* (July 25, 1960). "When the gun shot": MS. "had more athletes than spectators": Tricard. "seven other Tennessee State athletes": *The Tennessean* (February 18, 1960). "She needs somebody to push her": *The Tennessean* (February 23, 1960). "devoted to the gals": *Track and Field News* (Spring 1959). "A national coach": Temple. "Just having him there": Wilma. "He ruled the roost": Temple. "We wind up in the woods": Wilma. "I remember [Wilma] reading": Tricard. "I guess she would rather sleep": *New York Times* (September 6, 1960). "Here's where we really run": Temple.

CHAPTER 19

"I got off the bus": Boston pers int. "Venus Wasn't a Shot-Putter": *New York Times* (August 28, 1960). "It can't be emphasized enough": Temple. "On the charter plane": NHA. "a couple of tune-up track meets": Boston pers int. "You have to realize": Temple pers int. "The women's team has repeatedly": Davis. "Coaches were always asking me": Davis. "I've never had a girl": Temple. "The Russians were separate": Boston pers int. "A runner has to overcome": Temple. "The atmosphere in the Village": Wilma. "a kind of waltzy tune": Boston pers int. "I wouldn't have minded": Temple. "We were in popular demand": Wilma. "My girls had to be regular hepcats": Temple. "I just told them": Temple pers int. "Now Red decided": Temple. "Eventually, we started": Wilma. "Cab drivers were": Temple. "He came out and sat beside me": Temple pers int. "same that he was when the world": MS. "Fool, go someplace": *Palm Beach Post* (August 12, 2016). "Cassius was talking, talking": Edwina Temple pers int. "But I was more caught up": *Atlanta Journal-Constitution* (September 2, 2010). "I don't know too much": Temple pers int. "In this kind of competition": Temple. "I was depressed": Davis. "There would have been some trouble": Boston pers int. "Avery Brundage was such": HM. "Anything to help the program": Temple pers int. "controlled stammer": *Sports Illustrated* (November 14, 1960). "Somehow they put together": Boston pers int.

CHAPTER 20

"back in the kitchen": *Indianapolis Star* via Davis. "back in the classroom": Davis. "a girl never ran": Tricard. "I wasn't expecting to win": Davis. "Nothing compares": *Palm Beach Post* (August 12, 2016). "Chills running": MS. "The US delegation": Maraniss. "For the first time": Davis. "I'd never seen": Boston pers int. "The pressure of the Olympics": Temple. "built-in rooting section": *Nashville Banner* (August 26, 1960). "Victories are not": MS. "a Los Angeles housewife": *New York Times* (July 17, 1960). "I was ready for Rome": Davis. "If someone had walked up": HM. "For them, it was great to make": Boston pers int. "I stepped right into": Wilma. "they put her in the bottom": Temple. "When I got to the tunnel": Wilma. "When Wilma began": Temple.

CHAPTER 21

"Now any runner alive": Wilma. "By this time": Temple. "When we got out": Wilma. "swear off the Olympics": Temple. "Streaking in front": *New York Times* (September 3, 1960). "I wasn't expecting": Temple pers int. "Frances Kaszubski was walking": Tricard. "Hey, way to go": *Atlanta Journal-Constitution* (September 2, 2010). "There goes another": *The Tennessean* (September 3, 1960). "I could have jumped": *The Tennessean* (September 5, 1960). "Wilma said she did it": *Des Moines Tribune* (September 3, 1960). "going too much for wine": *Philadelphia Inquirer* (September 4, 1960). "insinuations of high-living": *The Tennessean* (September 6, 1960). "It was just like in the 100": *The Tennessean* (September 5, 1960). "Ray, sometimes" "I did awful": *The Tennessean* (September 5, 1960). "It was for each": *Nashville Banner* (September 3, 1960). "Wilma Rudolph": *Knoxville News Sentinel* (September 3, 1960). "Leave it to American": *Nashville Banner* (September 5, 1960). "When it rains on one": HM. "She had won all": Wilma. "Today when a gangling": *The Tennessean* (September 5, 1960). "Worst lane in the 200": NHA. "A little rain meant": Wilma. "I meant to run faster": *The Tennessean* (September 6, 1960). "limitless potential": *Nashville Banner* (September 6, 1960). "She has perfect": *Nashville Banner* (September 6, 1960). "Tennessee Tornado": *The Tennessean* (September 6, 1960). "There's not a nerve": *Nashville Banner* (September 6, 1960). "She won that": NHA. "I got six": *Nashville Banner* (September 6, 1960).

CHAPTER 22

"can run with any three": *The Tennessean* (September 6, 1960). "If Wilma can win": Lewis Int. "Get me the baton": NHA. "Ray can't fool": *The Knoxville News-Sentinel* (September 9, 1960). "Everyone always asks": Temple. "I kept saying" "I just gave her the stick": *The Tennessean* (September 8, 1960). "What does 44.4 seconds mean?": Davis. "We did it" "The Tennessee Tigerbelles": *The Tennessean* (September 8, 1960). "We had the TV": Murrell pers int. "Martha got out well": NHA. "Barbara was tough": Temple "As I approached": *Clarksville Leaf-Chronicle* (November 18, 1994). "The handoff was not": *Dayton Daily News* (February 2, 2021). "Lucinda went to pass": NHA. "Lucinda tried it again": Tricard. "My heart sank": Temple. "hit her a second time": NHA. "I yelled at her": *Clarksville Leaf-Chronicle* (November 18, 1994). "I knew that once": *Dayton Daily News* (February 2, 2021). "When she got that stick": Tricard. "She was so determined": Temple. "That child": Tricard. "bordered on hysterics": Temple. "Everybody ran their best": Wilma. "There was a lot": Gentry Jr. pers int. "When I saw Wilma run": Loretta Claiborne pers int. "We are four": *Dayton Daily News* (February 2. 2021). "They went up there": Temple pers int.

CHAPTER 23

"I'm breathing easy": *Nashville Banner* (September 9, 1960). "She's had tremendous competition": *Sports Illustrated* (November 14, 1960). "That's as far as we can go": *Nashville Banner* (September 7, 1960). "We've been running": *The Tennessean* (September 11, 1960). "Even tables were overturned": Temple. "Queen of the Olympics": *Clarksville Leaf-Chronicle* (November 18, 1994). "They claimed the clocks": *The Tennessean* (September 15, 1960). "soft living": *Post-Crescent* (September 15, 1960). "With a single voice": Davis. "High on Olympus": *New York Times* (September 8, 1960). "We kept running": *Sports Illustrated* (November 14, 1960). "The girls were tired": Edwina Temple pers int. "She was just Wilma": Murrell pers int. "BeeJay didn't ask": Boston pers int. "If I can overcome": Davis. "Wilma, I'm the president": Edwina Temple pers int. "simply on a hunch": *To Tell the Truth* on CBS (December 5, 1960). "She'd done more": *Sports Illustrated* (November 14, 1960). "We just came around": Edwina Temple pers int.

CHAPTER 24

"All the patting": NHA. "The legacy of the Tigerbelles": Gentry Jr. pers int. "I learned from Curry": Murrell pers int. "When my dad passed": Gentry Jr. pers int. "Sports is the greatest thing": Davis. "with a lot of character": Lewis Int. "I have had a remarkable life": Salisbury. "I didn't have obstacles": HM. "I had no regrets": Salisbury. "Had I not been in athletics": HM. "I remember when": *Thomaston Times* (July 15, 1996). "When I graduated": NHA. "prepared us for life": Lewis Int. "I have emulated": NHA. "I take it out of the case": Salisbury. "If she had two dresses": NHA. "She was the most giving": Lewis Int. "She would be the same": Van West. "In my opinion": Salisbury. "She, I suppose": Temple. "He was starting to get tired": Lewis Int. "If there's anybody in America": L&T. "I also feel": Temple. "I think the school": Lewis Int. "All of my Olympians": Temple pers int. "I was proud": Salisbury. "I miss him dearly": Lewis Int. "We've had many hardships": Temple. "They would sit and talk": Edwina Temple pers int.

Bibliography

Books

Ariail, Cat M. *Passing the Baton: Black Women Track Stars and American Identity*. Champaign: University of Illinois Press, 2020.

Cahn, Susan K. *Coming on Strong: Gender and Sexuality in Women's Sport*. Champaign: University of Illinois Press, 1994

Davis, Marianna W. *Contributions of Black Women to America*. Columbia, SC: Kenday Press, 1981.

Davis, Michael D. *Black American Women in Olympic Track and Field*. Jefferson, NC: McFarland & Company, Inc., 1992.

Etheridge, Eric. *Breach of Peace: Portraits of the 1961 Mississippi Freedom Riders*. Nashville, TN: Vanderbilt University Press, 2008.

Gentry, Carrie M. *A Life Worth Living: A Biography of Howard C. Gentry, Sr.* Nashville, TN: R. H. Boyd Publishing, 2010.

Halberstam, David. *The Children*. New York: Ballantine Publishing Group, 1999.

Haley, Alex. *Alex Haley: The Man Who Traced America's Roots*. New York: Reader's Digest Association, 2007.

Harper, Jo. *Wilma Rudolph: Olympic Runner*. New York: Aladdin Paperbacks, 2004.

Holston, Kezia Olivia. *Tweety and the Pig*. Bloomington, IN: Westbow Press, 2015.

Johnson, Dale A. *Vanderbilt Divinity School: Education, Contest, and Change*. Nashville, TN: Vanderbilt University Press, 2001.

Lewis, Dwight, and Susan Thomas. *A Will to Win*. Mount Juliet, TN: Cumberland Press, 1983.

———. *Temple's Tigerbelles*. Mount Juliet, TN: Cumberland Media, 2018.

Lewis, John, with Michael D'Orso. *Walking with the Wind: A Memoir of the Movement*. New York: Simon & Schuster, 1998.

Liberti, Rita, and Maureen M. Smith, *(Re)Presenting Wilma Rudolph*. Syracuse, NY: Syracuse University Press, 2015.

Maraniss, David. *Rome 1960: The Summer Olympics that Stirred the World*. New York: Simon & Schuster, 2008.

Miller, Patricia B., and David Kenneth Wiggins. *Sport and the Color Line: Black Athletes and Race Relations in Twentieth-Century America*. New York: Routledge, 2004.

Montillo, Roseanne. *Fire on the Track: Betty Robinson and the Triumph of the Early Olympic Women*. New York: Crown Publishing, 2017.

Plowden, Martha Ward. *Olympic Black Women*. New Orleans, LA: Pelican Publishing, 1995.

Rudolph, Wilma. *Wilma: The Story of Wilma Rudolph*. New York: Signet, 1977.

Salisbury, Tracey M. *First to the Finish Line: The Tennessee State Tigerbelles, 1944–1994*. Chapel Hill: University of North Carolina Press, 2009.

Schiot, Molly. *Game Changers: The Unsung Heroines of Sports History*. New York: Simon & Schuster, 2016.

Smith, Jessie Carney. *Notable Black American Women*. Farmington Hills, MI: Gale Research, Inc., 1996.

Smith, Maureen M. *Wilma Rudolph: A Biography*. Westport, CT: Greenwood Press, 2006.

Temple, Ed, with B'Lou Carter. *Only the Pure in Heart Survive: Glimpses into the Life of a World Famous Olympic Coach*. Nashville, TN: Boardman Press, 1980.

Tricard, Louise Mead. *American Women's Track and Field: A History, 1895 through 1980*. Jefferson, NC: McFarland & Company, Inc., 1985.

Tyus, Wyomia, and Elizabeth Terzakis. *Tigerbelle: The Wyomia Tyus Story*. New York: Akashic Books, 2018.

Wiggins, David K., and Ryan A. Swanson. *Separate Games: African American Sport Behind the Walls of Segregation*. Fayetteville, AR: University of Arkansas Press, 2016.

NEWSPAPERS AND PERIODICALS

Atlanta Journal-Constitution
Chicago Defender
Chicago Tribune
Clarksville Leaf-Chronicle
Commodore History Corner
Dayton Daily News
Des Moines Tribune
Indianapolis Recorder
Indianapolis Star
Jet magazine
Knoxville News Sentinel
Life magazine
Nashville Banner
Nashville Globe
Nashville Retrospect
Nashville Scene
Nashville Tennessean magazine
New York Herald Tribune
New York Times
Norfolk Journal and Guide
Northwest Indiana Times
Palm Beach Post

Philadelphia Inquirer
Post-Crescent
Runner's World
Sports Illustrated
Sun Herald (Mississippi)
The Tennessean
Thomaston Times
Track and Field News
Tri-State Chronicles

SPECIAL COLLECTIONS
Temple Family Archives—Personal archives, photos, and memorabilia
New Hope Academy Archives—Oral History Interview Series with Edward Temple, Barbara Jones, Edith McGuire
Dwight Lewis Interview Archives—Interviews with Barbara Jones, Samuel Abernathy, Isabelle Daniels, Charlene Rudolph, Margaret Matthews, Ralph Boston, John Lewis, C. T. Vivian, Lucinda Williams
History Makers—Archived interviews with Willye B. White
Visionary Project—Fisk University–sponsored projects collecting an oral history with Edward Temple, interviewed by Kenneth Thompson
Calvin "Monk" Jones Lecture Series, featuring Shirley Crowder Meadows

WEBSITES
Blackthen.com
Fulton County Government Facebook Page
Olympic.org
Sports-reference.com
TNState.edu/EdTemple
TSUNewsroom.com
TSUTigers.com
USAGym.org

PERSONAL INTERVIEWS
Samuel Abernathy
E. Roberts Alley
Ralph Boston
Chandra Cheeseborough
Loretta Claiborne
Howard Gentry Jr.
Christie Hauck
Dwight Lewis
Andrew Maraniss
Barbara Murrell

Bibliography

Bo Roberts
Tracey Salisbury
Carolyn Alley Simpson
Sharon Smith
Guy Tallent
Betty Jane Maples Taylor
Edward Temple
Edwina Temple

*Titles in bold are critical sources that have been quoted directly.

Index